D120263

LEADERSHIP

LEADERSHIP

Essential Selections on Power,
Authority, and Influence

Edited and with Commentary by
Barbara Kellerman

New York   Chicago   San Francisco
Lisbon   London   Madrid   Mexico City   Milan
New Delhi   San Juan   Seoul   Singapore
Sydney   Toronto

1 2 3 4 5 6 7 8 9 0   DOC/DOC   1 5 4 3 2 1 0

ISBN: 978-0-07-163384-0
MHID: 0-07-163384-7

Interior design by Lee Fukui and Mauna Eichner

This publication is designed to provide accurate and authoritative information in regard to the subject matter covered. It is sold with the understanding that the publisher is not engaged in rendering legal, accounting, or other professional service. If legal advice or other expert assistance is required, the services of a competent professional person should be sought.

> —*From a declaration of principles jointly adopted by a committee of the American Bar Association and a committee of publishers.*

McGraw-Hill books are available at special quantity discounts to use as premiums and sales promotions, or for use in corporate training programs. To contact a representative please visit the Contact Us pages at www.mhprofessional.com.

For Mela Lew and the others—
who shared my passion for the power of words.

Contents

PART 2

LITERATURE AS LEADERSHIP
117

PART 3

LEADERS IN ACTION
205

Acknowledgments

Great gratitude to Mela Lew—first student, then colleague, now friend.

And appreciation to Mike Leveriza, who gave assistance from day one.

Introduction

We ought to be grateful to language
for making life messier than ever.

—RICHARD POIRIER

I

What should leaders learn? Given the countless number of leadership courses, seminars, workshops, institutes, centers, books, films, exercises, experiences, teachers, coaches, and consultants, this is a question to which we would seem to have an answer. And we do—four at least: (1) leaders should develop certain skills, such as communications skills, negotiating skills, and decision-making skills, (2) leaders should acquire awareness—most obviously self-awareness and contextual awareness, (3) leaders should have practice in, for example, mobilizing, managing, and creating change, and (4) leaders should learn the difference between right and wrong.

There is another, a fifth, answer to the question, albeit one that is altogether different. This book is about what leaders should learn—but it is decidedly not, deliberately not, about what leadership education has lately come to look like. It is not, at least not directly, about skills; nor is it about awareness as currently construed; nor is it, for that matter, in the least experiential or focused especially on ethics. Rather, this book is a throwback—it is traditional. It asserts the importance of acquiring a fixed body of knowledge that is the leadership canon: the great leadership literature.

The question of what leaders need to learn is not new. Confucius had an answer, as did Plato and Machiavelli, and W. E. B. Du Bois and Mary Parker Follett. Moreover, this particular question merely mirrors the more general one: What do any of us need to learn? What, in this day and age, is the mark of a good education?

The debate about what should be taught and to whom tends to be contentious. In recent years, battle lines have been drawn between those who believe that a twenty-first-century education should be more practical than anything else and those who believe just the opposite—that, in the wry aside of academic gadfly Stanley Fish, "higher education, properly understood, is distinguished by the *absence* (italics mine) of a direct and designed relationship between its activities and measurable effects in the world." Students, in any case, especially students in college, are being pressured now to focus more on making a living and less on the meaning of life—which takes a toll on, among other things, the liberal arts, which for 30 years have been in steep decline. The number of courses on, say, Shakespeare's sonnets, or American diplomatic history, or modern French philosophy has diminished, in some cases to near the vanishing point. No wonder philosopher Martha Nussbaum bemoans the "loss of respect for the humanities as essential ingredients of democracy," literary critic Louis Menand wonders how to explain why what he does "is important," and Drew Gilpin Faust, a historian and the president of Harvard University, feels obliged to remind us that "human beings need meaning, understanding, and perspective, as well as jobs."

So far as leadership learning is concerned . . . well, it's nothing if not in keeping with the temper of the times. Overwhelmingly, twenty-first-century leadership education and development are about practice, not theory; about the present, not the past; about prose, not poetry; about evaluation, not meditation; about the real world, not the world of the imagination. Put directly, twenty-first-century leadership learning excludes the liberal arts almost entirely—literature, history, and philosophy, to take obvious examples—in favor of a focus on a practical purpose.

Again, this book is an exception to the general rule. To return to the Fish formulation, it *does* assume a "designed relationship between its activities," reading the great leadership literature, and "measurable effects in the world." But this relationship is not direct; it is *indirect*. That is, whatever the relationship between reading Machiavelli and Marx and Mandela to the actual act of leadership, it is circuitous and by osmosis— the result of a process that is more unconscious than conscious.

What exactly makes literature—in this case, the leadership literature— great? Is it enough to define it simply as seminal, as timeless and transcendent? Or is there more to be said?

More often than not, great works—or what at one time were considered great works—end in the dustbin of history. In nineteenth-century America, the classics, Greek and Roman in origin, were esteemed as paragons of literary and historic virtue, only to be exiled a hundred years later to the rough equivalent of academic Siberia. More recently, in the twentieth century, scholars at the University of Chicago assembled what they concluded were the classics (literary, scientific, and philosophical), all 443 of them, into 54 black leatherette volumes known ever since as the "Great Books." The concept caught on, at least for a time, but once dead white males surrendered their stranglehold, the idea of there being a finite number of "Great Books" seemed, perhaps, more quaint than anything else.

Our current conception of what is a classic is expansive, even elastic. Classics are still seen in context, but they should in some obvious way be pertinent to the here and now, relevant to different readers in different places, each with his or her own reactions and responses, insights and interpretations. Moreover, our assumptions about what has literary value have been revised, becoming similarly more expansive and inclusive. Leah Marcus and her colleagues came to the conclusion that in the past, the reputation of Queen Elizabeth I as a writer suffered on account of her gender. But they also found that her literary skills were demeaned because "her work did not seem to measure up to an idealized aesthetics of timeless literary greatness." Now, though, the rigid demarcation between literary and nonliterary texts no longer exists. We can appreciate Elizabeth as a writer who in certain situations used her way with words to enhance her influence as a leader.

This book, then, consists of the leadership classics as the word *classic* has come to be used. Every single selection either is about leadership or is, of itself, an act of leadership. Every single selection has literary value—not always aesthetic value, but always, necessarily, value in the use of language on leadership. Every single selection is seminal: it changed forever how and what we thought and/or how and what we did. And every single selection is universal—it can be appreciated anywhere by anyone, as long as he or she has an interest in leadership. I cannot yet confidently claim, however, that every single selection is timeless. Some are simply too recent to be certifiably enduring. Still, I would argue—I *am* arguing—that they belong. Not only have even the most recent selections already stood the test of time (at least a quarter century), but they are likely to linger because their impact was demonstrably great.

Having addressed what is included in this volume, I need similarly to address what is not. Inevitably, some of the good stuff ended up on the cutting room floor. The omissions fall into four categories. First, because of the constraints of space I had to leave out some leadership literature that indisputably is great. Omitted, for example, were the *Federalist Papers*, in which Alexander Hamilton, John Jay, and James Madison played such an eloquent role not only as political philosophers expounding on the virtues of constitutional democracy, but also as political leaders who were bound and determined to secure ratification of the proposed constitution.

Second, excluded from this volume (again, for lack of space) is leadership literature that is great, but is imagined rather than real. (The single exception is a brief excerpt from Tolstoy's *War and Peace*, which is part of the discussion on the "great man.") First and of course foremost there is is Shakespeare, some of whose plays, such as *Henry V* and *Julius Caesar*, are classics of the genre. Shakespeare was the supreme poet of power; an authority on authority, particularly authority derived from or associated with royalty; and an expert on influence, especially behind-the-scenes influence exerted by those who are weaker on those who are stronger.

There are other, less obvious, examples as well, such as Harriet Beecher Stowe's novel *Uncle Tom's Cabin*, which in mid-nineteenth-century America was the literary equivalent of a seismic event. Stowe was convinced that slavery was a calamity. But she was a woman of her time, and so she lacked both power and authority. She did not, however, necessarily lack influence, which is why she used her way with words to craft an antislavery story that was so highly wrought, so heart-rending and relentlessly compelling, that attention had to be paid. Her fictionalized account of man's inhumanity to man (first serialized in 1852) was an immediate sensation, with sky-high sales continuing for years—in America second only to those of the Bible. In fact, the impact of *Uncle Tom's Cabin* was so great that the debate on bondage seemed to center on Stowe's description of it, and on her depiction of what it did both to slaves and to slaveholders. Little wonder that President Abraham Lincoln allegedly said to Stowe as she stood before him at the White House years later, "So you're the little woman who wrote the book that made this Great War."

Third, while I did bring in Mary Parker Follett, I did not include any of the other handful of classics most closely associated with corporate leadership, simply because they are so readily available elsewhere. For instance, there is a well-known article by Abraham Zaleznik, first published in the *Harvard Business Review* in 1977, titled "Managers and Leaders: Are They Different?" Because the piece has been reissued and reprinted repeatedly over the years in various edited volumes and by the Harvard Business Press itself, which now designates it a "Harvard Business Review Classic," there is no need to include it here.

Finally, the last sort of omission from the present volume—leadership literature that is so hateful, so intolerant, that it is hurtful. I refer, for example, to Adolf Hitler's *Mein Kampf* (1925) and Sayyid Qutb's *Milestones* (1962). Both books are inarguably instructive, as they are important. *Mein Kampf* is more than an anti-Semitic rant; it is a prescient piece on the power of propaganda and on how to organize so that the powerless become the powerful. Similarly, *Milestones* is more than invective against infidels; for decades it has had deep resonance among some Muslims who are determined to do what they must to "change the course of human history in the direction ordained by Allah." Thus, these books are revolutionary tracts of considerable consequence. They describe destroying the decadent old, they anticipate the utopian new, and they pronounce on process, on how to get from here (the ignominious present) to there (the glorious future). Documents like these should never be dismissed as merely repellent, or as irrelevant or insignificant. But because leadership literature like this is offensive to so many, odious even, it is excluded here.

There was another kind of whittling down as well: since most of the selections are excerpts, most of them had to be pared to manageable size.

The implications of the different cuts are clear: choices of what to put in and what to take out were made at every turn—choices that were personal and political, substantive and aesthetic. This collection is not, then, etched in stone. I anticipate debate about what was included and what was excluded. But it does represent long years of leadership learning—my own—and it does consist only of leadership literature that is significant to the point of being seminal.

Though the book is divided into three parts—about which more later—the overarching arc is historical. To see the sweep of history as it pertains particularly to leaders and followers, each of the three parts is arranged chronologically. Margaret MacMillan observed that in recent years people have been more interested in history, "even in North America, where we have tended to look toward the future rather than the past." The question is, is it much use? MacMillan, herself a student of history, concludes that the answer is "probably yes." How, then, does history benefit leaders in particular?

First, it provides context. Context is critical, both to learning leadership and to exercising it. Second, knowing history, at least some history, makes us smarter and swifter. It encourages us to avoid easy generalizations, and it reminds us that courses of action have consequences, some of them unanticipated. But there is another reason to learn history—a reason that, for leaders at least, trumps the other two. For only by looking through the lens of history can we detect the all-important trajectory of power and influence: for hundreds of years at least, they have shifted *away* from leaders and *toward* followers, and they are continuing to do so even now.

In the beginning there were Lao Tsu, Confucius, Plato, and Plutarch, followed by Machiavelli, Thomas Hobbes, and of course Queen Elizabeth I. Each was concerned above all with those who had power, authority, and influence. Later, after John Locke, an entirely different cast of characters came along—Karl Marx and Friedrich Engels, for example—whose concern was equally with those who did *not* have power, authority, or influence. Finally, and only relatively recently, the balance of power between leaders and followers shifted altogether. Now the voices of those *without* power and authority are likely to be as insistent and sometimes as influential as the voices of those *with*. Put another way, by now the canon is replete with literature in which leadership was exercised not from the top down, but from the bottom up.

II

This book is full of big ideas, grand themes, and impossible dreams. They include, but are by no means limited to, the following.

The Importance of Instruction

The assumption that leadership can and should be taught is old, going back thousands of years. But there has never been much agreement either on *how* leadership should be taught or on *who* exactly should be the leadership learner. In fact, it's the differences that stand out. The range is from Lao Tsu's light hand at the one extreme to Machiavelli's heavy hand at the other; from Follett, who wrote about developing corporate leaders, to Alinsky, who focused on growing grassroots leaders; from Du Bois, who was intent on educating "the talented tenth," to Lenin, who was hell-bent on training revolutionary leaders, to Friedan, driven to get women to employ the education that already was theirs.

Still, differences notwithstanding, there is a common thread. By definition, the literature on learning leadership is based on the proposition that people can, and sometimes do, change. It is presumed, in other words, that we are able to learn leadership, to at least a degree, from adolescence all the way through, well into adulthood.

The View of Human Nature

Where you stand depends on where you sit. Every one of these writers, some of whom were, simultaneously, leaders, wrote as a consequence of what he or she considered to be the human condition. Most had a view best described as bleak. Not necessarily as bleak as that of Hobbes, who famously framed life as "solitary, poor, nasty, brutish, and short." But bleak nevertheless, which is why so much of the leadership literature is the consequence, if you will, of the conviction that no one can be trusted, neither leaders nor followers. The result? A literature that is filled with constraints, constraints not only on those *with* power and authority, but also on those *without*.

This lack of trust is everywhere in evidence, particularly among those who wrote to defy, who wrote as an act of rebellion by the powerless against the powerful. I include in this group not only writers who advocated violence when they deemed it necessary and appropriate, such as the anti-imperialist, anticolonialist Frantz Fanon, but also those like Martin Luther King, Jr., who, in "Letter from Birmingham Jail," does not at all seem the moderate that we thought we knew so well. King wrote in the "Letter": "We know through painful experience that freedom is never voluntarily given by the oppressor; it must be demanded by the oppressed." These are *not* the words of a man who has a whole lot of faith in the kindness of strangers. These are the words of a black man whose experience of white America was that we are, we *all* are, if not necessarily ill disposed, then not necessarily well disposed.

The Role of Rage and Outrage

Both rage and outrage fuel the fire of leadership, on occasion in those on the inside of a prison. In fact, writers who led and/or leaders who wrote were motivated more by anger and indignation than they were by anything else. Sometimes, as in the case of King, that anger, while crystal clear, was carefully controlled. His prose seethed, but it was measured. Similarly, in *Silent Spring*, Rachel Carson, though outraged by the despoiling of God's green earth, chose nevertheless to deflect her anger with her science.

But other writer-leaders were different. They were not in the least concerned with hiding their fury, or with tamping it down in any way. Their prose was fierce, militant, sometimes profane, and deliberately intended to incite. For example, gay activist Larry Kramer thrived on taking on anyone and everyone, blatantly and boisterously, including men who, like he, were gay. His piece, "1,112 and Counting" begins: "If this article doesn't scare the shit out of you, we're in real trouble. If this article doesn't rouse you to anger, fury, rage, and action, gay men may have no future on this earth."

The Attraction of the "Great Man"

Notwithstanding the push to be politically correct, the phrase "great man" is used still. It resurfaces whenever we argue about the role of the hero, the leader, in history. Is history, as Thomas Carlyle fervently believed, "the history of what man has accomplished in this world"? Or is history as Herbert Spencer insisted: the result of a confluence of forces in which leaders, like everyone else, are swept by the tide of human affairs? Or is it perhaps something else altogether? Is it, as Tolstoy came to conclude, the hand of God? In *War and Peace*, Tolstoy wrote that history is "involuntary" and "predestined from eternity."

No matter, at least not here, for the point I want to make is not that the great man, or woman, or leader, is either all-important or unimportant. Rather, it is that we obsess, and we always have, about him or her, no matter what the real explanation for historical causation may be. In short, we dwell on those who are dominant as opposed to those who are deferent.

The Growing Inclusiveness

It is impossible not to be struck by the changing nature of the leadership literature, the result of, among other things, who was literate—who actually could read what was being written and who could write.

To say that the ancient leadership literature was by and for dead white males is once more to say the obvious. What is less obvious is that in the distant past, this literature grew to include other voices, in particular those of women and people of color. And what is even less easy to see is that in the recent past, the leadership canon expanded still further, so that it now includes voices that previously were mute. I include in this second group poor people, wherever they are located and whatever their color; the colonized, those who for centuries were oppressed by their colonizers (often but by no means always Europeans); gays and lesbians, who until late in the last century did not (generally) dare blow their cover; and yes, I include in this group nonhuman animals, who until the last quarter of the twentieth century had never had an effective, enduring literary advocate. It took philosopher Peter Singer and his book *Animal Liberation* (1975), the bible of the animal rights movement, to speak for those who are unable to speak for themselves.

The Rise of the Follower

Since the Enlightenment and the emergence of modern democracy, this trend has been in evidence everywhere, at least in the West. Those without power or position have slowly but certainly come to be deemed worthy of attention. John Locke wrote of the right—yours and mine—to own property. Marx and Engels urged the workers of the world to unite, insisting that they had nothing to lose but their chains. Sojourner Truth, who could neither read nor write, used her voice instead, speaking and singing to fight for women and blacks. And John Stuart Mill authored *On Liberty*, which claimed that you have every right to captain your ship, so long as you do not intrude on my right to captain mine.

Because of the calamity that was the Holocaust, in the aftermath of the Second World War there was further interest in followers, as well as in leaders. Writers and researchers sensed, speculated, and ultimately proved that whatever had gone horribly wrong in Nazi Germany, it was not the fault of the Führer (the leader) alone. Hitler had to have had the support, active or passive, of millions of followers, from devoted disciples to bystanders to alienated isolates, all of whom were critical cogs in the Nazi machine. As Stanley Milgram's pioneering and still shocking experiments on obedience to authority demonstrated, because none of us can be trusted *not* to obey orders, even when to obey orders is to commit a crime, none of us is exempt from doing deeds that are contrary to our conscience.

The Power of the Big Idea

In his 1978 book, *Leadership*, James MacGregor Burns devoted an entire chapter to "intellectual leadership." It was an uncommon contribution because in the last half-century or so leadership has nearly always been equated with what people do, not with what they think. But Burns understood full well what in the present book becomes crystal clear: "intellectual leadership is transforming leadership." That is, intellectual leaders, perhaps more than any other kind of leaders, prepare the soil for great change—political, social, and economic. Among Burns's examples of intellectual leaders were several men included here, such as Thomas Hobbes and John Locke, who exercised "striking influence over the political ideas of an entire society and whole epoch," including, a century later, over other intellectual leaders an ocean away, such as the brilliant constitutionalist James Madison.

It is impossible to overestimate the leadership roles played by men as altogether different from each other as Karl Marx and Peter Singer, and for that matter by women as altogether different from each other as Elizabeth Cady Stanton and Rachel Carson. Singer and Stanton were activists, in addition to their being cutting-edge thinkers. But Marx and Carson did nearly all of their work at their desks, and still they were leaders of the utmost consequence.

To be sure, even the biggest of big ideas must be born at the right time. Articulated too early they fall on deaf ears; too late, their moment in the sun has come and gone. But when the time is right as in ripe, big ideas, intellectual leaders, have a power unlike any other.

The Power of the Pen

How exactly do big ideas get conveyed? How do they move from their point of origin to other places on the planet? Well, we've heard the line before—the pen is mightier than the sword. Still it's startling to see the extent to which ordinary words—written words or spoken words—are in and of themselves agents of change. At the most obvious level, language is merely a means of transport. We use it to send and receive information and ideas. But pens can be potent, in particular when the words they put to paper excite us, incite us, inspire us, and compel us to think and do things differently from the way we did before. (Now, of course, the visuals are different: a keyboard; a screen, not necessarily the printed page.)

This book is full of examples of people who used their pens to make their points—and in the process changed the world. Thomas Paine's slender work *Common Sense* lit the fire that lit the American Revolution. Winston Churchill's singular speeches before the Second World War led to his being prime minister of Great Britain after the war had started. And by all accounts it was Betty Friedan's *The Feminine Mystique* that motivated the modern women's movement. Is there another sort of leadership as astonishing? Have there ever, anywhere, been leaders greater than writers such as Paine, Churchill (who in 1953 won the Nobel Prize in Literature), and Friedan?

The Leadership Literature as Literature

Let me put this as plainly as I can: some of the leadership literature is gorgeous, a revelation to read and reread because of the beauty of the language. Consider Carson, describing in *Silent Spring* what it was like before life on earth was sullied:

> The town lay in the midst of a checkerboard of prosperous farms, with fields of grain and hillsides of orchards where, in spring, white clouds of bloom drifted above the green fields. In autumn, oak and maple and birch set up a blaze of color that flamed and flickered across a backdrop of pines. Then foxes barked in the hills and deer silently crossed the fields, half hidden in the mists of the fall mornings.
>
> Along the roads, laurel, viburnum and alder, great ferns and wildflowers delighted the traveler's eye throughout much of the year. Even in winter the roadsides were places of beauty, where countless birds came to feed on the berries and on the seed heads of the dried weeds rising above the snow.

Or listen to Lincoln speaking at the cemetery at Gettysburg:

> But, in a larger sense, we can not dedicate—we can not consecrate—we can not hallow—this ground. The brave men, living and dead, who struggled here, have consecrated it, far above our poor power to add or detract. The world will little note, nor long remember what we say here, but it can never forget what they did here.

Of course, most of the leadership literature is not in the least "gorgeous." But it can be compelling in another way—so urgent it is impossible to resist. Here are the women at Seneca Falls, led by Elizabeth Cady Stanton, who drafted the "Declaration of Sentiments" to demand for women greater equity with men:

> The history of mankind is a history of repeated injuries and usurpations on the part of man toward woman, having in direct object the establishment of an absolute tyranny over her. . . .
>
> He has compelled her to submit to laws, in the formulation of which she had no voice.
>
> He has withheld from her rights which are given to the most ignorant and degraded men. . . .
>
> He has endeavored, in every way that he could to destroy her confidence in her own powers, to lessen her self-respect, and to make her willing to lead a dependent and abject life.

III

Writing this book has been a whole other kind of leadership learning—even for me. I say "even for me" because I have studied leadership and, more recently, followership all my professional life. Moreover, I have understood all my professional life that leadership is, and must be, an area of intellectual inquiry that is interdisciplinary. How can we know leadership, how can we know the relationship between leaders and followers without knowing history, philosophy, psychology, politics, sociology, anthropology, literature, art, and so on?

Of course, knowing enough about enough to know leadership in full is impossible. But, as soon as I moved to greater intellectual inclusiveness in the classroom, with a course I developed at the Harvard Kennedy School titled "Leadership Literacy," I knew that some number of students thought as I did, that, in Drew Faust's phrase, learning is "about a great deal more than measurable utility."

Still, for the reasons suggested earlier, in the beginning I had my doubts. I wondered whether students at the school, which is, after all, a professional school, would elect to take a course that was as much about literature as it was about leadership. Why—with limited time and all the other available leadership courses, courses that were more obviously practical—would students choose to take "Leadership Literacy"? If you want to be a real-world leader, what's the point of Plato? If you want to be a twenty-first-century leader, why consider Elizabeth I? If you want to be a business leader, why take time with Gandhi? Or for that matter, if you want to be a political leader, why invest as much as a minute in Mary Parker Follett?

In the beginning, the numbers were small. The first time "Leadership Literacy" was offered, only a few students showed up—16, as I recall—but then word got around and the numbers grew. Now, some six years later, many more than before have come to realize the relevance of the leadership literature—of words, written or spoken—to the course of human affairs. This at a time when professional schools, business schools in particular, are adding "lessons that fit the times" (in the words of the *Wall Street Journal*), that is, lessons about what happened five minutes ago, while subtracting lessons about what happened five years ago, not to mention five hundred years ago.

Like "Leadership Literacy," this book digs all the way down to ideas that have been at the core, at the heart of leadership since time immemorial. Put another way, in response to the question of what leaders should learn, it looks at leadership as an area of inquiry in the liberal arts, as opposed to only as an exercise in professional development.

The subject is power: some of the readings are by writers who are satisfied to use force as one of the instruments of leadership. The subject is also authority: some of the readings are by writers who are concerned primarily with position, with how, for instance, to lead as president or prince. Finally, the subject is influence: some of the readings are by writers who conceive of change as requiring no more than a compelling case.

As mentioned, the book is organized chronologically, but it is chronological within each of the three different parts. Part 1, "About Leadership," consists of writings *on the subject of leadership*. Part 2, "Literature as Leadership," consists of writings that are *in and of themselves acts of leadership*. And Part 3, "Leaders in Action," is the *sound of voices*, either literally, as in the spoken word, or figuratively, as in the written word, of seven men and two women who themselves were great leaders.

Each selection is preceded by an introductory note, and then followed by my somewhat more extended commentary and analysis. This sequence enables the reader to enter, or to reenter, the world of the writer fresh, without being told beforehand by me—by the editor, by the so-called expert—what to think or how to feel about works that are considered classic. (For the sake of simplicity, footnotes in the original text have been removed; the information is of course available in the original sources.)

Historian Tony Judt laments that most of us who are in a position to do so are wary of so much as suggesting that some readings are essential and should be required. We lack "cultural self-confidence," Judt argues, and so "we've lacked the ability to say, 'This is a good book and should be taught, this isn't and shouldn't.'" *This* book—this collection of essential selections—reflects no such defect. It contains not *good* leadership literature but *great* leadership literature—with which anyone with even a passing interest in leadership should have, at least, a passing acquaintance.

LEADERSHIP

1

ABOUT LEADERSHIP

*Ideas, both when they are right
and when they are wrong,
are more powerful
than is commonly understood.
Indeed, the world is ruled by little else.*

—JOHN MAYNARD KEYNES

T HE EVIDENCE IS IN: the interest is endless. Leaders—and, for that matter, followers—have occupied and preoccupied great minds since the beginning of recorded history.

As the Keynes quote would seem to suggest, this section contains selections from works by those who thought about leadership and followership, then wrote about them in so clever and creative a way that their work is considered classic.

Lao Tsu, Confucius, Plato, and Plutarch, each in different ways, ruminated on leadership and advised leaders, directly or indirectly, on what to do to achieve the ideal, or at least come as close to it as possible. Machiavelli provided counsel as well, but to one particular leader, the prince, and in his case, this counsel was pragmatic: how to preserve power in the here and now.

Hobbes, Locke, and Mill are of a piece in a way; each was writing about governance, but each reached different conclusions about who should lead and how and who should follow and how, based on his view of the human condition. Similarly, Carlyle, Spencer, James, and Tolstoy constitute a group, at least for this purpose, although they did not concur in the least on whether man makes history, whether it's the other way around, or whether history is something else altogether, the hand of God.

Weber and Freud, scientists both, applied their science to their study of leadership, with Freud additionally, at the end of his life, bringing to his work on leadership his experience as an exile. Follett's contribution was primarily but by no means exclusively directed toward leadership in business; Burns's was primarily but by no means exclusively directed toward leadership in government. This section, "About Leadership," ends with a discussion of followership in works by Milgram and Arendt, both of whom turned trauma into the study of power and authority as it pertains to those who are not at the top.

To those among us who are drawn to dominance and deference like moths to the proverbial flame, these writers are an irresistible group. From sages in ancient China to researchers in present-day America, they put their stamp on understanding leadership and followership forevermore.

~

LAO TSU

CIRCA 6TH CENTURY BCE

The following 9 chapters—each "chapter" is no more than several lines—
were selected from a total of 81. They are, legend has it, from Lao Tsu's
2,500-year-old work, the *Tao Te Ching*, translated as "The Way and Its
Powers." The chapters, numbered as they are in the book, address the
question of how to lead. Invariably, the suggestion is to lead lightly, even
to the point of not leading or seeming not to lead at all.

Taoism as a political philosophy can be considered in contrast to
Confucianism. Whereas the latter is concerned with rules and rituals, the
former is more elusive, more mystical, and more paradoxical. Lao Tsu
writes: "The Tao abides in non-action. Yet nothing is left undone."

---- FROM TAO TE CHING ----

CIRCA 6TH CENTURY BCE

SEVEN

Heaven and earth last forever.
Why do heaven and earth last forever?
They are unborn,
So ever living.
The sage stays behind, thus he is ahead.
He is detached, thus at one with all.
Through selfless action, he attains fulfillment.

EIGHT

The highest good is like water.
Water gives life to the ten thousand things and does not strive.
It flows in places men reject and so is like the Tao.

In dwelling, be close to the land.
In meditation, go deep in the heart.
In dealing with others, be gentle and kind.
In speech, be true.
In ruling, be just.
In business, be competent.
In action, watch the timing.

No fight: No blame.

NINE

Better stop short than fill to the brim.
Oversharpen the blade, and the edge will soon blunt.
Amass a store of gold and jade, and no one can protect it.
Claim wealth and titles, and disaster will follow.
Retire when the work is done.
This is the way of heaven.

TEN

Carrying body and soul and embracing the one,
Can you avoid separation?
Attending fully and becoming supple,
Can you be as a newborn babe?
Washing and cleansing the primal vision,
Can you be without stain?
Loving all men and ruling the country,
Can you be without cleverness?
Opening and closing the gates of heaven,
Can you play the role of woman?
Understanding and being open to all things,
Are you able to do nothing?
Giving birth and nourishing,
Bearing yet not possessing,
Working yet not taking credit,
Leading yet not dominating,
This is the Primal Virtue.

TWELVE

The five colors blind the eye.
The five tones deafen the ear.
The five flavors dull the taste.
Racing and hunting madden the mind.
Precious things lead one astray.

Therefore the sage is guided by what he feels and not by what he sees.
He lets go of that and chooses this.

THIRTEEN

Accept disgrace willingly.
Accept misfortune as the human condition.

What do you mean by "Accept disgrace willingly"?
Accept being unimportant.
Do not be concerned with loss or gain.
This is called "accepting disgrace willingly."

What do you mean by "Accept misfortune as the human condition"?
Misfortune comes from having a body.
Without a body, how could there be misfortune?

Surrender yourself humbly; then you can be trusted to care for all things.
Love the world as your own self; then you can truly care for all things.

FIFTEEN

The ancient masters were subtle, mysterious, profound, responsive.
The depth of their knowledge is unfathomable.
Because it is unfathomable,
All we can do is describe their appearance.
Watchful, like men crossing a winter stream.
Alert, like men aware of danger.
Courteous, like visiting guests.
Yielding, like ice about to melt.

Simple, like uncarved blocks of wood.
Hollow, like caves.
Opaque, like muddy pools.

Who can wait quietly while the mud settles?
Who can remain still until the moment of action?
Observers of the Tao do not seek fulfillment.
Not seeking fulfillment, they are not swayed by desire for change.

SEVENTEEN

The very highest is barely known by men.
Then comes that which they know and love,
Then that which is feared,
Then that which is despised.

He who does not trust enough will not be trusted.

When actions are performed
Without unnecessary speech,
People say, "We did it!"

SIXTY-SIX

Why is the sea king of a hundred streams?
Because it lies below them.
Therefore it is the king of a hundred streams.

If the sage would guide the people, he must serve with humility.
If he would lead them, he must follow behind.
In this way when the sage rules, the people will not feel oppressed;
When he stands before them, they will not be harmed.
The whole world will support him and will not tire of him.

Because he does not compete,
He does not meet competition.

Comment

We in the West are divided on the East. On the one hand, Eastern theory and practice on mind and body have never been more widely accepted or readily adopted. But on the other hand, Western leaders and managers, in both business and government, remain largely immune to Eastern influences.

Above all, this applies to doing nothing, a notion that is familiar in the East and unthinkable in the West, and to doing something, an option in the East and a requirement in the West. Leaders in the West think that they must act—they must do something. They think that they cannot *not* act and be, simultaneously, a leader. However Lao Tsu, the Old Master, who is believed to have lived in China some six centuries before the Christian era, thought differently. In fact, he thought quite the opposite. As far as he was concerned, inaction was nearly always preferable to action, even for "kings and lords."

The historical record on Lao Tsu is as meager as it is vague. Even his masterpiece, or what is reputedly his masterpiece, the *Tao Te Ching*, is cloaked in the mist of the distant past. We cannot even be sure that it is the work of one man as opposed to more than one who, for whatever reasons, chose to use a single pen name. What we do know is this: other than the Bible, the *Tao Te Ching* is the most widely translated book ever. Through the millennia, it has been read not only in China and in Asia, but also in the West, at least since the eighteenth century, when a Latin translation was first brought to England. In other words, whatever its precise provenance, the *Tao Te Ching* is like other classics of the leadership literature: it is timeless and transcendent.

The *Tao Te Ching* is difficult to decipher. It is open to interpretation, which is to say that it means different things to different people. Some see it as mystical. Others read it as they would a philosophical treatise. And still others consider it a document designed to secure the social order. The problem of translation further compounds the difficulties: the Chinese language contains characters with multiple meanings.

Professor Jacob Needleman looked at the layers of the *Tao* this way: The *Tao* is metaphysical—it describes the way things are. The *Tao* is psychological—it interprets human nature. The *Tao* is ethical—it tells us what we ought to know about how to treat others. And the *Tao* is spiritual—it guides us in our search for truth. Of course, all these meanings fuse ultimately into one: a vision of the good life and of how to achieve it.

Lao Tsu wrote in a time in which social and political unrest were ubiquitous, so the *Tao Te Ching* speaks of strife, struggle, and sacrifice. Still, the work describes leadership as a balancing act between being in the real, external world and being, simultaneously, in the ideal, internal world. While scholars have long argued about what precisely the sage meant when he preached inaction, or "not doing," there is nevertheless agreement that "doing nothing, achieving everything" is the heart of Lao Tsu's political thought.

The idea is to think of doing less, or even of not doing anything, as an alternative to excessive exertion. For on the assumption that this text was intended primarily for the ruler or the ruling elite (as literacy was limited at the time), it can be presumed that the "transformative power of nonaction" was intended to result in both personal fulfillment and political order.

Given that wise rulers never oblige the ruled to do anything, it can be argued that Lao Tsu thought that followers were in some sense the equals of their leaders. They are, in any case, to be led only by the lightest of hands, hands so light to the touch that they seem less real than imagined.

∼

CONFUCIUS
551–479 BCE

It is impossible to overestimate the impact of Confucius on Chinese history and culture. As scholar and translator Simon Leys put it in his introduction to *Analects*, "No book in the entire history of the world has exerted, over a longer period of time, a greater influence on a larger number of people than this slim little volume." However, the short text that constitutes Confucius's literary legacy was crafted not by him, but rather by his disciples, who took it upon themselves, as did the disciples of Jesus, to ensure that Confucius would endure. His primary passions were politics, governance, and leadership, but these were embedded in educating for ethics, which was his primary purpose.

Confucius, then, is at the start of a long literary tradition that assumes that good leadership and, yes, good followership can, at least to some extent, be taught. The teacher is presumed to be a sage, or at least older and wiser, and the pupil is presumed to have a capacity for change. The instruction on governance takes many forms and persists to this day—which is to say that now as before there is the assumption that leadership can be learned.

ANALECTS

CIRCA 475–221 BCE

CHAPTER 1

1.1. The Master said: "To learn something and then to put it into practice at the right time: is this not a joy? To have friends coming from afar: is this not a delight? Not to be upset when one's merits are ignored: is this not the mark of a gentleman?"

1.2. Master You said: "A man who respects his parents and his elders would hardly be inclined to defy his superiors. A man who is not inclined to defy his superiors will never foment a rebellion. A gentleman works at the root. Once the root is secured, the Way unfolds. To respect parents and elders is the root of humanity."

1.3 The Master said: "Clever talk and affected manners are seldom signs of goodness."

1.4. Master Zeng said: "I examine myself three times a day. When dealing on behalf of others, have I been trustworthy? In intercourse with my friends, have I been faithful? Have I practiced what I was taught?"

1.5. The Master said: "To govern a state of middle size, one must dispatch business with dignity and good faith; be thrifty and love all men; mobilize the people only at the right times."

1.6. The Master said: "At home, a young man must respect his parents; abroad, he must respect his elders. He should talk little, but with good faith; love all people, but associate with the virtuous. Having done this, if he still has energy to spare, let him study literature."

1.7. Zixia said: "A man who values virtue more than good looks, who devotes all his energy to serving his father and mother, who is willing to give his life for his sovereign, who in intercourse with friends is true to his word—even though some may call him uneducated, I still maintain he is an educated man."

1.8. The Master said: "A gentleman who lacks gravity has no authority and his learning will remain shallow. A gentleman puts loyalty and faithfulness foremost; he does not befriend his moral inferiors. When he commits a fault, he is not afraid to amend his ways."

1.9. Master Zeng said: "When the dead are honored and the memory of remote ancestors is kept alive, a people's virtue is at its fullest."

1.10. Ziqin asked Zigong: "When the Master arrives in another country, he always becomes informed about its politics. Does he ask for such information, or is it given him?" Zigong replied: "The Master obtains it by being cordial, kind, courteous, temperate, and deferential. The Master has a way of enquiring which is quite different from other people's, is it not?" . . .

1.16. The Master said: "Don't worry if people don't recognize your merits; worry that you may not recognize theirs."

Chapter 2

2.1. The Master said: "He who rules by virtue is like the polestar, which remains unmoving in its mansion while all the other stars revolve respectfully around it."

2.2. The Master said: "The three hundred *Poems* are summed up in one single phrase: 'Think no evil.'"

2.3. The Master said: "Lead them by political maneuvers, restrain them with punishments: the people will become cunning and shameless. Lead them by virtue, restrain them with ritual: they will develop a sense of shame and a sense of participation."

2.4. The Master said: "At fifteen, I set my mind upon learning. At thirty, I took my stand. At forty, I had no doubts. At fifty, I knew the will of Heaven. At sixty, my ear was attuned. At seventy, I follow all the desires of my heart without breaking any rule." . . .

2.19. Duke Ai asked: "What should I do to win the hearts of the people?" Confucius replied: "Raise the straight and set them above the crooked, and you will win the hearts of the people. If you raise the crooked and set them above the straight, the people will deny you their support."

2.20. Lord Ji Kang asked: "What should I do in order to make the people respectful, loyal, and zealous?" The Master said: "Approach them with dignity and they will be respectful. Be yourself a good son and a kind father, and they will be loyal. Raise the good and train the incompetent, and they will be zealous."

2.21. Someone said to Confucius: "Master, why don't you join the government?" The Master said: "In the *Documents* it is said: 'Only culti-vate filial piety and be kind to your brothers, and you will be contributing to the body politic.' This is also a form of political action; one need not nec-essarily join the government." . . .

CHAPTER 13

13.1. Zilu asked about government. The Master said: "Guide them. Encourage them." Zilu asked him how to develop these precepts. The Master said: "Untiringly."

13.2. Ran Yong was steward of the Ji Family. He asked about govern-ment. The Master said: "Guide the officials. Forgive small mistakes. Pro-mote men of talent." "How does one recognize that a man has talent and deserves to be promoted?" The Master said: "Promote those you know. Those whom you do not know will hardly remain ignored."

13.3. Zilu asked: "If the ruler of Wei were to entrust you with the gov-ernment of the country, what would be your first initiative?" The Master said: "It would certainly be to rectify the names." Zilu said: "Really? Isn't this a little farfetched? What is this rectification for?" The Master said: "How boorish can you get! Whereupon a gentleman is incompetent, thereupon he should remain silent. If the names are not correct, language is without an object. When language is without an object, no affair can be effected. When no affair can be effected, rites and music wither. When rites and music wither, punishments and penalties miss their target, the people do not know where they stand. Therefore, whatever a gentleman conceives of, he must be able to say; and whatever he says, he must be able to do. In the matter of language a gentleman leaves nothing to chance."

13.4. Fan Chi asked Confucius to teach him agronomy. The Master said: "Better ask an old farmer." Fan Chi asked to be taught gardening. The Master said: "Better ask an old gardener."

Fan Chi left. The Master said: "What a vulgar man! If their betters cultivate the rites, the people will not dare to be disrespectful. If their betters cultivate justice, the people will not dare to be disobedient. If their betters cultivate good faith, the people will not dare to be mendacious. To such a country, people would flock from everywhere with their babies strapped to their backs. What is the use of agronomy?"

13.5. The Master said: "Consider a man who can recite the three hundred *Poems*; you give him an official post, but he is not up to the task; you send him abroad on a diplomatic mission, but he is incapable of simple repartee. What is the use of all his vast learning?"

13.6. The Master said: "He is straight: things work out by themselves, without his having to issue orders. He is not straight: he has to multiply orders, which are not being followed anyway."

13.7. The Master said: "In politics, the states of Lu and Wei are brothers."

13.8. The Master commented on Prince Jing of Wei: "He knows how to live. As he began to have a little wealth, he said 'This is quite adequate.' As his wealth increased, he said 'This is quite comfortable.' When his wealth became considerable, he said 'This is quite splendid.'"

13.9. The Master was on his way to Wei, and Ran Qiu was driving. The Master said: "So many people!" Ran Qiu said: "Once the people are many, what next should be done?"—"Enrich them."—"Once they are rich, what next should be done?"—"Educate them."

13.10. The Master said: "If a ruler could employ me, in one year I would make things work, and in three years the results would show."

13.11. The Master said: "'When good men have been running the country for a hundred years, cruelty can be overcome, and murder extirpated.' How true is this saying!"

13.12. The Master said: "Even with a true king, it would certainly take one generation for humanity to prevail."

13.13. The Master said: "If a man can steer his own life straight, the tasks of government should be no problem for him. If he cannot steer his own life straight, how could he steer other people straight?"

13.14. Ran Qiu was returning from court. The Master said: "What kept you so long?" The other replied: "There were affairs of state." The Master said: "You mean private affairs. Had there been any affairs of state, even though I am not in office, I would have heard of them."

13.15. Duke Ding asked: "Is there one single maxim that could ensure the prosperity of a country?" Confucius replied: "Mere words could not achieve this. There is this saying, however: 'It is difficult to be a prince, it is not easy to be a subject.' A maxim that could make the ruler understand the difficulty of his task would come to ensuring the prosperity of the country."

"Is there one single maxim that could ruin a country?"

Confucius replied: "Mere words could not achieve this. There is this saying, however: 'The only pleasure of being a prince is never having to suffer contradiction.' If you are right and no one contradicts you, that's fine; but if you are wrong and no one contradicts you—is this not almost a case of 'one single maxim that could ruin a country'?" . . .

CHAPTER 20

20.2. Zizhang asked Confucius: "How does one qualify to govern?" The Master said: "He who cultivates the five treasures and eschews the four evils is fit to govern." Zizhang said: "What are the five treasures?" The Master said: "A gentleman is generous without having to spend; he makes people work without making them groan; he has ambition but no rapacity; he has authority but no arrogance; he is stern but not fierce." Zizhang said: "How can one be 'generous without having to spend'?" The Master said: "If you let the people pursue what is beneficial for them, aren't you being generous without having to spend? If you make people work only on tasks that are reasonable, who will groan? If your ambition is humanity, and if you accomplish humanity, what room is there left for rapacity? A gentleman treats equally the many and the few, the humble and the great, he gives the same attention to all: has he not authority without arrogance? A gentleman dresses correctly, his gaze is straight, people look at him with awe: is he not stern without being fierce?"

Zizhang said: "What are the four evils?" The Master said: "Terror, which rests on ignorance and murder. Tyranny, which demands results without proper warning. Extortion, which is conducted through contradictory orders. Bureaucracy, which begrudges people their rightful entitlements."

20.3 Confucius said: "He who does not understand fate is incapable of behaving as a gentleman. He who does not understand the rites is incapable of taking his stand. He who does not understand words is incapable of understanding men."

Comment

For most of the past 2,000 years, China has been elusive, distant from the West—literally, obviously, but figuratively as well. Now, though, the planet is shrinking, and China has emerged from an inscrutable past into a formidable present.

This then is the time, high time, to consider, or reconsider, Confucius, who for more than two millennia has had an incalculable impact on Chinese culture and consciousness. As Yale professor Annping Chin observed, "Until the mid-twentieth century, China was so inseparable from the idea of Confucius that her scheme of government and society, her concept of the self and human relationships, and her construct of culture and history all seemed to have originated from his mind alone." Put another way, because Confucius's world seems somehow complete and self-contained, the Chinese people have found in his scant body of work most of the answers to most of their questions. He provided a guidebook of sorts—an instruction on good conduct and on a life well lived.

When China began to modernize, especially under Communism and the tyrannical reign of Mao Zedong (from the 1950s to the 1970s), Confucius fell out of favor. He was associated with the past, not with the present, and certainly not with the future, so in their zeal the zealots threw out the Master—"the first teacher." But he did not vanish, was not banished, for long. Not long after Mao was dead and buried, Confucius resurfaced to resume something resembling his traditional place in China's collective consciousness. By the end of the twentieth century, he was once again honored: China's ostensibly orthodox Communist government sponsored a symposium on Confucius in celebration of the 2,545th anniversary of his birth.

In twenty-first century China, there is debate about whether and how Confucianism should be revived on a wider scale and in a more systematic way. Confucius is no longer seen as a symbol of a distant past. Rather, in some circles at least, he has become a harbinger, a forerunner of the new China, one that is more open to the world and, by and large, more eager to engage it. As Daniel Bell has noted, Confucian intellectuals are currently involved in educational reform, and Confucian values permeate thousands of social experiments, particularly those promoting harmony and compassion.

Like many of history's great political philosophers, Confucius lived during a time of trouble. The old order was collapsing, and the new order was yet to be determined. So Confucius committed himself to public service and, especially, to education. His mission was to teach an elite corps of leaders how to govern wisely and well.

Confucius considered education to be of paramount importance. The educated governor was the necessary precursor to good governance, which, in turn, was the necessary precursor to public order. More specifically, Confucius believed in the need to cultivate leaders who were "gentlemen," who possessed *de*, which is to say, virtue.

This was not, in other words, leadership by lineage. Rather, in theory at least, any man could learn to lead, so long as he was willing and able to become the moral exemplar that Confucius deemed to be of highest importance. The point is made at the start of the *Analects*: "Master Zeng said: 'I examine myself three times a day. When dealing on behalf of others, have I been trustworthy? In intercourse with my friends, have I been faithful? Have I practiced what I was taught?'"

Notwithstanding the theoretical possibility of social mobility, however, in Confucius's world, the social order was secured through a hierarchy that was rigidly fixed. Higher education was ostensibly available to all, but, as the following admonition makes clear, each man had his place, and each man was expected to remain in his place: "Good government consists in the ruler being a ruler, the minister being a minister, the father being a father, and the son being a son." Thus it was not only good leadership that mattered to Confucius, but good followership as well. "A man who respects his parents and his elders would hardly be inclined to defy his superiors. A man who is not inclined to defy his superiors will never foment a rebellion."

The world of Confucius is one in which the Master gets what he needs and wants not by using force, but by employing a set of skills that today might be termed "social intelligence." For example, when the Master treads on foreign soil, he secures his interests by being "cordial, kind, courteous, temperate, and deferential." The Master, the leader, is, in short, a role model, a gentleman who is to be emulated because he is older and wiser and familiar with the ways of the world. His capacity to lead is based on moral suasion, which is to say that he attracts followers first by setting an example, and then by presiding over the rites and rituals that are considered signs and symbols of stability and security.

As evidenced in the exchanges between Confucius and his disciples, the Master is not otherworldly. By cautioning against bad leadership, against terror and tyranny, as he did toward the end of his discourse, Confucius signaled that while aspiring always to a better world, he was, inevitably and ineluctably, a part of this one.

~

PLATO
427–347 or 348 BCE

Plato is one of the great *writers* in the Western literary tradition, and one of the most brilliant and influential of all *philosophers*. His primary impact has been on political thought. But his intellectual interests were so wide-ranging and far-flung that they encompassed nearly every aspect of the human condition: religion, reality, ethics, governance, happiness and, of course, leadership and followership. *The Republic*, which is excerpted here, has been described variously as a "timeless philosophical masterpiece," the "first great work of Western political philosophy," and "matchless as an introduction to the basic issues that confront human beings as citizens." Because the book is long and complex, the following two excerpts, imagined dialogues between Plato's great mentor, Socrates, and Plato's older brother, Glaucon, were chosen in part for their brevity and simplicity. The first selection is from Book V and focuses on the ideal—it is a rueful reflection on the philosopher-king. The second is from Book IX and is all too real. It speaks of tyranny, of the leader as tyrant, and of his followers as victims.

---------- THE REPUBLIC ----------

CIRCA 380 BCE

BOOK V

Now we trust to find out what it is that causes our cities to be so badly governed and what prevents them from being governed well. What might be the last change that would transform bad government into good government? It would surely be preferable to manage this with a single change. If not one change, then two; if not two, then the fewest and most moderate changes possible.

Proceed.

I think there is one change that could bring about the transformation we desire. It is no small change, nor would it be easy to implement. But it is possible.

What is it?

So. At last I come face to face with what I have called the greatest of the waves. But I will speak even if it break over my head and drown me in a flood of laughter and derision. Mark my words.

I am all attention.

Unless philosophers become kings in our cities, or unless those who now are kings and rulers become true philosophers, so that political power and philosophic intelligence converge, and unless those lesser natures who run after one without the other are excluded from governing, I believe there can be no end to troubles, my dear Glaucon, in our cities or for all mankind. Only then will our theory of the state spring to life and see the light of day, at least to the degree possible. Now you see why I held back so long from speaking out about so troublesome a proposition. For it points to a vexing lesson: whether in private or public life there is no other way to achieve happiness.

Socrates, after launching such an assault you must expect to be attacked by hordes of our leading men of learning. They will at once cast off their garments and strip for action—metaphorically speaking, of course.

Snatching the first handy weapon, they will rush at you full tilt, fully prepared to do dreadful deeds. If you can't find arguments to fend them off and make your escape, you will learn what it means to be scorned and despised.

It was you who got me into this.

A good thing, too. But I won't desert you; I'll help defend you as best I can. My good will and encouragement may be of use, and perhaps I shall be able to offer more suitable answers than others. With such a helpmate at your side you should be able to be at your best in convincing the unbelievers that you are right.

Your invaluable offer of assistance obliges me to try. If we are going to find some way to elude our assailants, I think we must explain what we mean by our daring suggestion that philosophers ought to be rulers. First, we must make clear what it is to be a philosopher. Then, we should be able to vindicate ourselves by explaining that philosophy and political leadership are inherent qualities of the philosopher's nature, so that it behooves the others to let philosophy alone and to follow the leaders.

It is high time that you come forward with your explanation.

Then let us proceed along the following lines to see if we can clarify our position.

Go ahead.

Need I remind you—or do you remember—that we said if a man loves something, he ought to show his love for all of it? It will not do for him to say that some of it he likes and some not.

It is well that you remind me because I really don't understand what you are saying.

Such an answer would come from another better than from you, Glaucon. As a lover, you should know how everyone in the flower of youth somehow stirs and arouses emotion in the lover's breast, and all appear desirable and worthy of his attentions. Is that not the way you respond to the fair? You will describe the one with the snub nose as having nerve. A hook nose confers on another a royal countenance. He whose nose is neither snub nor hooked is endowed with regularity of proportion. To be dark-skinned is manly, while the fair are children of the gods. As for the "honey-colored," what is the term itself but a euphemism invented by some lover who is willing to put up with a pallid complexion if only it is coupled with blooming youth? In short, you will employ any pretense and any fair word rather than risk losing a single one of the young flowers.

If you want to make me your example of a lover's traits, I admit to them for the sake of the argument.

What do you say to the lovers of wine? Do they not do the same thing? Are they not eager to consume every kind of wine on any pretext?

They are.

The same again with men of ambition. If they can't manage to become commanding generals, they are still willing to give commands as lieutenants. If the high and mighty will not honor them, they are willing to accept honors from lesser folk. But honors they must have.

All too true.

Then I have a proposition for you to accept or reject. When we say that a man desires something, do we say he desires all that pertains to it or only one part and not another?

He will desire the whole of it.

So we can say of the philosopher that he loves all wisdom and not just fragments of it.

Yes.

Then any student who is half-hearted in his studies—especially when he is young and lacks the understanding to judge between what is useful and what is not—cannot be called a philosopher or a lover of wisdom. He is like one who picks at his food. We say that he is not really hungry and has no appetite. We say that he is a poor eater and no lover of the table.

Rightly.

But he who is inclined to sample all studies, who gladly addresses himself to the task of learning and cannot get enough of it, he is the one we shall rightly call philosopher and lover of wisdom?

But Glaucon demurred: Not so. You will be conferring these titles on a strange and motley crew. For example, all the lovers of entertainments and other splendors become what they are, I suppose, because they delight in learning something. And those who are always clamoring to hear something new are queer fish to be counted among philosophers. They can't be induced to attend a serious debate or similar entertainment, but they run to all the festivals celebrating Dionysus as if they were paid to lend their ears to every chorus in the land. No difference whether the show is in town or country village, they never miss a one. Are we really to regard these and their like and all the practitioners of the minor arts as philosophers?

No, but they do bear a likeness to philosophers.

Who, then, are the true philosophers?

Those who come to love the spectacle of truth. . . .

BOOK IX

We must still consider the tyrannical man himself. How does he evolve from the democratic man? What kind of life does he lead? Is he happy or miserable?

You are right. These are questions we still haven't answered.

I think we have neglected one thing in particular.

What?

We have not yet given a full accounting of human desires, nor have we sufficiently described their nature. We must consider these matters; otherwise our inquiry will remain incomplete.

Don't we still have time to look into them?

By all means. One of their aspects I should particularly like to examine. I think all of us harbor within ourselves unnecessary pleasures and appetites. Some are also lawless. But in some men, when the laws are supported by reason and by the better desires, lawless propensities can be eradicated or at least marvelously reduced in number and intensity. To be sure, in others these kinds of desires remain strong and numerous.

What desires do you mean?

Those that stir when the soul is otherwise asleep, when the dominating characteristics of gentleness and rationality slumber. Then the wild and brutish part, sated with food and drink, becomes restless and goes on the prowl in search of anything that will satisfy its instincts. You know that in such a state it will shrink from nothing because it has been released from reason and a sense of shame. It will not hold back from contemplating intercourse with a mother or lying together with anyone else, whether man, god, or beast. Foul murder is no crime, and no flesh is forbidden. In sum, shamelessness and folly have their way.

That is the truth.

On the other hand, I can imagine a healthy man who lives in harmony with himself. He goes to sleep only after he has summoned up the rational element in his soul, nourishing it with fair thoughts and precepts. So he achieves clarity in consciousness of self. So, too, he neither sates nor starves his appetites in order that they may rest and that their related pains or pleasures may not subvert the soul's excellence. Then the soul is left free to reach out and seek to comprehend things as yet unknown to it, things that have been, are now, or are yet to be. And if a man does not permit a quarrel to keep anger awake after he has fallen asleep, he will have tamed the spirited part of his soul as well. Hence he will have calmed two of the elements in his soul and quickened the third where reason governs. You must agree one who goes to his rest in so temperate a manner is most likely to behold truth and is least likely to be visited by dreams of lawlessness.

Exactly.

Well, we have been too much diverted by this issue. But the point we need to keep in mind is this: every one of us—even those accorded the highest degree of respectability—harbors a fierce brood of savage and imperious appetites that reveal themselves most readily in dreams. Reflect on what I have said and see if you agree.

I do agree. . . .

Lesser evils they may be if there are only a few who inflict them.

That is because small things are small only when compared to the great. All together such petty crimes produce a degree of corruption and evil in the city that, as the saying goes, comes nowhere near hailing distance of the ruin the tyrant brings. But when these kinds of men and their followers become many, when they become conscious of their numbers and fasten on the folly of the multitude, that is the moment of the tyrant's entrance. He will be the one among them who harbors within himself the greatest and most ruthless tyrant of all.

Of course. His tyranny will be absolute.

If the city willingly submits to him. But if the city resists he will punish his fatherland just as he tormented his own father and mother. He will import a new set of companions to help him enslave what he once reverenced as his fatherland or, as the Cretans say, his motherland. These will surely be his intentions.

Exactly.

Is not the public character of such men shaped in private life before they ever come to power in the state? Will they not associate with flatterers ready to stoop to any service? Conversely, should they want favors from others, will they not themselves play the flunky, cringing and fawning while pledging their love? Having once gained their object, however, they behave quite differently.

That is right.

So they live their whole lives without friends. They are always one man's master or another man's slave. Tyrants never learn friendship or freedom.

You are right.

Would we also be right to say that these are men without honor?

We would.

And if our agreement holds true about the nature of justice, could we not say that they are entirely unjust?

The agreement surely holds.

Then let us draw some conclusions about the nature of the man who is supremely evil. His waking behavior, I presume, will resemble the traits we observed in his dreams.

I agree.

He is the joint product of his tyrannical nature and his despotic rule, and the longer he rules, the more oppressive his tyranny.

At this point Glaucon took up the argument: Inevitably, he said. . . .

First off, will you say that a city ruled by a tyrant is free or slave?

Altogether slave.

Yet you see free men as well as masters in this very city.

I see that a few are masters. But the many, who are also the most decent, are deprived of honor and shamefully enslaved.

Then, if man is like the city, won't these same relationships prevail in him? In the main, won't he be servile and ungenerous? Won't the better parts of his nature be enthralled, while a small part, frenzied and evil, plays the master?

Inevitably.

Will you say that such a soul is slave or free?

Slave.

Will you not also say that the city enslaved by the tyrant is least able to attain what it really wants?

Yes.

So, too, a man's soul, wholly enslaved by its inner tyrant, will be least able to do what it wants. Instead it will be maddened by disorder and frenzy and full of remorse.

Unquestionably.

Will the tyrannical city be rich or poor?

Poor.

So then will the tyrannical man be ever in want.

So he will be.

Will not the city and the man resound with terror and alarms?

They will.

Do you think you could find any other kind of man more burdened with such ills than the tyrannical man, crazed by his own passions and appetites?

Never.

As far as the tyrant's city is concerned, I take it all these considerations persuade you that is the most miserable of all cities.

Am I not rightly persuaded?

Indeed you are. And when you behold the same evils in the tyrannical man, what do you say of him?

He is by far the unhappiest of men.

Here we must disagree.

Why?

I do not think he is the most wretched of all.

Then who is?

I have in mind a man whose afflictions you might think are greater still.

What man is he?

A man tyrannical by nature who does not live a private life; he has the misfortune of becoming a tyrant over the city.

From what has already been said, I suppose you may be right.

Yes, but at this high point of the argument supposing such things is not enough; they require more serious examination. After all, we are here addressing the greatest of all questions: the difference between the good life and the bad.

That is true.

Then see if there is anything in what I have to say. An illustration might help to put the matter in perspective.

What is your illustration?

Consider the private men living in the cities who are very rich and have many slaves. They resemble the tyrant in that they rule over many, although the number governed by the tyrant is much greater.

The resemblance is there.

You know that they feel secure, that they are not frightened of their servants.

What should they fear?

Nothing. But do you know why?

Yes. The private citizen can rely on the entire city to protect him.

Very true. But supposing some god should lay hold of a man with fifty slaves and carry him off together with his wife and children. Supposing he and all his property and servants were set down in some lonely place where there were no free men to come to his aid. What do you think he would fear—how much would he fear—that he and his wife and children would be murdered by the slaves of his household?

I think he would be desperate with fear.

Would he not at once feel constrained to truckle to some of his slaves, going against his own and making them promises and even free them? Would he not be compelled to be the flatterer of his own servants?

Either that or perish.

But now suppose that the god surrounded him with many neighbors who would not allow any man's claim to be master of another. Could they lay hands on him, he would suffer harsh punishment.

Then I think his situation would become still more precarious. He would be alone among enemies.

Is this not the kind of prison to which the tyrant is condemned, the man we described with so many fears and so many appetites? He is pleasure-loving and greedy, but alone among the men of the city there is no place he dares go. What all men want to see he may not see. For the most part he lives like a woman, cowering in his house and envying those who can enjoy the pleasures of travel abroad.

That is certain.

Such a crop of evils reveals how much more wretched is the existence of the tyrannical man—the very man whom you judged the most miserable. Not only is he ill governed within himself, but once misfortune removes him from private life and establishes him in the tyrant's place, he must try to control others when he cannot control himself. He is like a sick man who is unable to exercise self-restraint and yet is not permitted to pass his days in cloistered privacy; instead, he is obliged to engage adversaries in never-ending rivalry and discord.

A telling and exact comparison, Socrates.

Is this not utter misery? Is not the life of the tyrant governing the city more miserable even than that life which you earlier judged to be so wretched?

No doubt about it.

Then he who is completely the tyrant is completely the slave. That is the truth, though some may deny it. More than all the others he must cringe and truckle. He must flatter the worst of men. Unable to obtain even a modicum of satisfaction for his desires, he must suffer more deprivation than any other. So he is a poor man, as anyone who knows how to judge souls can tell. He is fear's victim his whole life long, beset by convulsions and tumults. In sum, he resembles the city he rules, and the resemblance holds, does it not?

Yes.

Comment

The works that are included in this volume have been chosen on the basis of both content and literary merit. Plato in particular should be read as a writer as well as a political philosopher.

What a clever conceit to put *The Republic* in dialogue form! Dialogue per se was nothing new, of course. Confucius employed exchange to make his case, and theater and drama were important components of cultural life in ancient Athens. But Plato's decision to cast what otherwise would have been long treatises in the form of lively conversations was a stroke of genius. The dialogues bring his ideas to life in a way that would have been impossible without them, and they introduce us to a cluster of characters, some of whom were real. The dialogues are not necessarily historically accurate; rather, they are the medium through which Plato chose to send his message.

Paramount among the players is, of course, Socrates, whose influence on Plato was enormous. (At no point does Plato himself speak.) It is Socrates' voice we hear over and over again, his ideas that matter most, and his quest for truth that we presume reflects Plato's own. To be sure, there is evidence that the real, historical Socrates was not as perfect as Plato presented him. The playwright Aristophanes, for example, depicted Socrates quite differently, and less favorably. Still, he remained a lodestar throughout Plato's work, described by him as the wisest of thinkers, a great mentor and pedagogue, and a paragon of virtue.

"Socratic dialogue" is a literary device used by Plato to maximum effect. It is also a way of teaching that is specially suited to subjects that elude easy answers. Plato seems for a time to have been a teacher of young men, in particular those preparing to be leaders. This explains at least in good part his interest in leadership education, which he concluded should be lifelong and should include literature, music, physical exercise, elementary and advanced mathematics, philosophy and metaphysics, and real-world experience in both the civil service and the military. Plato's use of dialogue was, then, a way to enliven his text and enlist his audience. It was also a way of instruction that deliberately was other than from the top down.

In the end, though, Plato was a political philosopher more than he was anything else. In particular, *The Republic* is a dive deep into the realm of political thought. It is divided into 10 different books, all of which in some way explore the question of whether it is better always to be just rather than unjust. Of special interest here is Plato on leadership—although to a twenty-first-century democrat, his views on the subject are not heartening. That is, notwithstanding our romantic conceptions of Athenian democracy, Plato himself was an autocrat, not a democrat; an elitist, not a populist. In his view, leaders should, nearly without exception, come from the ruling class. And in his view, exceptional education should be available only to these exceptional men and not to the rest, who belonged either to the small middle class, which consisted of civilian and military administrators, or to the large lower class, which included everyone else. Finally, the planned state that was Plato's preference was supposed to assign to everyone a place to which everyone was supposed willingly to accede.

To the modern ear, this sounds stifling—some would say totalitarian. But Plato is better portrayed as a well-intentioned authoritarian. He was an idealist, perhaps even a mystic, who sought to create the perfect state, given the exigencies of the human condition. His admittedly imagined ideal of the philosopher-king is in many ways as benign as it is familiar: the ruler who is a philosopher or the philosopher who rules, either one of whom would lead wisely and well in a realm of truth and beauty. In Book V of *The Republic*, Socrates makes the point plain—and sounds a note of warning: "Unless philosophers become kings in our cities, or unless those who are now kings and rulers become true philosophers . . . I believe there can be no end to troubles, my dear Glaucon, in our cities or for all mankind."

As the dialogue moves back and forth, between point and counterpoint, so Plato contrasts the philosopher-king with the tyrant, who is the philosopher-king's more fully realized counterpart. For if the former was destined always to be elusive, if not impossible actually to realize, the tyrant was not. Tyrants were real—in fact, Plato's descent into the depths of what tyrants think and feel and do is grounded not only in his knowledge but in his experience.

His depiction of bad or even evil leadership is, of all things, psychological, even psychoanalytical, in its disposition. Plato recognizes that "all of us harbor in ourselves unnecessary pleasures and appetites." But while some of us can and do tame such impulses, others of us succumb to "the wild and brutish part," so that when we are "released from reason and a sense of shame," we do all manner of dreadful deeds. Indeed Plato connects what we dream to what we do in a manner more reminiscent of Freud than of anyone else—a tyrant is torn between his superego (his "reason") and his id (those "wild and brutish" desires that drive him to distraction). Plato's tyrant can never be content. He is condemned forever to be frustrated, insatiable because he is obsessed with what he does not have, rather than grateful for what he does. Counterintuitively, the tyrant is also enslaved, victimized by a self that is impossible to control.

Finally there are the followers. To Plato, they are of minor importance, but they are not ignored altogether. In Book IX, in which Socrates and Glaucon talk about tyrants, they also discuss, at least fleetingly, those who are tyrannized. Glaucon asks if a city that is governed by a tyrant is free or enslaved. Socrates replies that such a city is "altogether slave." When Glaucon then proceeds to try to catch him on the fine point of an argument, Socrates responds by saying, with what we imagine is some passion, that the unfortunates who live in such a city "are deprived of honor and shamefully enslaved." This is Plato—taking the measure of more than most.

∽

PLUTARCH

CIRCA 46–120 CE

Life stories have been the most durable and popular of our literary forms. But, so far as we know, Plutarch, a Greek, was the first formal biographer. He penned portraits that survive still, revealing that reading about great men can provide personal pleasure while serving a pedagogical purpose.

The *Lives* is composed of 50 short studies of Greek and Roman statesmen, soldiers, and orators. Of the studies, 46 are arranged roughly chronologically and in pairs, the better to contrast and compare Greeks with Romans. Plutarch is not a reliable historian—he did not always hew to the facts. However, his *Lives* live because his eye was trained on the individual as opposed to the collective, and because the men they portray seem somehow as fresh and vibrant now as they did then, some two thousand years in the past.

The selection that follows is a comparison between Dion, a Greek, and Brutus, that great, flawed Roman, drawn in full by Shakespeare in his tragedy *Julius Caesar*.

———— LIVES ————
CIRCA 100–120
THE COMPARISON OF DION AND BRUTUS

There are noble points in abundance in the characters of these two men, and one to be first mentioned is their attaining such a height of greatness upon such inconsiderable means; and on this score Dion has by far the advantage. For he had no partner to contest his glory, as Brutus had in Cassius, who was not, indeed, his equal in proved virtue and honour, yet contributed quite as much to the service of the war by his boldness, skill, and activity, and some there be who impute to him the rise and beginning of the whole enterprise, saying that it was he who roused Brutus, till then indisposed to stir, into action against Caesar. Whereas Dion seems of himself to have provided not only arms, ships, and soldiers, but likewise friends and partners for the enterprise. Neither did he, as Brutus, collect money and forces from the war itself, but, on the contrary, laid out of his own substance, and employed the very means of his private sustenance in exile for the liberty of his country. Besides this, Brutus and Cassius, when they fled from Rome, could not live safe or quiet, being condemned to death and pursued, and were thus of necessity forced to take arms and haz-ard their lives in their own defence, to save themselves, rather than their country. On the other hand, Dion enjoyed more ease, was more safe, and his life more pleasant in his banishment, than was the tyrant's who had banished him, when he flew to action, and ran the risk of all to save Sicily.

Take notice, too, that it was not the same thing for the Sicilians to be freed from Dionysius, and for the Romans to be freed from Caesar. The for-mer owned himself a tyrant, and vexed Sicily with a thousand oppressions; whereas Caesar's supremacy, certainly, in the process for attaining it, had inflicted no trouble on its opponents, but, once established and victorious, it had indeed the name and appearance, but fact that was cruel or tyran-nical there was none. On the contrary, in the malady of the times and the need of a monarchical government, he might be thought to have been sent as the gentlest physician, by no other than a divine intervention. And thus the common people instantly regretted Caesar, and grew enraged and implacable against those that killed him. Whereas Dion's chief offense in the eyes of his fellow-citizens was his having let Dionysius escape, and not having demolished the former tyrant's tomb.

In the actual conduct of war, Dion was a commander without fault improving to the utmost those counsels which he himself gave, and where others led him into disaster correcting and turning everything to the best. But Brutus seems to have shown little wisdom in engaging in the final battle, which was to decide everything, and when he failed not to have done his business in seeking a remedy; he gave all up, and abandoned his hopes, not venturing against fortune even as far as Pompey did, when he had still means enough to rely on in his troops, and was clearly master of all the seas with his ships.

The greatest thing charged on Brutus is, that he, being saved by Caesar's kindness, having saved all the friends whom he chose to ask for, he moreover accounted a friend, and preferred above many, did yet lay violent hands upon his preserver. Nothing like this could be objected against Dion; quite the contrary; whilst he was of Dionysius's family and his friend, he did good service and was useful to him; but driven from his country, wronged in his wife, and his estate lost, he openly entered upon a war just and lawful. Does not, however, the matter turn the other way? For the chief glory of both was their hatred of tyranny, and abhorrence of wickedness. This was unmixed and sincere in Brutus; for he had no private quarrel with Caesar, but went into the risk singly for the liberty of his country. The other, had he not been privately injured, had not fought. This is plain from Plato's epistles, where it is shown that he was turned out, and did not forsake the court to wage war upon Dionysius. Moreover, the public good made Brutus Pompey's friend (instead of his enemy as he had been) and Caesar's enemy; since he proposed for his hatred and his friendship no other end and standard but justice. Dion was very serviceable to Dionysius whilst in favour; when no longer trusted, he grew angry and fell to arms. And, for this reason, not even were his own friends all of them satisfied with his undertaking, or quite assured that, having overcome Dionysius, he might not settle the government on himself, deceiving his fellow-citizens by some less obnoxious name than tyranny. But the very enemies of Brutus would say that he had no other end or aim, from first to last, save only to restore to the Roman people their ancient government.

And apart from what has just been said, the adventure against Dionysius was nothing equal with that against Caesar. For none that was famil-
iarly conversant with Dionysius but scorned him for his life of idle
amusement with wine, women, and dice; whereas it required an heroic
soul and a truly intrepid and unquailing spirit so much as to entertain the
thought of crushing Caesar, so formidable for his ability, his power, and
his fortune, whose very name disturbed the slumbers of the Parthian and
Indian kings. Dion was no sooner seen in Sicily but thousands ran in to
him and joined him against Dionysius; whereas the renown of Caesar,
even when dead, gave strength to his friends; and his very name so heightened the person that took it, that from a simple boy he presently became
the chief of the Romans; and he could use it for a spell against the enmity
and power of Antony. If any object that it cost Dion great trouble and difficulties to overcome the tyrant, whereas Brutus slew Caesar naked and unprovided, yet this itself was the result of the most consummate policy and
conduct, to bring it about that a man so guarded around, and so fortified
at all points, should be taken naked and unprovided. For it was not on the
sudden, nor alone, nor with a few, that he fell upon and killed Caesar, but
after long concerting the plot, and placing confidence in a great many
men, not one of whom deceived him. For he either at once discerned the
best men, or by confiding in them made them good. But Dion, either making a wrong judgment, trusted himself with ill men, or else by his employing them made ill men of good; either of the two would be a reflection on
a wise man. Plato also is severe upon him, for choosing such for friends as
betrayed him.

Besides, when Dion was killed, none appeared to revenge his death.
Whereas Brutus, even amongst his enemies, had Antony that buried him
splendidly; and Caesar also took care his honours should be preserved.
There stood at Milan in Gaul, within the Alps, a brazen statue, which Caesar in aftertimes noticed (being a real likeness, and a fine work of art), and
passing by it presently stopped short, and in the hearing of many commanded the magistrates to come before him. He told them their town had
broken their league, harbouring an enemy. The magistrates at first simply
denied the thing, and not knowing what he meant, looked one upon another, when Caesar, turning towards the statue and gathering his brows,

said, "Pray, is not that our enemy who stands there?" They were all in confusion, and had nothing to answer, but he, smiling, much commended the Gauls, as who had been firm to their friends, though in adversity, and ordered that the statue should remain standing as he found it.

Comment

Plutarch was a man much to be admired. He was a moralist, a philosopher as biographer who judged his subjects—leaders all—more on the content of their character than on anything else. He also practiced what he preached: he was gentle in his disposition and generous to those who most needed it. He believed that kindness and beneficence should be extended to all living things, pointedly praising the people of Athens who spared the lives of spent animals by putting them out to pasture rather than putting them to death.

Plutarch's portraits were intended as instruction. Think of them as an ancient form of leadership education, in which learning about leadership is derived from the close study of great men. These, though, are studies of a very special sort, for, as Plutarch made plain, he was less interested in glorious exploits than he was in minor moments, including fleeting expressions and casual jests. In his preface to the life of Alexander, Plutarch writes that it was better to be informed about men's "characters and inclinations than the most famous sieges, the greatest armaments, or the bloodiest battles." Plutarch famously likened himself to a painter of portraits: he, like they, was more focused on the lines and features of the face than on the rest of the body, for it is the face "in which character is seen."

As James Atlas observed in his recent introduction to Lives, one of their most notable features is how, for all the differences, the scenes they depict resemble our own. "Plutarch's evocation of the texture of Greek and Roman life has an utterly familiar feel. The architecture of homes, the contrast between city and country; the rituals of meals: all this information is conveyed with a freshness that makes it seem as if we could be reading about the civic culture of twenty-first-century Rome—or of New York City." Still, Plutarch's work is timeless primarily because he trains his lens on personality rather than on politics, on private dispositions as opposed to public deeds, and on the importance of character in addition to capacity.

"The Comparison of Dion and Brutus" is Plutarch at his best. In the writer's equivalent of what for a painter would be just a few short strokes, we learn what we need to know about the two men, and we learn what we need to know about what Plutarch considered important. To be sure, this clipped comparison of the two men follows lengthier essays on each of them separately, the first on Dion and the second on Marcus Brutus. But "The Comparison of Dion and Brutus" is in its own right a telling tale, sympathetic and judgmental at once.

To those who have read Shakespeare's *Julius Caesar*, Brutus is, of course, a familiar figure. What is not so well known (at least not now) is that Shakespeare drew on Plutarch for his portrayal of Brutus. As depicted by Shakespeare, Brutus is a complicated mix of good and bad, well-intentioned on the one hand but weak on the other. Among his deficits, he is too easily led (or, more precisely, misled) by others. Cassius in particular entices Brutus into a murderous scheme—which constitutes a near copy of the story as told centuries earlier by Plutarch.

Brutus is described by Plutarch, and for that matter by Shakespeare, as being of exemplary character. But Brutus is also deeply flawed. Lesser charges emerge from the comparison between him and Dion, such as Dion's accomplishments being his alone, while Brutus had help from others. And then there was Brutus's final battle, which he badly mismanaged, whereas Dion, in contrast, was "a commander without fault." But more than anything else, Plutarch faults Brutus for slaying Caesar, his friend and mentor as well as his superior: "The greatest thing charged on Brutus is that he, being saved by Caesar's kindness . . . did yet lay violent hands upon his preserver." Then the inevitable comparison: "Nothing like this could be objected against Dion."

Still there are shadings and subtleties that enable Plutarch to portray Brutus as highly conflicted and richly textured. So Plutarch writes of Brutus that even his enemies would admit "he had no other end or aim, from first to last, save only to restore to the Roman people their ancient government." This is exactly the Brutus we find in Shakespeare—a noble man with inspired ends, who accedes nevertheless to dastardly means.

Plutarch is not so much read now as he was even 50 years ago. As pedagogical fashions change (the Western canon is less dominant and less prevalent than it used to be), some of the classics recede. But

Plutarch's descriptions of leaders long gone and his unfailingly sharp assessments of what they did and why seem somehow fresh, and as true now as they were before.

~

NICCOLÒ MACHIAVELLI
1469–1527

Machiavelli was a political theorist—and a political actor. His classic, *The Prince*, written in 1513, mirrors this double life. It is both a reflection on the human condition and an instruction on how to lead given the human condition. Described by Harvard professor Harvey Mansfield as "the most famous book on politics ever written," *The Prince* is ubiquitous and has been so nearly from the time it was written, five centuries ago.

The following selections are from 4 different chapters, out of a total of 26. As will become apparent, to use the word *Machiavellian* simply as a pejorative is as misleading as it is commonplace. For Machiavelli's mind was far more nuanced, more complex, than the charge "Machiavellian" would seem to suggest.

---------- THE PRINCE ----------
1513

XVII
OF CRUELTY AND MERCY, AND WHETHER IT IS BETTER TO BE LOVED THAN FEARED, OR THE CONTRARY

Descending next to the other qualities cited before, I say that each prince should desire to be held merciful and not cruel; nonetheless he should take care not to use this mercy badly. Cesare Borgia was held to be cruel; nonetheless his cruelty restored the Romagna, united it, and reduced it to peace and to faith. If one considers this well, one will see that he was much more merciful than the Florentine people, who so as to escape a name for cruelty, allowed Pistoia to be destroyed. A prince, therefore, so as to keep his subjects united and faithful, should not care about the infamy of cruelty, because with very few examples he will be more merciful than

Machiavelli, Niccolò. *The Prince*. Translated and with an introduction by Harvey Mansfield. Chicago: University of Chicago Press, 1998.

those who for the sake of too much mercy allow disorders to continue, from which come killings or robberies; for these customarily hurt "a whole community."...

Nonetheless, he should be slow to believe and to move, nor should he make himself feared, and he should proceed in a temperate mode with prudence and humanity so that too much confidence does not make him incautious and too much diffidence does not render him intolerable.

From this a dispute arises whether it is better to be loved than feared, or the reverse. The response is that one would want to be both the one and the other; but because it is difficult to put them together, it is much safer to be feared than loved, if one has to lack one of the two. For one can say this generally of men: that they are ungrateful, fickle, pretenders and dissemblers, evaders of danger, eager for gain. While you do them good, they are yours, offering you their blood, property, lives, and children, as I said above, when the need for them is far away; but, when it is close to you, they revolt. And that prince who has founded himself entirely on their words, stripped of other preparation, is ruined; for friendships that are acquired at a price and not with greatness and nobility of spirit are bought, but they are not owned and when the time comes they cannot be spent. And men have less hesitation to offend one who makes himself loved than one who makes himself feared; for love is held by a chain of obligation, which, because men are wicked, is broken at every opportunity for their own utility, but fear is held by a dread of punishment that never forsakes you.

The prince should nonetheless make himself feared in such a mode that if he does not acquire love, he escapes hatred, because being feared and not being hated can go together very well. This he will always do if he abstains from the property of his citizens and his subjects, and from their women; and if he also needs to proceed against someone's life, he must do it when there is suitable justification and manifest cause for it. But above all, he must abstain from the property of others, because men forget the death of a father more quickly than the loss of a patrimony. Furthermore, causes for taking away property are never lacking, and he who begins to live by rapine always finds cause to seize others' property; and, on the contrary, causes for taking life are rarer and disappear more quickly.

But when the prince is with his armies and has a multitude of soldiers under his government, then it is above all necessary not to care about a name for cruelty, because without this name he never holds his army united, or disposed to any action. Among the admirable actions of Hannibal is numbered this one: that when he had a very large army, mixed with infinite kinds of men, and had led it to fight in alien lands, no dissension ever arose in it, neither among themselves nor against the prince, in bad as well as in his good fortune. This could not have arisen from anything other than his inhuman cruelty which, together with his infinite virtues, always made him venerable and terrible in the sight of his soldiers; and without it, his other virtues would not have sufficed to bring about this effect. And the writers, having considered little in this, on the one hand admire this action of his but on the other condemn the principal cause of it. . . .

I conclude, then, returning to being feared and loved, that since men love at their convenience and fear at the convenience of the prince, a wise prince should found himself on what is his, not on what is someone else's; he should only contrive to avoid hatred, as was said.

XIX
OF AVOIDING CONTEMPT AND HATRED

But because I have spoken of the most important of the qualities mentioned above, I want to discourse on the others briefly under this generality, that the prince, as was said above in part, should think how to avoid those things that make him hateful and contemptible. When he avoids them, he will have done his part and will find no danger in his other infamies. What makes him hated above all, as I said, is to be rapacious and a usurper of the property and the women of his subjects. From these he must abstain, and whenever one does not take away either property or honor from the generality of men, they live content and one has only to combat the ambition of the few which may be checked in many modes and with ease. What makes him contemptible is to be held variable, light, effeminate, pusillanimous, irresolute, from which a prince should guard himself as from a shoal. He should contrive that greatness, spiritedness, gravity, and strength are recognized in his actions, and he should insist that his judgments in the private concerns of his subjects be irrevocable. And he should maintain such an opinion of himself that no one thinks either of deceiving him or getting around him.

The prince who gives this opinion of himself is highly reputed, and against whoever is reputed it is difficult to conspire, difficult to mount an attack, provided it is understood that he is excellent and revered by his own subjects. For a prince should have two fears: one within, on account of his subjects; the other outside, on account of external powers. From the latter one is defended with good arms and good friends; and if one has good arms, one will always have good friends. And things inside will always remain steady, if things outside are steady, unless indeed they are disturbed by a conspiracy; and even if things outside are in motion, provided he has ordered and lived as I said, as long as he does not forsake himself he will always withstand every thrust, as I said Nabis the Spartan did. But, as to subjects, when things outside are not moving, one has to fear that they may be conspiring secretly. From this the prince may secure himself sufficiently if he avoids being hated or despised and keeps the people satisfied with him; this is necessary to achieve, as was said above at length. And one of the most powerful remedies that a prince has against conspiracies is not to be hated by the people generally. For whoever conspires always believes he will satisfy the people with the death of the prince, but when he believes he will offend them, he does not get up the spirit to adopt such a course, because the difficulties on the side of the conspirators are infinite. And one sees from experience that there have been many conspiracies, but few have had a good end. For whoever conspires cannot be alone, but he cannot find company except from those he believes to be malcontents; and as soon as you disclose your intent to a malcontent, you give him the matter with which to become content, because manifestly he can hope for every advantage from it. So, seeing sure gain on this side, and on the other, dubious gain full of danger, he must indeed either be a rare friend, or an altogether obstinate enemy of the prince, to observe his faith with you. And to reduce this to brief terms, I say that on the part of the conspirator there is nothing but fear, jealousy, and the anticipation of terrifying punishment; but on the part of the prince there is the majesty of the principality, the laws, the protection of friends and of the state which defend him, so that when popular good will is added to all these things, it is impossible that anyone should be so rash as to conspire. . . .

XXI
What a Prince Should Do to Be Held in Esteem

Nothing makes a prince so much esteemed as to carry on great enterprises and to give rare examples of himself. . . .

. . . A prince should also show himself a lover of the virtues, giving recognition to virtuous men, and he should honor those who are excellent in an art. Next, he should inspire his citizens to follow their pursuits quietly, in trade and in agriculture and in every other pursuit of men, so that one person does not fear to adorn his possessions for fear that they be taken away from him, and another to open up a trade for fear of taxes. But he should prepare rewards for whoever wants to do these things, and for anyone who thinks up any way of expanding his city or his state. Besides this, he should at suitable times of the year keep the people occupied with festivals and spectacles. And because every city is divided into guilds or into clans, he should take account of those communities, meet with them sometimes, and make himself an example of humanity and munificence, always holding firm the majesty of his dignity nonetheless, because he can never want this to be lacking in anything.

XXIII
In What Mode Flatterers Are to Be Avoided

I do not want to leave out an important point and an error from which princes defend themselves with difficulty, unless they are very prudent or make good choices. And these are the flatterers of whom courts are full; for men take such pleasure in their own affairs and so deceive themselves there that they defend themselves with difficulty from this plague, and in trying to defend oneself from it one risks the danger of becoming contemptible. For there is no other way to guard oneself from flattery unless men understand that they do not offend you in telling you the truth; but when everyone can tell you the truth, they lack reverence for you. Therefore, a prudent prince must hold to a third mode, choosing wise men in his state; and only to these should he give freedom to speak the truth to him, and of those things only that he asks about and nothing else. But he should ask them about everything and listen to their opinions; then he should decide by himself, in his own mode; and with these councils and with each member of them he should behave in such a mode that everyone knows that the more freely he speaks, the more he will be accepted. Aside from these, he should not want to hear anyone; he should move directly to the thing that was decided and be obstinate in his decisions. Whoever does otherwise either falls headlong because of flatterers or changes often because of the variability of views, from which a low estimation of him arises. . . .

A prince, therefore, should always take counsel, but when he wants, and not when others want it; on the contrary, he should discourage everyone from counseling him about anything unless he asks it of them. But he should be a very broad questioner, and then, in regard to the things he asked about, a patient listener to the truth; indeed, he should become upset when he learns that anyone has any hesitation to speak it to him. And since many esteem that any prince who establishes an opinion of himself as prudent is so considered not because of his nature but because of the good counsel he has around him, without doubt they are deceived. For this is a general rule that never fails: that a prince who is not wise by himself cannot be counseled well, unless indeed by chance he should submit himself to one alone to govern him in everything, who is a very prudent man. In this case he could well be, but it would not last long because that governor would in a short time take away his state. But by taking counsel from more than one, a prince who is not wise will never have united counsel, nor know how to correct them or understand them. And they cannot be found otherwise, because men will always turn out bad for you unless they have been made good by a necessity. So one concludes that good counsel, from wherever it comes, must arise from the prudence of the prince, and not the prudence of the prince from good counsel.

Comment

One of Machiavelli's biographers, Albert Russell Ascoli, referred to *The Prince* as "a scandal that Western political thought and practice has been gazing at in horror and in fascination since its first publication." Scandal or no, *The Prince* is remarkable, both for its protracted pertinence and popularity and for its abiding insights and influence. To this day,

Machiavelli's manifesto remains assigned reading in schools all over the world, and sells well of itself, to be discovered and dissected by different people in different places. This inevitably raises the question: what is it about *The Prince* that accounts for its endurance? After all, it was written hundreds of years ago, and in a setting remote from our own, Florentine Italy. How then to explain its attraction through the ages and its appeal even now?

The great leadership literature is two things simultaneously: it is particular, and it is universal. By telling transcendent truths, it speaks to the situation immediately at hand—and extends beyond it. *The Prince* is a perfect example of this duality. It is a subjective reflection, based on Machiavelli's experience as a politician and diplomat who fell out of favor to the point of being imprisoned and, briefly, tortured. At the same time, it is an objective consideration of governance, and of the nature of the human condition.

Like some of his esteemed predecessors and many of his esteemed successors, Machiavelli believed that rulers require education of a special sort and training of a certain kind. So think of *The Prince* as a primer, a how-to book, if you will, in particular for Lorenzo de'Medici, who became duke of Urbino in 1516. The immediate context was conflict, to the point of murder and mayhem. Assuming the past and present as prologue, then, Machiavelli imagined the new prince as being in need of a manual on how to lead in a time of continuing crisis.

The Prince is without guile. It is direct and utterly pragmatic, and it assumes that the prince—any prince, for that matter—wants to secure three things: first, the preservation of power, specifically, his own; second, the preservation of his principality; and third, the preservation of peace, or at least, order. Everything in *The Prince* is written with these three ends in mind. It is the means to these ends that have proved so controversial for so long, and that have resulted in the erroneous impression that Machiavelli's primary purpose was to espouse a heavy hand.

It is true that *The Prince* was the first major treatise on governance that deliberately distanced itself from a moral code of any kind. God is absent from Machiavelli, as is the rule of law, as is any other sort of moral compass. Machiavelli's political universe is grounded in the here and now—it is in every aspect pragmatic. It is, further, self-contained; immune to outside influence, historical or contemporaneous; and concerned above all with the exercise of power. The prince, then, the ruler, the governor, the leader, is responsible to himself and to his people, but not to a higher power of any sort.

Note the contrast to the conventional wisdom: Machiavelli is sensitive not only to the needs and wants of the leader, but to those of his followers as well. Repeatedly he instructs the prince to take his subjects into account, recommending that he treat them well unless he has no choice but to do otherwise. Chapter XXI, "What a Prince Should Do to Be Held in Esteem," speaks to this very point. A prince should not only show himself to be a lover of virtues, but recognize virtue in others. He should enable his subjects to "follow their pursuits quietly," and at "suitable times of the year" keep them "occupied with festivals and spectacles." In addition, while "holding firm the majesty of his dignity," the prince should "make himself an example of humanity and munificence." In other words, Machiavelli's perfect prince understands that it is in his own interest to give as well as to take.

Still, when writing about Machiavelli, there's no avoiding the unavoidable: the prince should do what he must, from being good to being bad, even to the point, if necessary, of being brutal. In Chapter XV (not included here), Machiavelli maintained that the prince must "learn to be able not to be good, and to use this and not use it according to necessity." However, the key phrase here is "according to necessity." Machiavelli was careful about cruelty; he did not recommend its gratuitous use. Rather, cruelty was to be employed sparingly—and strategically. It was to be employed only when it was essential for the purposes of, again, preserving the prince's personal power, preserving the principality, and/or preserving the peace. Moreover, Machiavelli understood full well the costs to leaders of harming followers. As he wrote elsewhere in *The Prince*, if injuries are deemed necessary, they should be done "all at a stroke." Why? Because injuries done at a stroke will "taste less" and therefore offend less. Benefits, on the other hand, should be doled out "little by little" Why? So that they, in turn, "may be tasted better." This careful and crafty calculation—*this* is Machiavellian!

∽

THOMAS HOBBES
1588–1679

Hobbes is the author of one of the most important and influential of all books in English, *Leviathan*. He is of special interest to those who are as concerned with followership as with leadership, for he was among the first to direct his attention not only to the rights and privileges of the high and mighty, but also to the rights—or, more precisely put, to a single right—of ordinary people, that is, the right to life.

Hobbes concluded that in order to stay safe and secure, it is in our interest—in our self-interest—to submit to the state, to the Leviathan of the title, in the form of an absolute ruler. While such an authoritarian, even totalitarian, leader might seem at odds with Hobbes's concern for the common man, it does nevertheless follow from his bleak view of the human condition. For it was, after all, Hobbes who famously declared that life was "solitary, poor, nasty, brutish, and short." How then to preserve it, and preserve ourselves, absent a protector, however fearsome and fierce?

──── LEVIATHAN ────
1651

OF THE NATURAL CONDITION OF MANKIND AS CONCERNING THEIR FELICITY AND MISERY

Nature hath made men so equal in the faculties of body and mind as that, though there be found one man sometimes manifestly stronger in body or of quicker mind than another, yet when all is reckoned together the difference between man and man is not so considerable as that one man can thereupon claim to himself any benefit to which another may not pretend as well as he. For as to the strength of body, the weakest has strength enough to kill the strongest, either by secret machination or by confederacy with others that are in the same danger with himself.

And as to the faculties of the mind, setting aside the arts grounded upon words, and especially that skill of proceeding upon general and infallible rules, called science, which very few have and but in few things, as being not a native faculty born with us, nor attained, as prudence, while we look after somewhat else, I find yet a greater equality amongst men than that of strength. For prudence is but experience, which equal time equally bestows on all men in those things they equally apply themselves unto. That which may perhaps make such equality incredible is but a vain conceit of one's own wisdom, which almost all men think they have in a greater degree than the vulgar; that is, than all men but themselves, and a few others, whom by fame, or for concurring with themselves, they approve. For such is the nature of men that howsoever they may acknowledge many others to be more witty, or more eloquent or more learned, yet they will hardly believe there be many so wise as themselves; for they see their own wit at hand, and other men's at a distance. But this proveth rather that men are in that point equal, than unequal. For there is not ordinarily a greater sign of the equal distribution of anything than that every man is contented with his share.

From this equality of ability ariseth equality of hope in the attaining of our ends. And therefore if any two men desire the same thing, which nevertheless they cannot both enjoy, they become enemies; and in the way to their end (which is principally their own conservation, and sometimes their delectation only) endeavour to destroy or subdue one another. And from hence it comes to pass that where an invader hath no more to fear than another man's single power, if one plant, sow, build, or possess a convenient seat, others may probably be expected to come prepared with forces united to dispossess and deprive him, not only of the fruit of his labour, but also of his life or liberty. And the invader again is in the like danger of another.

And from this diffidence of one another, there is no way for any man to secure himself so reasonable as anticipation; that is, by force, or wiles, to master the persons of all men he can so long till he see no other power great enough to endanger him: and this is no more than his own conservation requireth, and is generally allowed. Also, because there be some that, taking pleasure in contemplating their own power in the acts of conquest, which they pursue farther than their security requires, if others, that otherwise would be glad to be at ease within modest bounds, should not by invasion increase their power, they would not be able, long time, by standing only on their defence, to subsist. And by consequence, such augmentation of dominion over men being necessary to a man's conservation, it ought to be allowed him.

Again, men have no pleasure (but on the contrary a great deal of grief) in keeping company where there is no power able to overawe them all. For every man looketh that his companion should value him at the same rate he sets upon himself, and upon all signs of contempt or undervaluing naturally endeavours, as far as he dares (which amongst them that have no common power to keep them in quiet is far enough to make them destroy each other), to extort a greater value from his contemners, by damage; and from others, by the example. So that in the nature of man, we find three principal causes of quarrel. First, competition; secondly, diffidence; thirdly, glory. The first maketh men invade for gain; the second, for safety; and the third, for reputation. The first use violence, to make themselves masters of other men's persons, wives, children, and cattle; the second, to defend them; the third, for trifles, as a word, a smile, a different opinion, and any other sign of undervalue, either direct in their persons or by reflection in their kindred, their friends, their nation, their profession, or their name. Hereby it is manifest that during the time men live without a common power to keep them all in awe, they are in that condition which is called war; and such a war as is of every man against every man. For war consisteth not in battle only, or the act of fighting, but in a tract of time, wherein the will to contend by battle is sufficiently known: and therefore the notion of time is to be considered in the nature of war, as it is in the nature of weather. For as the nature of foul weather lieth not in a shower or two of rain, but in an inclination thereto of many days together: so the nature of war consisteth not in actual fighting, but in the known disposition thereto during all the time there is no assurance to the contrary. All other time is peace.

Whatsoever therefore is consequent to a time of war, where every man is enemy to every man, the same [is] consequent to the time wherein men live without other security than what their own strength and their own invention shall furnish them withal. In such condition there is no place for industry, because the fruit thereof is uncertain: and consequently no culture of the earth; no navigation, nor use of the commodities that may be imported by sea; no commodious building; no instruments of moving and removing such things as require much force; no knowledge of the face of the earth; no account of time; no arts; no letters; no society; and which is worst of all, continual fear, and danger of violent death; and the life of man, solitary, poor, nasty, brutish, and short.

It may seem strange to some man that has not well weighed these things that Nature should thus dissociate and render men apt to invade and destroy one another: and he may therefore, not trusting to this inference, made from the passions, desire perhaps to have the same confirmed by experience. Let him therefore consider with himself: when taking a journey, he arms himself and seeks to go well accompanied; when going to sleep, he locks his doors; when even in his house he locks his chests; and this when he knows there be laws and public officers, armed, to revenge all injuries shall be done him; what opinion he has of his fellow subjects, when he rides armed; of his fellow citizens, when he locks his doors; and of his children, and servants, when he locks his chests. Does he not there as much accuse mankind by his actions as I do by my words? But neither of us accuse man's nature in it. The desires, and other passions of man, are in themselves no sin. No more are the actions that proceed from those passions till they know a law that forbids them; which till laws be made they cannot know, nor can any law be made till they have agreed upon the person that shall make it.

It may peradventure be thought there was never such a time nor condition of war as this; and I believe it was never generally so, over all the world: but there are many places where they live so now. For the savage people in many places of America, except the government of small families, the concord whereof dependeth on natural lust, have no government at all, and live at this day in that brutish manner, as I said before. Howsoever, it may be perceived what manner of life there would be, where there were no common power to fear, by the manner of life which men that have formerly lived under a peaceful government use to degenerate into a civil war. But though there had never been any time wherein particular men were in a condition of war one against another, yet in all times kings and persons of sovereign authority, because of their independency, are in continual jealousies, and in the state and posture of gladiators, having their weapons pointing, and their eyes fixed on one another; that is, their forts, garrisons, and guns upon the frontiers of their kingdoms, and continual spies upon their neighbours, which is a posture of war. But because they uphold thereby the industry of their subjects, there does not follow from it that misery which accompanies the liberty of particular men.

To this war of every man against every man, this also is consequent; that nothing can be unjust. The notions of right and wrong, justice and injustice, have there no place. Where there is no common power, there is no law; where no law, no injustice. Force and fraud are in war the two cardinal virtues. Justice and injustice are none of the faculties neither of the body nor mind. If they were, they might be in a man that were alone in the world, as well as his senses and passions. They are qualities that relate to men in society, not in solitude. It is consequent also to the same condition that there be no propriety, no dominion, no mine and thine distinct; but only that to be every man's that he can get, and for so long as he can keep it. And thus much for the ill condition which man by mere nature is actually placed in; though with a possibility to come out of it, consisting partly in the passions, partly in his reason.

The passions that incline men to peace are: fear of death; desire of such things as are necessary to commodious living; and a hope by their industry to obtain them. And reason suggesteth convenient articles of peace upon which men may be drawn to agreement. These articles are they which otherwise are called the laws of nature, whereof I shall speak more particularly in the two following chapters.

Comment

In important ways, Machiavelli and Hobbes were of a piece. Both developed their political philosophies during a time of turmoil (Hobbes amidst the civil strife in, among other countries, mid-seventeenth-century England). Both were concerned with the here and now, not with the Kingdom of Heaven. Both were pragmatists rather than idealists, less interested than most of their counterparts in developing character and virtue and more interested than they in effective governance. And finally, both were preoccupied with preservation, in the first case primarily with the preservation of power, and in the second primarily with the preservation of life.

However, for all his pathbreaking work, Machiavelli came out of a tradition in which the constant concern was with the person in power.

Hobbes, in contrast, broke the mold. His concern was as much with the led as with the leader, and in particular with everyone's right to life. This shift constituted a sea change. Here is twentieth-century philosopher Leo Strauss on precisely this point: "The fundamental change from an orientation by natural duties to an orientation by natural rights finds its clearest and most telling expression in the teaching of Hobbes, who squarely made an unconditional natural right [the right to life] the basis of all natural duties, the duties being therefore only conditional."

Hobbes was nearly Darwinian in his approach. That is, as did Darwin centuries later, Hobbes relied on his powers of observation. And, as did Darwin centuries later, Hobbes studied his subject, the human animal, in what he at least considered to be the state of nature. Of course, Darwin was a scientist and Hobbes was not. So Hobbes's findings were based in the main on what he witnessed in his own time and place—which was not pretty. It was a time of war, both religious and civil, that led to defeat for the English monarchy and triumph for Oliver Cromwell, Lord Protector of the new "commonwealth."

What Hobbes deduced from the hard times was that man was not to be trusted, ever. He was by nature (in the state of nature) fearful and rapacious, selfish and dangerous, and hell-bent on his own safety and security to the exclusion of nearly everyone else. Moreover, man's self-interest was understandable, even justifiable, for in a state of nature, no one had much of an advantage over anyone else. Hobbes noted that "the weakest has strength enough to kill the strongest, either by secret machination or by confederacy with others." Given this, given that men by nature are nearly equal and are disposed to the lawless, limitless competition that results, ineluctably, in strife and even in war, the key question for Hobbes was: what is the optimum form of government for the maximum number of people?

In the twenty-first century, Hobbes's response to the question seems counterintuitive—and disappointing. For Hobbes claimed that it was in our own best interest to surrender autonomy to autocracy. In his view, only leaders who were autocrats had the power and authority to save us from ourselves, from our own natural, dreadful instincts and impulses. "Where there is no common power, there is no law: where no law, no injustice. Force and fraud are in war the two cardinal virtues."

Hobbes's autocrat is not, however, imposed from above. Rather, in keeping with his fledgling ideas on the social contract, free and equal persons should willingly and freely give absolute power to an absolute sovereign. What they get in return is protection, the stability and certainty that they require to lead a life that is "commodious" and occasionally even "delightful."

Therefore, although Hobbes was arguing for authoritarianism, as Blair Worden points out, he "nonetheless broke with the premises on which the run of seventeenth century authoritarian thought rested. His location of the origins of sovereignty in the people's consent was but one aspect of his rejection of the halo of power." In fact, Hobbes's absolute ruler was expected to meet a high standard: to rule reasonably, not capriciously. But if he did not, if the leader did turn tyrant, the led had no recourse. In the interest of their own protection, they had no choice but to submit.

The word *Hobbesian* has become part of the English language. To use it as an adjective is to suggest that life is as Hobbes had it—solitary, poor, nasty, and brutish, if now not particularly short. Lest you think this view extreme, think again. For as it happens, this bleak view of the human condition is by no means confined to the seventeenth century, any more than it is to the England that was Hobbes's home.

～

JOHN LOCKE
1632–1704

Thomas Hobbes and John Locke have long been compared—and they do in fact concur on several particulars. But it is the differences between them that stand out. Locke was more concerned than was Hobbes with natural law, and less concerned than was Hobbes with natural rights. Hobbes was fixed on the right to life, while Locke expanded the notion of rights to include liberty and, nearly as notably, property. On this point there is in any case consensus: Locke's contribution constituted so great a departure from his great predecessor(s) that it amounted to no less than a sea change in political theory.

Locke's logic concerning the right to hold private property; his conception of social contract theory, which claims that governments derive their legitimacy from the consent of the governed; and his insistence that this consent be applied to the leader as well as to the led—all were breakthroughs. In fact, Locke's insistence that if the leader does not sufficiently satisfy the led, he may be recalled, by force if necessary, puts him finally completely at odds with Hobbes, who, except in matters of life and death, would have us surrender to an absolute authority with absolute power.

The following three selections are from Locke's *Second Treatise of Government*. The first is an excerpt on property, the next is on the separation of powers, and the last is on different kinds of leaders—"paternal, political, and despotical."

SECOND TREATISE OF GOVERNMENT
1690

Sec. 27. Though the earth, and all inferior creatures, be common to all men, yet every man has a property in his own person: this no body has any right to but himself. The labour of his body, and the work of his hands, we may say, are properly his. Whatsoever then he removes out of the state that nature hath provided, and left it in, he hath mixed his labour with, and joined to it something that is his own, and thereby makes it his property. It being by him removed from the common state nature hath placed it in, it hath by this labour something annexed to it, that excludes the common right of other men: for this labour being the unquestionable property of the labourer, no man but he can have a right to what that is once joined to, at least where there is enough, and as good, left in common for others.

Sec. 28. He that is nourished by the acorns he picked up under an oak, or the apples he gathered from the trees in the wood, has certainly appropriated them to himself. No body can deny but the nourishment is his. I ask then, when did they begin to be his? when he digested? or when he ate? or when he boiled? or when he brought them home? or when he picked them up? and it is plain, if the first gathering made them not his, nothing else could. That labour put a distinction between them and common: that added something to them more than nature, the common mother of all, had done; and so they became his private right. And will any one say, he had no right to those acorns or apples, he thus appropriated, because he had not the consent of all mankind to make them his? Was it a robbery thus to assume to himself what belonged to all in common? If such a consent as that was necessary, man had starved, notwithstanding the plenty God had given him. We see in commons, which remain so by compact, that it is the taking any part of what is common, and removing it out of the state nature leaves it in, which begins the property; without which the common is of no use. And the taking of this or that part, does not depend on the express consent of all the commoners. Thus the grass my horse has bit; the turfs my servant has cut; and the ore I have digged in any place, where I have a right to them in common with others, become my property, without the assignation or consent of any body. The labour that was mine, removing them out of that common state they were in, hath fixed my property in them.

Sec. 29. By making an explicit consent of every commoner, necessary to any one's appropriating to himself any part of what is given in common, children or servants could not cut the meat, which their father or master had provided for them in common, without assigning to every one his peculiar part. Though the water running in the fountain be every one's, yet who can doubt, but that in the pitcher is his only who drew it out? His labour hath taken it out of the hands of nature, where it was common, and belonged equally to all her children, and hath thereby appropriated it to himself. . . .

Sec. 149. Though in a constituted common-wealth, standing upon its own basis, and acting according to its own nature, that is, acting for the preservation of the community, there can be but one supreme power, which is the legislative, to which all the rest are and must be subordinate, yet the legislative being only a fiduciary power to act for certain ends, there remains still in the people a supreme power to remove or alter the legislative, when they find the legislative act contrary to the trust reposed in them: for all power given with trust for the attaining an end, being limited by that end, whenever that end is manifestly neglected, or opposed, the trust must necessarily be forfeited, and the power devolve into the hands of those that gave it, who may place it anew where they shall think best for their safety and security. And thus the community perpetually retains a supreme power of saving themselves from the attempts and designs of any body, even of their legislators, whenever they shall be so foolish, or so wicked, as to lay and carry on designs against the liberties and properties of the subject: for no man or society of men, having a power to deliver up their preservation, or consequently the means of it, to the absolute will and arbitrary dominion of another; when ever any one shall go about to bring them into such a slavish condition, they will always have a right to preserve, what they have not a power to part with; and to rid themselves of those, who invade this fundamental, sacred, and unalterable law of self-preservation, for which they entered into society. And thus the community may be said in this respect to be always the supreme power, but not as considered under any form of government, because this power of the people can never take place till the government be dissolved. . . .

Sec. 151. In some commonwealths, where the legislative is not always in being, and the executive is vested in a single person, who has also a share in the legislative; there that single person in a very tolerable sense may also be called supreme: not that he has in himself all the supreme power, which is that of law-making; but because he has in him the supreme execution, from whom all inferior magistrates derive all their several subordinate powers, or at least the greatest part of them: having also no legislative superior to him, there being no law to be made without his consent, which cannot be expected should ever subject him to the other part of the legislative, he is properly enough in this sense supreme. But yet it is to be observed, that tho' oaths of allegiance and fealty are taken to him, it is not to him as supreme legislator, but as supreme executor of the law, made by a joint power of him with others; allegiance being nothing but an obedience according to law, which when he violates, he has no right to obedience, nor can claim it otherwise than as the public person vested with the power of the law, and so is to be considered as the image, phantom, or representative of the common-wealth, acted by the will of the society, declared in its laws; and thus he has no will, no power, but that of the law. But when he quits this representation, this public will, and acts by his own private will, he degrades himself, and is but a single private person without power, and without will, that has any right to obedience; the members owing no obedience but to the public will of the society.

Sec. 152. The executive power, placed any where but in a person that has also a share in the legislative, is visibly subordinate and accountable to it, and may be at pleasure changed and displaced; so that it is not the supreme executive power, that is exempt from subordination, but the supreme executive power vested in one, who having a share in the legislative, has no distinct superior legislative to be subordinate and accountable to, farther than he himself shall join and consent; so that he is no more subordinate than he himself shall think fit, which one may certainly conclude will be but very little. . . .

Sec. 169. THOUGH I have had occasion to speak of these separately before, yet the great mistakes of late about government, having, as I suppose, arisen from confounding these distinct powers one with another, it may not, perhaps, be amiss to consider them here together.

Sec. 170. First, then, Paternal or parental power is nothing but that which parents have over their children, to govern them for the children's good, till they come to the use of reason, or a state of knowledge, wherein they may be supposed capable to understand that rule, whether it be the law of nature, or the municipal law of their country, they are to govern themselves by: capable, I say, to know it, as well as several others, who live as freemen under that law. The affection and tenderness which God hath planted in the breast of parents towards their children, makes it evident, that this is not intended to be a severe arbitrary government, but only for the help, instruction, and preservation of their offspring. But happen it as it will, there is, as I have proved, no reason why it should be thought to extend to life and death, at any time, over their children, more than over any body else; neither can there be any pretence why this parental power should keep the child, when grown to a man, in subjection to the will of his parents, any farther than having received life and education from his parents, obliges him to respect, honour, gratitude, assistance and support, all his life, to both father and mother. And thus, 'tis true, the paternal is a

natural government, but not at all extending itself to the ends and juris-
dictions of that which is political. The power of the father doth not reach at
all to the property of the child, which is only in his own disposing.

Sec. 171. Secondly, Political power is that power, which every man
having in the state of nature, has given up into the hands of the society,
and therein to the governors, whom the society hath set over itself, with
this express or tacit trust, that it shall be employed for their good, and the
preservation of their property: now this power, which every man has in
the state of nature, and which he parts with to the society in all such cases
where the society can secure him, is to use such means, for the preserving of his own property, as he thinks good, and nature allows him; and to
punish the breach of the law of nature in others, so as (according to the
best of his reason) may most conduce to the preservation of himself, and
the rest of mankind. So that the end and measure of this power, when in
every man's hands in the state of nature, being the preservation of all of
his society, that is, all mankind in general, it can have no other end or
measure, when in the hands of the magistrate, but to preserve the members of that society in their lives, liberties, and possessions; and so cannot be an absolute, arbitrary power over their lives and fortunes, which are
as much as possible to be preserved; but a power to make laws, and
annex such penalties to them, as may tend to the preservation of the
whole, by cutting off those parts, and those only, which are so corrupt, that
they threaten the sound and healthy, without which no severity is lawful.
And this power has its original only from compact and agreement, and the
mutual consent of those who make up the community.

Sec. 172. Thirdly, Despotical power is an absolute, arbitrary power one
man has over another, to take away his life, whenever he pleases. This is a
power, which neither nature gives, for it has made no such distinction
between one man and another; nor compact can convey: for man not
having such an arbitrary power over his own life, cannot give another man
such a power over it; but it is the effect only of forfeiture, which the aggressor makes of his own life, when he puts himself into the state of war
with another: for having quitted reason, which God hath given to be the
rule betwixt man and man, and the common bond whereby human kind
is united into one fellowship and society; and having renounced the way
of peace which that teaches, and made use of the force of war, to compass

his unjust ends upon another, where he has no right; and so revolting from his own kind to that of beasts, by making force, which is their's, to be his rule of right, he renders himself liable to be destroyed by the injured person, and the rest of mankind, that will join with him in the execution of justice, as any other wild beast, or noxious brute, with whom mankind can have neither society nor security. . . .

Sec. 173. Nature gives the first of these, viz. paternal power to parents for the benefit of their children during their minority, to supply their want of ability, and understanding how to manage their property. (By property I must be understood here, as in other places, to mean that property which men have in their persons as well as goods.)

Voluntary agreement gives the second, viz. political power to governors for the benefit of their subjects, to secure them in the possession and use of their properties. And forfeiture gives the third despotical power to lords for their own benefit, over those who are stripped of all property.

Sec. 174. He, that shall consider the distinct rise and extent, and the different ends of these several powers, will plainly see, that paternal power comes as far short of that of the magistrate, as despotical exceeds it; and that absolute dominion, however placed, is so far from being one kind of civil society, that it is as inconsistent with it, as slavery is with property. Paternal power is only where minority makes the child incapable to manage his property; political, where men have property in their own disposal; and despotical, over such as have no property at all.

Comment

To point to property, as John Locke did, may seem a small thing. It is, after all, merely a material matter, a matter of the pocketbook. However, to consider Locke on property is to come to see him for what he was: a political philosopher supremely important to the development of modern democracy—and of capitalism.

Locke did more than argue that man had a natural right to appropriate what he could cultivate (although this claim would, by itself, be revolutionary). By introducing money into the discussion, he provided a means for people to accrue more, theoretically much more, than what they could consume on their own. To quote C. B. Macpherson, a preeminent (though not undisputed) expert on Locke, "The introduction of money by tacit consent has removed the previous natural limitations of rightful appropriation [earlier set by Locke himself], and in so doing has invalidated the natural provision that everyone should have [only] as much as he could make use of."

Locke's decision to distinguish between the right to own only as much as will not spoil, and the right to own still more, was due, in part, to events on the American continent. On the one hand, the English generally believed that Native Americans should have only what they needed to sustain themselves; but on the other hand, they believed that English colonists, in spite of their not living or laboring on the land, were entitled to own more. This distinction reflected the imperial mindset for which England later became famous (or infamous); additionally, it foreshadowed the rise of capitalism and the political and economic inequities that inevitably ensue. As Locke himself observed on the earlier use of gold and silver as currency, "Men have agreed to disproportionate and unequal Possession of the Earth."

What exactly Locke thought should be the relationship between labor and property (ownership) remains in dispute. What is not in dispute is that Locke believed that even the lowliest of men was entitled to reap what he sowed, which among other things implied an entirely new, much more equitable relationship between leaders and followers. Locke was not, of course, oblivious to the dangers of disorder, dangers that had shaped the thinking of philosopher predecessors such as Thomas Hobbes. So he assumed, as did they, that the individual had to be subordinate to the collective. But whereas this assumption seemed to constrain the thinking of others, it freed Locke to insist that the leader should be like the led: he should have imposed on him some limits.

First, Locke argued that the social contract—the contract between the governors and the governed—should preserve as much individual freedom as was possible. Second, Locke proposed that a social contract be drawn up between equals or, better, equals of sorts. At a minimum, leaders, people in positions of authority, were to be limited in the power they were permitted to exercise. Third, Locke insisted on decision making by majority rule, a sea change from decision making either by a single leader or by an all-powerful political elite. Fourth, though he was not alone in developing the doctrine of the separation of powers, the fact that Locke made a case for "balancing the power of government by placing several parts of it in different hands" made him the right man for the right time, particularly in what would become, a century later, the United States. Finally, Locke claimed the ultimate constraint—the right of those *without* power or authority to unseat those *with* it, by force if necessary.

As Thomas Peardon has pointed out, nowhere was Locke more widely read and greatly appreciated than on the American continent. His books were widely circulated in the colonies, New England clergy drew on them for Sunday sermons, and they provided continuing grist for the revolutionary mill. In fact, "so close is the Declaration of Independence to Locke in form, phraseology, and content, that Jefferson was accused of copying the *Second Treatise*."

Ultimately John Locke got what he deserved: a place in the pantheon of those who forever, and for the better, changed relations between leaders and led.

⌒

THOMAS CARLYLE
1795–1881

HERBERT SPENCER
1830–1903

WILLIAM JAMES
1842–1910

LEO TOLSTOY
1828–1910

Each of these four writers weighed in on the knottiest of all leadership questions: does the man (or woman) make history, or does history make the man? The so-called great man in history debate has been around, it seems, forever. But it vaulted to permanent prominence with a book by the English "prophet" Thomas Carlyle, titled *On Heroes, Hero-Worship, and the Heroic in History*. Carlyle's position on this issue was extreme. He claimed that history was no more and no less than—indeed, was tantamount to—the history of "the Great Men who have worked here." Herbert Spencer, in turn, the English philosopher who was closely associated with Charles Darwin's theory of evolution, took strong exception to Carlyle's view. Spencer thought that history was altogether independent of the actions of individual actors, no matter how clever or competent those actors might be. In fact, in *The Study of Sociology*, Spencer went so far as to dismiss, even to denigrate those who thought that men made a difference, insisting instead that the great man theory was "utterly incoherent." It was left to the American philosopher William James to play diplomat. Although he criticized Spencer for being an absolutist, he was not unsympathetic to his position. At the least, in "Great Men and Their Environment," James admitted, "not every 'man' fits every 'hour.'" Finally, there is Leo Tolstoy, who beat his own path to the door of the discussion by telling an epic tale, *War and Peace*, in which his position on the great man was made abundantly clear.

THOMAS CARLYLE
ON HEROES, HERO-WORSHIP, AND THE HEROIC IN HISTORY
1841

We have undertaken to discourse here for a little on Great Men, their manner of appearance in our world's business, how they have shaped themselves in the world's history, what ideas men formed of them, what work they did;—on Heroes, namely, and on their reception and performance; what I call Hero-worship and the Heroic in human affairs. Too evidently this is a large topic; deserving quite other treatment than we can expect to give it at present. A large topic; indeed, an illimitable one; wide as Universal History itself. For, as I take it, Universal History, the history of what man has accomplished in this world, is at bottom the History of the Great Men who have worked here. They were the leaders of men, these great ones; the modellers, patterns, and in a wide sense creators, of whatsoever the general mass of men contrived to do or to attain; all things that we see standing accomplished in the world are properly the outer material result, the practical realisation and embodiment, of Thoughts that dwelt in the Great Men sent into the world: the soul of the whole world's history, it may justly be considered, were the history of these. Too clearly it is a topic we shall do no justice to in this place!

One comfort is, that Great Men, taken up in any way, are profitable company. We cannot look however imperfectly, upon a great man, without gaining something by him. He is the living light-fountain, which it is good and pleasant to be near. The light which enlightens, which has enlightened the darkness of the world: and this not as a kindled lamp only, but rather as a natural luminary shining by the gift of Heaven; a flowing light-fountain, as I say, of native original insight, of manhood and heroic nobleness;—in whose radiance all souls feel that it is well with them. On any terms whatsoever, you will not grudge to wander in such neighbourhood for a while. These Six classes of Heroes, chosen out of widely distant countries and epochs, and in mere external figure differing altogether, ought, if we look faithfully at them to illustrate several things for us. Could we see *them* well, we should get some glimpses into the very marrow of the world's history. How happy, could I but, in any measure, in such times as these, make manifest to you the meanings of Heroism; the divine relation (for I may well call it such) which in all times unites a Great Man to other men; and thus, as it were, not exhaust my subject, but so much as break ground on it! At all events, I must make the attempt.

HERBERT SPENCER
———— THE STUDY OF SOCIOLOGY ————
1873

The great-man-theory of History finds everywhere a ready prepared conception—is, indeed, but the definite expression of that which is latent in the thoughts of the savage, tacitly asserted in all early traditions, and taught to every child by multitudinous illustrations. The glad acceptance it meets with has sundry more special causes. There is, first, this universal of personalities, which, active in the aboriginal man, dominates still—a love seen in the urchin who asks you to tell him a story, somebody's adventures; a love gratified in adults by police-reports, court-news, divorce-cases, accounts of accidents, and lists of births, marriages, and deaths; a love displayed even by conversations in the streets, where fragments of dialogue, heard in passing, show that mostly between men, and always between women, the personal pronouns recur every instant. If you want roughly to estimate any one's mental calibre, you cannot do it better than by observing the ratio of generalities to personalities in his talk—how far simple truths about individuals are replaced by truths abstracted from numerous experiences of men and things. And when you have thus measured many, you find but a scattered few likely to take anything more than a biographical view of human affairs. In the second place, this great-man-theory commends itself as promising instruction along with amusement. Being already fond of hearing about people's sayings and doings, it is pleasant news that, to understand the course of civilization, you have only to read diligently the lives of distinguished men. What can be a more acceptable doctrine than that while you are satisfying an instinct not very remotely allied to that of the village gossip—while you are receiving through print instead of orally, remarkable facts concerning notable persons, you are gaining that knowledge which will make clear to you why things have happened thus or thus in the world, and will prepare you for forming a right opinion on each question coming before you as a citizen. And then, in the third place, the interpretation of things thus given is so beautifully simple—seems so easy to comprehend. Providing you are content with conceptions that are out of focus, as most people's conceptions are, the solutions it yields appear quite satisfactory. Just as that theory of the Solar System which supposes the planets to have been launched into their orbits by the hand of the Almighty, looks feasible so long as you do not insist on knowing exactly what is meant by the hand of the Almighty; and just as the special creation of plants and animals seems a tenable hypothesis until you try and picture to yourself definitely the process by which one of them is brought into existence; so the genesis of societies by the actions of great men, may be comfortably believed so long as, resting in notions, you do not ask for particulars.

But now, if, dissatisfied with vagueness, we demand that our ideas shall be brought into focus and exactly defined, we discover the hypothesis to be utterly incoherent. If, not stopping at the explanation of social progress as due to the great man, we go back a step and ask whence comes the great man, we find that the theory breaks down completely.

WILLIAM JAMES
GREAT MEN AND
THEIR ENVIRONMENT
1880

And this brings us at last to the heart of our subject. The causes of production of great men lie in a sphere wholly inaccessible to the social philosopher. He must simply accept geniuses as data, just as Darwin accepts his spontaneous variations. For him, as for Darwin, the only problem is, these data being given, how does the environment affect them, and how do they affect the environment? Now, I affirm that the relation of the visible environment to the great man is in the main exactly what it is to the "variation" in the Darwinian philosophy. It chiefly adopts or rejects, preserves or destroys, in short *selects* him. And whenever it adopts and preserves the great man, it becomes modified by his influence in an entirely original and peculiar way. He acts as a ferment, and changes its constitution, just as the advent of a new zoological species changes the faunal and floral equilibrium of the region in which it appears. We all recollect Mr. Darwin's famous statement of the influence of cats on the growth of clover in their neighbourhood. We all have read of the effects of the European rabbit in New Zealand, and we have many of us taken part in the controversy about the English sparrow here—whether he kills most canker-worms or drives away most native birds. Just so the great man, whether he can be an importation from without like Clive in India or Agassiz here, or whether he spring from the soil like Mahomet or Franklin, brings about a rearrangement, on a large or small scale, of the pre-existing social relations.

The mutations of societies, then, from generation to generation, are in the main due directly or indirectly to the acts or the example of individuals whose genius was so adapted to the receptivities of the moment, or whose accidental position of authority was so critical that they became ferments, initiators of movement, setters of precedent or fashion, centres of corruption, or destroyers of other persons, whose gift, had they had free play, would have led society in another direction. . . .

But the indeterminism is not absolute. Not every "man" fits every "hour." Some incompatibilities there are. A given genius may come either too early or too late. Peter the Hermit would now be sent to a lunatic asylum. John

Mill in the tenth century would have lived and died unknown. Cromwell and Napoleon need their revolutions, Grant his civil war. An Ajax gets no fame in the day of telescopic-sighted rifles; and, to express differently an instance which Spencer uses, what could a Watt have effected in a tribe which no precursive genius had taught to smelt iron or to turn a lathe? . . .

Thus social evolution is a resultant of the interaction of two wholly distinct factors—the individual, deriving his peculiar gifts from the play of the physiological and infrasocial forces, but bearing all the power of initiative and origination in his hands; and, second, the social environment, with its power of adopting or rejecting both him and his gifts. Both factors are essential to change. The community stagnates without the impulse of the individual. The impulse dies away without the sympathy of the community.

LEO TOLSTOY
———— WAR AND PEACE ————
1869

From the close of the year 1811 an intensified arming and concentrating of the forces of Western Europe began, and in 1812 these forces—millions of men reckoning those transporting and feeding the army—moved from the west eastwards to the Russian frontier, towards which since 1811 Russian forces had been similarly drawn. On the 12th of June 1812 the forces of Western Europe crossed the Russian frontier and war began, that is, an event took place opposed to human reason and to human nature. Millions of men perpetrated against one another such innumerable crimes, frauds, treacheries, thefts, forgeries, issues of false money, burglaries, incendiarisms, and murders, as in whole centuries are not recorded in the annals of all the law courts of the world, but which those who committed them did not at the time regard as being crimes.

What produced this extraordinary occurrence? What were its causes? The historians tell us with naïve assurance that its causes were the wrongs inflicted on the Duke of Oldenburg, the nonobservance of the Continental System, the ambition of Napoleon, the firmness of Alexander, the mistakes of the diplomatists, and so on.

Excerpt from pages 645–648 from *War and Peace,* by Leo Tolstoy (1983). Reprinted by permission of Oxford University Press.

Consequently it would only have been necessary for Metternich, Rumyantsev, or Talleyrand, between a levée and an evening party, to have taken proper pains and written a more adroit note, or for Napoleon to have written to Alexander: "My respected Brother, I consent to restore the duchy to the Duke of Oldenburg"—and there would have been no war.

We can understand that the matter seemed like that to contemporaries. . . . [But] to us their descendants, who are not historians and are not carried away by the process of research and can therefore regard the event with unclouded common sense, an incalculable number of causes present themselves. The deeper we delve in search of these causes the more of them we find; and each separate cause or whole series of causes appears to us equally valid in itself and equally false by its insignificance compared to the magnitude of the events, and by its impotence—apart from the co-operation of all the other coincident causes—to occasion the event. To us the wish or objection of this or that French corporal to serve a second term appears as much a cause as Napoleon's refusal to withdraw his troops beyond the Vistula and to restore the duchy of Oldenburg; for had he not wished to serve, and had a second, a third, and a thousandth corporal and private also refused, there would have been so many less men in Napoleon's army and the war could not have occurred.

Had Napoleon not taken offence at the demand that he should withdraw beyond the Vistula, and not ordered his troops to advance, there would have been no war; but had all his sergeants objected to serving a second term then also there could have been no war. Nor could there have been a war had there been no English intrigues and no Duke of Oldenburg, and had Alexander not felt insulted, and had there not been an autocratic government in Russia, or a Revolution in France and a subsequent dictatorship and Empire, or all the things that produced the French Revolution, and so on. Without each of these causes nothing could have happened. So all these causes—myriads of causes—coincided to bring it about. And so there was no one cause for that occurrence, but it had to occur because it had to. Millions of men, renouncing their human feelings and reason, had to go from west to east to slay their fellows, just as some centuries previously hordes of men had come from the east to the west slaying their fellows.

The actions of Napoleon and Alexander, on whose words the event seemed to hang, were as little voluntary as the actions of any soldier who was drawn into the campaign by lot or by conscription. This could not be otherwise, for in order that the will of Napoleon and Alexander (on whom the event seemed to depend) should be carried out, the concurrence of innumerable circumstances was needed without any one of which the event could not have taken place. It was necessary that millions of men in whose hands lay the real power—the soldiers who fired, or transported provisions and guns—should consent to carry out the will of these weak individuals, and should have been induced to do so by an infinite number of diverse and complex causes.

We are forced to fall back on fatalism as an explanation of irrational events (that is to say, events the reasonableness of which we do not understand). The more we try to explain such events in history reasonably, the more unreasonable and incomprehensible do they become to us.

Each man lives for himself, using his freedom to attain his personal aims, and feels with his whole being that he can now do or abstain from doing this or that action; but as soon as he has done it, that action performed at a certain moment in time becomes irrevocable and belongs to history, in which it has not a free but a predestined significance.

There are two sides to the life of every man, his individual life which is the more free the more abstract its interests, and his elemental swarm-life in which he inevitably obeys laws laid down for him.

Man lives consciously for himself, but is an unconscious instrument in the attainment of the historic, universal, aims of humanity. A deed done is irrevocable, and its result coinciding in time with the actions of millions of other men assumes an historic significance. The higher a man stands on the social ladder, the more people he is connected with and the more power he has over others, the more evident is the predestination and inevitability of his every action.

"The king's heart is in the hands of the Lord."

A king is history's slave.

... When an apple has ripened and falls why does it fall? Because of its attraction to the earth, because its stalk withers, because it is dried by the sun, because it grows heavier, because the wind shakes it, or because the boy standing below wants to eat it?

Nothing is the cause. All this is only the coincidence of conditions in which all vital organic and elemental events occur. And the botanist who finds that the apple falls because the cellular tissue decays and so forth, is equally right with the child who stands under the tree and says the apple fell because he wanted to eat it and prayed for it. Equally right or wrong is he who says that Napoleon went to Moscow because he wanted to, and perished because Alexander desired his destruction, and he who says that an undermined hill weighing a million tons fell because the last navvy struck it for the last time with his mattock. In historic events the so-called great men are labels giving names to events, and like labels they have but the smallest connexion with the event itself.

Every act of theirs, which appears to them an act of their own will, is in an historical sense involuntary, and is related to the whole course of history and predestined from eternity.

Comment

In 1943, an American philosopher by the name of Sidney Hook published a book titled *The Hero in History: A Study in Limitation and Possibility.* Earlier in his life, Hook had been a Marxist who thought that history was "determined" or strongly "conditioned" by class or class differences. But Hook later changed his mind. He concluded that great men in the guise of great leaders—Lenin was his preferred example—do make history. In fact, in *The Hero in History,* Hook goes a step further, arguing that there are two different types of heroes: one the "eventful man" and the other the "event-making man."

Hook described the *eventful man* (his italics) as one "whose actions influenced subsequent developments along a quite different course than would have been followed if these actions had not been taken." The *event-making man,* in turn, is an eventful man "whose actions are the consequences of outstanding capacities of intelligence, will, and character rather than accidents of position." Why did Hook make the distinction? Because he thought it important to separate those who led on the basis of their position from those who led on the basis of their personality. As he framed it, by formulating the two types, he did "justice to the general belief that a hero is great not merely in virtue of what he does but in virtue of what he is."

In his discussion of the hero in history, Hook took on Carlyle, Spencer, and James, finding fault with each, but acknowledging nevertheless that they preceded in key ways his own attempt to unravel the role of the leader in history. Hook considered Carlyle an extremist in his view—and he was right. Carlyle's book on heroes grew out of a series of lectures, which he delivered with all the fervor and conviction of a prophet straight out of the Bible. As one of his contemporaries put it, "If we take the word [prophet] in its largest sense he [Carlyle] truly deserved the name. . . . He was a prophet most of all in the emphatic utterance of truths which no-one else, or hardly anyone else, ventured to deliver."

Carlyle's view of the great man was expansive and creative all at the same time: he was ecumenical in his conception of who the hero was and what the hero did. In fact, he expanded the traditional view of the hero as conqueror, ruler, or governor to include another cast of characters altogether. Alongside the king was the poet as leader. Alongside the god was the priest as leader. And alongside the revolutionary was the man of letters as leader. Each was a hero, a creator "of whatsoever the general mass of men contrived to do or to attain."

Precisely because Spencer's name is closely associated with the theory of evolution, it is easy to see why he would object strongly to Carlyle's view of leaders as men who so dominate the world they inhabit that they "baffle all attempts at explanation and classification." As Hector Macpherson noted, Spencer's work "foreshadowed a conception of biography in which the great man would no longer be viewed as an incomprehensible incarnation of supernatural energy, but as the product of certain interpretable forces." What seems clear, especially given the short-tempered tone of Spencer's prose, is that he was driven to distraction by the drama of Carlyle. Had Carlyle been less extreme in his position, Spencer might have been more moderate in his own.

James is one among a handful of American thinkers—his work crossed conventional disciplinary lines, from physiology to psychology, to philosophy, and back—who are widely considered to be great. A member of one of America's most illustrious and intellectual families (his brother was the novelist Henry James), James's contributions to various areas of academic inquiry were enormous. His interest in the issue of historical causation, though, seems almost incidental, as if he simply could not resist injecting himself into the great man in history debate, which at the time was particularly lively. James was more sympathetic to Carlyle than to Spencer, a reflection of his intellectual proclivities. But if he inclined to Carlyle, he was not, if you will, Carlyle-like. James was more moderate in his disposition, and so developed his opinion without what Hook referred to as "the Carlylean fantasy that the great man was responsible for the very conditions of his emergence and effectiveness." In other words, James charted the course of human history by mixing the man and the moment in a way that most students of leadership have since found persuasive.

The preeminent literary critic Harold Bloom has written of Tolstoy that he combines "the incomparable powers of the two strongest ancient authors, the poet of the *Iliad* and the original teller of the stories of Abraham, Jacob, Joseph, and Moses in Genesis and Exodus." It happened that in one of his masterpieces, the novel *War and Peace*, Tolstoy posed the question that we pose here: Is history predetermined—the inevitable result of ineffable forces? Or does man have free will and the capacity therefore to create intended change? Given his strong belief in God, and given that *War and Peace* depicts a drama of infinite complexity (Napoleon's war against Russia), Tolstoy concludes, perhaps inevitably, that the great man theory has no merit. To quote the master directly, "A king is history's slave."

~

JOHN STUART MILL
1806–1873

"Certainly no one has ever been so right about so many things so much of the time as John Stuart Mill, the nineteenth-century English philosopher, politician, and know-it-all nonpareil." So opined critic Adam Gopnik about one of the greatest champions of complete equality ever—between the sexes, among races and classes, and among all individuals, no matter whether they were members of a majestic majority or meager minority.

Mill's life could have been calamitous. He was born in London to the prominent Scottish philosopher and economist James Mill, who, along with his mentor, utilitarian philosopher Jeremy Bentham, force-fed the boy information and ideas from the age of three. First Greek, then Latin, then the rest until at age 12 young John was poised to enter university. By the age of 20, he was a clerk at the East India Company, a popular writer of radical inclinations, and victim of a nervous breakdown. (Today the diagnosis would probably be clinical depression.) But two years later he dug out, gradually to create a life full of love and work.

Mill's *On Liberty*, an excerpt from which follows, is not directly about leadership, nor is it directly about followership. What it is instead is an ode—arguably the finest—to human freedom. Mill's insistence that "over himself, over his own body and mind, the individual is sovereign" could be the consequence of his own oppressive upbringing. It is, in the event, as compelling a claim as there is of your right to captain your ship, and mine to captain mine.

---------- ON LIBERTY ----------
1859

The struggle between Liberty and Authority is the most conspicuous feature in the portions of history with which we are earliest familiar, particularly in that of Greece, Rome, and England. But in old times this contest was between subjects, or some classes of subjects, and the Government. By liberty, was meant protection against the tyranny of the political rulers. The rulers were conceived (except in some of the popular governments of Greece) as in a necessarily antagonistic position to the people whom they ruled. They consisted of a governing One, or a governing tribe or caste, who derived their authority from inheritance or conquest, who, at all events, did not hold it at the pleasure of the governed, and whose supremacy men did not venture, perhaps did not desire, to contest, whatever precautions might be taken against its oppressive exercise. Their power was regarded as necessary, but also as highly dangerous; as a

John Stuart Mill: *On Liberty and Other Essays*, edited by John Gray (OWC, 1991): pp. 5–9, 18–19, 62–63, 84–85, 127–128. Reproduced by permission of Oxford University Press.

weapon which they would attempt to use against their subjects, no less than against external enemies. To prevent the weaker members of the community from being preyed on by innumerable vultures, it was needful that there should be an animal of prey stronger than the rest, commissioned to keep them down. But as the king of the vultures would be no less bent upon preying upon the flock than any of the minor harpies, it was indispensable to be in a perpetual attitude of defence against his beak and claws. The aim, therefore, of patriots was to set limits to the power which the ruler should be suffered to exercise over the community; and this limitation was what they meant by liberty. It was attempted in two ways. First, by obtaining a recognition of certain immunities, called political liberties or rights, which it was to be regarded as a breach of duty in the ruler to infringe, and which, if he did infringe, specific resistance, or general rebellion, was held to be justifiable. A second, and generally a later expedient, was the establishment of constitutional checks, by which the consent of the community, or of a body of some sort, supposed to represent its interests, was made a necessary condition to some of the more important acts of the governing power. To the first of these modes of limitation, the ruling power, in most European countries, was compelled, more or less, to submit. It was not so with the second; and, to attain this, or when already in some degree possessed, to attain it more completely, became everywhere the principal object of the lovers of liberty. And so long as mankind were content to combat one enemy by another, and to be ruled by a master, on condition of being guaranteed more or less efficaciously against his tyranny, they did not carry their aspirations beyond this point.

A time, however, came, in the progress of human affairs, when men ceased to think it a necessity of nature that their governors should be an independent power, opposed in interest to themselves. It appeared to them much better that the various magistrates of the State should be their tenants or delegates, revocable at their pleasure. In that way alone, it seemed, could they have complete security that the powers of government would never be abused to their disadvantage. By degrees this new demand for elective and temporary rulers became the prominent object of the exertions of the popular party, wherever any such party existed; and superseded, to a considerable extent, the previous efforts to limit the power of rulers. As the struggle proceeded for making the ruling power emanate from the periodical choice of the ruled, some persons began to think that too much importance had been attached to the limitation of the power itself. *That* (it might seem) was a resource against rulers whose interests were habitually opposed to those of the people. What was now wanted was, that the rulers should be identified with the people; that their interest and will should be the interest and will of the nation. The nation did not need to be protected against its own will. There was no fear of its tyrannizing over itself. Let the rulers be effectually responsible to it, promptly removable by it, and it could afford to trust them with power of which it could itself dictate the use to be made. . . .

In time, however, a democratic republic came to occupy a large portion of the earth's surface, and made itself felt as one of the most powerful members of the community of nations; and elective and responsible government became subject to the observations and criticisms which wait upon a great existing fact. It was now perceived that such phrases as "self-government," and "the power of the people over themselves," do not express the true state of the case. The "people" who exercise the power are not always the same people with those over whom it is exercised; and the "self-government" spoken of is not the government of each by himself, but of each by all the rest. The will of the people, moreover, practically means the will of the most numerous or the most active *part* of the people; the majority, or those who succeed in making themselves accepted as the majority; the people, consequently, *may* desire to oppress a part of their number; and precautions are as much needed against this as against any other abuse of power. The limitation, therefore, of the power of government over individuals loses none of its importance when the holders of power are regularly accountable to the community, that is, to the strongest party therein. This view of things, recommending itself equally to the intelligence of thinkers and to the inclination of those important classes in European society to whose real or supposed interests democracy is adverse, has had no difficulty in establishing itself; and in political speculations "the tyranny of the majority" is now generally included among the evils against which society requires to be on its guard.

Like other tyrannies, the tyranny of the majority was at first, and is still vulgarly, held in dread, chiefly as operating through the acts of the public authorities. But reflecting persons perceived that when society is itself the tyrant—society collectively, over the separate individuals who compose it—its means of tyrannizing are not restricted to the acts which it may do by the hands of its political functionaries. Society can and does execute its own mandates: and if it issues wrong mandates instead of right, or any mandates at all in things with which it ought not to meddle, it practises a social tyranny more formidable than many kinds of political oppression, since, though not usually upheld by such extreme penalties, it leaves fewer means of escape, penetrating much more deeply into the details of life, and enslaving the soul itself. Protection, therefore, against the tyranny of the magistrate is not enough: there needs protection also against the tyranny of the prevailing opinion and feeling; against the tendency of society to impose, by other means than civil penalties, its own ideas and practices as rules of conduct on those who dissent from them. . . .

SUCH being the reasons which make it imperative that human beings should be free to form opinions, and to express their opinions without reserve; and such the baneful consequences to the intellectual, and through that to the moral nature of man, unless this liberty is either conceded, or asserted in spite of prohibition; let us next examine whether the same reasons do not require that men should be free to act upon their opinions— to carry these out in their lives, without hindrance, either physical or moral, from their fellow-men, so long as it is at their own risk and peril. This last proviso is of course indispensable. No one pretends that actions should be as free as opinions. On the contrary, even opinions lose their immunity, when the circumstances in which they are expressed are such as to constitute their expression a positive instigation to some mischievous act. An opinion that corn-dealers are starvers of the poor, or that private property is robbery, ought to be unmolested when simply circulated through the press, but may justly incur punishment when delivered orally to an excited mob assembled before the house of a corn-dealer, or when handed about among the same mob in the form of a placard. Acts of whatever kind, which, without justifiable cause, do harm to others, may be, and in the more important cases absolutely require to be, controlled by the unfavourable sentiments, and, when needful, by the active interference of mankind. The liberty of the individual must be thus far limited; he must not make himself a nuisance to other people. But if he refrains from molesting others in what concerns them, and merely acts according to his own inclination and judgment in things which concern himself, the same reasons which show that opinion should be free, prove also that he should be allowed, without molestation, to carry his opinions into practice at his own cost. That mankind are not infallible; that their truths, for the most part, are only half-truths; that unity of opinion, unless resulting from the fullest and freest comparison of opposite opinions, is not desirable, and diversity not an evil, but a good, until mankind are much more capable than at present of recognizing all sides of the truth, are principles applicable to men's modes of action, not less than to their opinions. As it is useful that while mankind are imperfect there should be different opinions, so is it that there should be different experiments of living; that free scope should be given to varieties of character, short of injury to others; and that the worth of different modes of life should be proved practically, when any one thinks fit to try them. It is desirable, in short, that in things which do not primarily concern others, individuality should assert itself. . . .

Neither one person, nor any number of persons, is warranted in saying to another human creature of ripe years, that he shall not do with his life for his own benefit what he chooses to do with it. He is the person most interested in his own well-being: the interest which any other person, except in cases of strong personal attachment, can have in it, is trifling, compared with that which he himself has; the interest which society has in him individually (except as to his conduct to others) is fractional, and altogether indirect: while, with respect to his own feelings and circumstances, the most ordinary man or woman has means of knowledge immeasurably surpassing those that can be possessed by any one else. The interference of society to overrule his judgment and purposes in what only regards himself, must be grounded on general presumptions; which may be altogether wrong, and even if right, are as likely as not to be misapplied to individual cases, by persons no better acquainted with the circumstances of such cases than those are who look at them merely from without. In this department, therefore, of human affairs, Individuality has its proper field of action . . . individual spontaneity is entitled to free exercise. Considerations to aid his judgment, exhortations to strengthen his will, may be offered to him, even obtruded on him, by others; but he himself is the final judge. All errors which he is likely to commit against advice and warning, are far outweighed by the evil of allowing others to constrain him to what they deem his good.

Comment

By the time John Stuart Mill penned *On Liberty*, the United States of America was a nation-state. There were, moreover, other democracies by then, other countries in which the high and mighty had surrendered at least some power and some influence to ordinary people. Why, then, was Mill motivated to craft a tract on individual rights?

Like his father, Mill was a disciple of Jeremy Bentham, a family friend and mentor. Mill was, in other words, a Utilitarian, who, like his two prominent elders, held the view that we ought to provide the greatest happiness to the greatest number. But Mill took Bentham's original proposition one step—a large step—further. Mill argued that the realm of human happiness, which involved the pursuit of pleasure as well as the absence of suffering, should be extended from the public to the private, from the political to the personal. Put another way, he expanded the sphere of noninterference by insisting that so long as we do no harm, one to another (known as the "harm principle"), we should be allowed to do more or less as we will. We have the right, Mill argued, to secure our own individual happiness unimpeded by people in positions of authority, or by the laws of the land, or even by "prevailing opinion," known otherwise as the "tyranny of the majority."

Mill's conception of the tyranny of the majority was far ahead of its time, almost as if it were lifted from a twenty-first-century text on social psychology. He had a preternatural understanding of the human condition, particularly of our proclivity to conform, to go along with what others conceive of as correct. Thus his railing against the power of public opinion, and thus his insistence that power can be exercised over members of a civilized community against their will "only to prevent harm to others." As Robert Devigne pointed out, Mill was persuaded that liberty is lost not only on account of coercion and conformity, but as well on account of inaction and alienation.

Mill championed human rights—*individual rights*—in every aspect. In part this was the product of his own history and disposition, and in part it was the product of his partnership with, and passion for, Harriet Taylor. Mill met Taylor in 1830, over dinner with friends. She was married, with two small children. Notwithstanding the conventions and constraints that would exist even now, they were, then and there, taken with each other, smitten. And so began one of the great collaborations, and great loves, in literary history. During most of their nearly three decades together, Mill and Taylor were furtive in their arrangements—it was only after Mr. Taylor died that Mrs. Taylor and Mr. Mill finally married. Their marriage would be short-lived, though. Within eight years Harriet Taylor died, to be mourned and extolled by her bereaved husband for the rest of his life. *On Liberty* was dedicated to the author's deceased wife: "To the beloved and deplored memory of her who was the inspirer, and in part the author, of all that is best in my writings—the friend and wife whose exalted sense of truth and right was my strongest incitement."

Taylor was a philosopher and activist in her own right, in particular on behalf of women. While Mill tended to credit Taylor with more than she deserved—in his autobiography, he wrote that his own most valuable ideas "originated with her; were emanations from her mind"—we can say with certainty that one of his greatest works, *The Subjugation of Women*, an ardent argument for equality between the sexes, was a consequence of her influence. The Essay, as Mill called it, begins as follows: "The principle which regulates the existing social relations between the two sexes—the legal subordination of one sex to the other—is wrong in itself. ... It ought to be replaced by a principle of perfect equality, admitting no power or privilege on the one side, nor disability on the other."

With Taylor by his side for nearly 30 years, Mill emerged as a most vigorous and optimistic defender of the better angels of our nature. He ignored the dark side of the human condition, which in a way is a fault, since our flaws are everywhere in evidence. But by assuming and accentuating the positive, Mill extolled the virtue of individual liberty with unalloyed intelligence and integrity. Had he formulated a maxim to fit this book, it would have read, "Neither a follower nor a leader be."

~

MAX WEBER
1864–1920

German-born Max Weber is considered among the foremost social theorists of the twentieth century. While he is best known for developing sweeping theories on the rise of capitalism, it is his groundbreaking work on leadership that is of interest here. Weber's work on the role of the individual in increasingly structured societies led him to distinguish among three different types of leaders, whose right to lead was derived from one of "three pure types of legitimate authority."

The first such type is *rational:* leaders lead because they are seen by their followers as having the legal right to do so. The second type is *traditional:* leaders lead because they are seen by their followers as being the legitimate heir to a legitimate tradition, as, for example, when a prince inherits a throne from his father, the king. And the third type of legitimate authority is *charismatic:* leaders lead because they are seen by their followers as being so exceptional as to merit their extreme dedication and devotion.

While the three types may seem simple, they emerge from Weber's complex and highly sophisticated analysis of the relationship between the leaders and the led. His conception of charismatic leadership was, in any case, so persuasive that it became pervasive—not only in the academy, but in the popular culture as well. Thus the selection that follows focuses primarily on charisma, as opposed to law or tradition.

THE THEORY OF SOCIAL AND ECONOMIC ORGANIZATION
1921

There are three pure types of legitimate authority. The vitality of their claims to legitimacy may be based on:

1. **Rational grounds**—resting on a belief in the "legality" of patterns of normative rules and the right of those elevated to authority under such rules to issue commands (legal authority);

2. *Traditional grounds*—resting on an established belief in the sanctity of immemorial traditions and the legitimacy of the status of those exercising authority under them (traditional authority); or finally,

3. *Charismatic grounds*—resting on devotion to the specific and exceptional sanctity, heroism or exemplary character of an individual person, and of the normative patterns or order revealed or ordained by him (charismatic authority).

In the case of legal authority, obedience is owed to the legally established impersonal order. It extends to the persons exercising the authority of office under it only by virtue of the formal legality of their commands and only within the scope of authority of the office. In the case of traditional authority, obedience is owed to the *person* of the chief who occupies the traditionally sanctioned position of authority and who is (within its sphere) bound by tradition. But here the obligation of obedience is not based on the impersonal order, but is a matter of personal loyalty within the area of accustomed obligations. In the case of charismatic authority, it is the charismatically qualified leader as such who is obeyed by virtue of personal trust in him and his revelation, his heroism or his exemplary qualities so far as they fall within the scope of the individual's belief in his charisma. . . .

The term "charisma" will be applied to a certain quality of an individual personality by virtue of which he is set apart from ordinary men and treated as endowed with supernatural, superhuman, or at least specifically exceptional powers or qualities. These are such as are not accessible to the ordinary person, but are regarded as of divine origin or as exemplary, and on the basis of them the individual concerned is treated as a leader. In primitive circumstances this peculiar kind of deference is paid to prophets, to people with a reputation for therapeutic or legal wisdom, to leaders in the hunt, and heroes in war. It is very often thought of as resting on magical powers. How the quality in question would be ultimately judged from any ethical, aesthetic, or other such point of view is naturally entirely indifferent for purposes of definition. What is alone important is how the individual is actually regarded by those subject to charismatic authority, by his "followers" or "disciples."

For present purposes it will be necessary to treat a variety of different types as being endowed with charisma in this sense. It includes the state of a "berserker" whose spells of maniac passion have, apparently wrongly, sometimes been attributed to the use of drugs. In Medieval Byzantium a group of people endowed with this type of charismatic war-like passion were maintained as a kind of weapon. It includes the "shaman," the kind of magician who in the pure type is subject to epileptoid seizures as a means of falling into trances. Another type is that of Joseph Smith, the founder of Mormonism, who, however, cannot be classified in this way with absolute certainty since there is a possibility that he was a very sophisticated type of deliberate swindler. Finally it includes the type of intellectual, such as Kurt Eisner, who is carried away with his own demagogic success. Sociological analysis, which must abstain from value judgments, will treat all these on the same level as the men who, according to conventional judgments, are the "greatest" heroes, prophets, and saviours.

1. It is recognition on the part of those subject to authority which is decisive for the validity of charisma. This is freely given and guaranteed by what is held to be a "sign" or proof, originally always a miracle, and consists in devotion to the corresponding revelation, hero worship, or absolute trust in the leader. But where charisma is genuine, it is not this which is the basis of the claim to legitimacy. This basis lies rather in the conception that it is the *duty* of those who have been called to a charismatic mission to recognize its quality and to act accordingly. Psychologically this "recognition" is a matter of complete personal devotion to the possessor of the quality, arising out of enthusiasm, or of despair and hope.

   No prophet has ever regarded his quality as dependent on the attitudes of the masses toward him. No elective king or military leader has ever treated those who have resisted him or tried to ignore him otherwise than as delinquent in duty. Failure to take part in a military expedition under such leader, even though recruitment is formally voluntary, has universally been met with disdain.

2. If proof of his charismatic qualification fails him for long, the leader endowed with charisma tends to think his god or his magical or heroic powers have deserted him. If he is for long unsuccessful, above all if

his leadership fails to benefit his followers, it is likely that his charismatic authority will disappear. This is the genuine charismatic meaning of the "gift of grace. . . ."

3. The corporate group which is subject to charismatic authority is based on an emotional form of communal relationship. The administrative staff of a charismatic leader does not consist of "officials," at least its members are not technically trained. It is not chosen on the basis of social privilege nor from the point of view of domestic or personal dependency. It is rather chosen in terms of the charismatic qualities of its members. The prophet has his disciples; the war lord his selected henchmen; the leader, generally, his followers. There is no such thing as "appointment" or "dismissal," no career, no promotion. There is only a "call" at the instance of the leader on the basis of the charismatic qualification of those he summons. There is no hierarchy; the leader merely intervenes in general or in individual cases when he considers the members of his staff inadequate to a task with which they have been entrusted. There is no such thing as a definite sphere of authority and of competence, and no appropriation of official powers on the basis of social privileges. There may, however, be territorial or functional limits to charismatic powers and to the individual's "mission." There is no such thing as a salary or a benefice. Disciples or followers tend to live primarily in a communistic relationship with their leader on means which have been provided by voluntary gift. There are no established administrative organs. In their place are agents who have been provided with charismatic authority by their chief or who possess charisma of their own. There is no system of formal rules, of abstract legal principles, and hence no process of judicial decision oriented to them. But equally there is no legal wisdom oriented to judicial precedent. Formally concrete judgments are newly created from case to case and are originally regarded as divine judgments and revelations. From a substantive point of view, every charismatic authority would have to subscribe to the proposition, "It is written . . . , but I say unto you. . . ." The genuine prophet, like the genuine military leader and every true leader in this sense, preaches, creates, or demands *new* obligations. In the pure type of charisma, these are imposed on the authority of revolution

by oracles, or of the leader's own will, and are recognized by the members of the religious, military, or party group, because they come from such a source. Recognition is a duty. When such an authority comes into conflict with the competing authority of another who also claims charismatic sanction, the only recourse is to some kind of a contest, by magical means or even an actual physical battle of the leaders. In principle, only one side can be in the right in such a conflict; the other must be guilty of a wrong which has to be expiated.

Charismatic authority is thus specifically outside the realm of everyday routine and the profane sphere. In this respect, it is sharply opposed both to rational, and particularly bureaucratic, authority, and to traditional authority, whether in its patriarchal, patrimonial, or any other form. Both rational and traditional authority are specifically forms of everyday routine control of action; while the charismatic type is the direct antithesis of this. Bureaucratic authority is specifically rational in the sense of being bound to intellectually analysable rules; while charismatic authority is specifically irrational in the sense of being foreign to all rules. Traditional authority is bound to the precedents handed down from the past and to this extent is also oriented to rules. Within the sphere of its claims, charismatic authority repudiates the past, and is in this sense a specifically revolutionary force. It recognizes no appropriation of positions of power by virtue of the possession of property, either on the part of a chief or of socially privileged groups. The only basis of legitimacy for it is personal charisma, so long as it is proved; that is, as long as it receives recognition and is able to satisfy the followers or disciples. But this lasts only so long as the belief in its charismatic inspiration remains.

Comment

Weber's interest in leadership grew out of his interest in the bureaucratization of modern life. He looked to charismatic leaders, leaders whose right to lead emanated from the power of their personalities, to correct for rational leaders, whose right to lead emanated from the power of their positions. For charismatic leaders, unlike rational leaders (leaders, in the main, of large organizations), provide their followers with purpose and meaning, with what seem to them to be transcendent ties, both among themselves and to the larger universe they together inhabit.

Traditional leaders are by no means obsolete—think, for example, of the continuing role in American politics played by the families of John F. Kennedy, George Herbert Walker Bush, and Bill Clinton. One brother seems properly to inherit the mantle of leadership from another brother; similarly, leadership can devolve from father to son, and even, as in the case of the Clintons, from husband to wife. But for a range of reasons, including the now more equitable distribution of money and property, leaders who depend on traditional connections are on the wane.

Over the last two centuries, rational leaders—leaders who provide increasingly complex societies with stability and security—have become the norm, increasingly in the East as well as in the West. Such leaders derive their authority from the positions they hold, positions that entitle them to preside over organizations governed by rules and regulations and staffed by managers charged with carrying out clearly defined tasks.

Still, it is the charismatic leader who seems to speak to the temper of modern times. Charismatic leaders provide their followers with more than purpose and meaning—they lend excitement as well. By holding out hope for a perfect world, or at least one far better than the one we live in now, they capture our hearts as well as our minds.

To be sure, there is a distinction between the way we understand charismatic leadership now and the way Weber intended it. His conception was purer or, better, more extreme. Weber's charismatic leaders were so powerful they posed a challenge to the existing order. In other words, originally charismatic leadership was a kind of revolutionary leadership, in which the charismatic leader took on other, more ordinary leaders, whose authority was derived from the hidebound sources of law and tradition.

Charismatic leaders have strong emotional connections to their followers, who, in turn, are deeply devoted to them. Their devotion derives from the "specific . . . sanctity, heroism or exemplary character of an individual person." As Ann Ruth Wilner observed in her book on charismatic leadership, "In the charismatic relationship, followers believe their leader to have superhuman qualities or to possess to an extraordinary degree the qualities highly esteemed in their culture." As a result of this belief, they "comply because for them it is sufficient that their leader has given the command. If *he* has ordered, it is their duty to obey."

By now the notion of charismatic leadership has been adulterated and diluted. The word *charisma* is used freely now, applied almost indiscriminately to leaders, indeed to famous people generally, who are considered unusually attractive or appealing. Moreover, today we use the word to describe an individual, rather than a relationship; charisma is no longer defined necessarily as a dynamic involving a leader and at least one follower.

Withal, the conception of charisma has taken hold. It is as much a part of our contemporary culture as is celebrity itself—although Weber, the most serious of social scientists, would be unlikely to approve.

∾

SIGMUND FREUD
1856–1939

Freud had one of the most fertile minds in human history. While his influence has diminished in recent decades—traditional psychoanalysis is practiced less often than it was, and theories rivaling Freud's, such as feminism and structuralism, have gained currency—his talking cure and his seminal thinking on human behavior, from making love to making war, seem to be stamped forever on our collective consciousness.

It happens that among Freud's particular interests were leadership and followership. In his later life, as the Nazis came to control first Germany and then Austria, Freud's interest in power and authority was easy enough to understand. But his fascination with why some people lead and others follow preceded as well as prognosticated the totalitarian regimes of Hitler and Stalin.

Some have argued that Freud's study of the dynamic between the leaders and the led grew in the main out of the nature of psychoanalytic theory and practice. Freud, who was trained as a physician, recognized early on that his particular treatment of neurosis depended in good part on having his patients trust him absolutely, on having them look to him, even surrender to him, as they would to a parent or other strong authority figure. But to read excerpts from *Group Psychology and the Analysis of the Ego* and *Civilization and Its Discontents* (published in 1921 and 1930, respectively), and then from *Moses and Monotheism* (1939), is to come to recognize that Freud's interest in the relationships between those with power and authority and those without was long-standing as well as wide-ranging.

GROUP PSYCHOLOGY AND
THE ANALYSIS OF THE EGO
1921

We may recall from what we know of the morphology of groups that it is possible to distinguish very different kinds of groups and opposing lines in their development. There are very fleeting groups and extremely lasting ones; homogeneous ones, made up of the same sorts of individuals, and unhomogeneous ones; natural groups, and artificial ones, requiring an external force to keep them together; primitive groups, and highly organized ones with a definite structure. But for reasons which remain to be explained we should like to lay particular stress upon a distinction to which writers on the subject have been inclined to give too little attention; I refer to that between leaderless groups and those with leaders. And, in complete opposition to the usual practice, we shall not choose a relatively simple group formation as our point of departure, but shall begin with highly organized, lasting and artificial groups. The most interesting example of such structures are Churches—communities of believers—and armies.

A Church and an army are artificial groups—that is, a certain external force is employed to prevent them from disintegrating and to check alterations in their structure. As a rule a person is not consulted, or is given no choice, as to whether he wants to enter such a group; any attempt at leaving it is usually met with persecution or with severe punishment, or has quite definite conditions attached to it. It is quite outside our present interest to enquire why these associations need such special safeguards. We are only attracted by one circumstance, namely that certain facts, which are far more concealed in other cases, can be observed very clearly in those highly organized groups which are protected from dissolution in the manner that has been mentioned. In a Church (and we may with advantage take the Catholic Church as a type) as well as in an army, however different the two may be in other respects, the same illusion holds good of there being a head—in the Catholic Church Christ, in an army its Commander-in-Chief—who loves all the individuals in the group with an equal love. Everything depends upon this illusion; if it were to be dropped, then both Church and army would dissolve, so far as the external force permitted them to. This equal love was expressly enunciated by Christ: "Inasmuch as ye have done it unto one of the least of these my brethren, ye have done it unto me." He stands to the individual members of the group of believers in the relation of a kind elder brother; he is their substitute father. All the demands that are made upon the individual are derived from this love of Christ's. A democratic strain runs through the Church, for the very reason that before Christ everyone is equal, and that everyone has an equal share in his love.

It is not without a deep reason that the similarity between the Christian community and a family is invoked, and that believers call themselves brothers in Christ, that is, brothers through the love which Christ has for them. There is no doubt that the tie which unites each individual with Christ is also the cause of the tie which unites them with one another. The like holds good of an army. The Commander-in-Chief is a father who loves all soldiers equally, and for that reason they are comrades among themselves. The army differs structurally from the Church in being built up of a series of such groups. Every captain is, as it were, the Commander-in-Chief and the father of his company, and so is every non-commissioned officer of his section.

It is true that a similar hierarchy has been constructed in the Church, but it does not play the same part in it economically; for more knowledge and care about individuals may be attributed to Christ than to a human Commander-in-Chief.

An objection will justly be raised against this conception of the libidinal structure of an army on the ground that no place has been found in it for such ideas as those of one's country, of national glory, etc., which are of such importance in holding an army together. The answer is that that is a different instance of a group tie, and no longer such a simple one; for the examples of great generals, like Caesar, Wallenstein, or Napoleon, show that such ideas are not indispensable to the existence of an army. We shall presently touch upon the possibility of a leading idea being substituted for a leader and upon the relations between the two. The neglect of this libidinal factor in an army, even when it is not the only factor operative, seems to be not merely a theoretical omission but also a practical danger. Prussian militarism, which was just as unpsychological as German science, may have had to suffer the consequences of this in the [first] World War. We know that the war neuroses which ravaged the German army have been recognized as being a protest of the individual against the part he was expected to play in the army; and according to the communication of Simmel (1918), the hard treatment of the men by their superiors may be considered as foremost among the motive forces of the disease. If the importance of the libido's claims on this score had been better appreciated, the fantastic promises of the American President's Fourteen Points would probably not have been believed so easily, and the splendid instrument would not have broken in the hands of the German leaders.

It is to be noticed that in these two artificial groups each individual is bound by libidinal ties on the one hand to the leader (Christ, the Commander-in-Chief) and on the other hand to the other members of the group. How these two ties are related to each other, whether they are of the same kind and the same value, and how they are to be described psychologically—these questions must be reserved for subsequent enquiry. But we shall venture even now upon a mild reproach against earlier writers for not having sufficiently appreciated the importance of the leader in the psychology of the group, while our own choice of this as a first subject for investigation has brought us into a more favourable position. It would appear as though we were on the right road towards an explanation of the principal phenomenon of group psychology—the individual's lack of freedom in a group. If each individual is bound in two directions by such an intense emotional tie, we shall find no difficulty in attributing to that circumstance the alteration and limitation which have been observed in his personality. . . .

The uncanny and coercive characteristics of group formations, which are shown in the phenomena of suggestion that accompany them, may therefore with justice be traced back to the fact of their origin from the primal horde. The leader of the group is still the dreaded primal father; the group still wishes to be governed by unrestricted force; it has an extreme passion for authority; in Le Bon's phrase, it has a thirst for obedience.

CIVILIZATION AND
ITS DISCONTENTS
1930

The last, but certainly not the least important, of the characteristic features of civilization remains to be assessed: the manner in which the relationships of men to one another, their social relationships, are regulated—relationships which affect a person as a neighbour, as a source of help, as another person's sexual object, as a member of a family and of a State. Here it is especially difficult to keep clear of particular ideal demands and to see what is civilized in general. Perhaps we may begin by explaining that the element of civilization enters on the scene with the first attempt to regulate these social relationships. If the attempt were not made, the relationships would be subject to the arbitrary will of the individual: that is to say, the physically stronger man would decide them in the sense of his own interests and instinctual impulses. Nothing would be changed in this if this stronger man should in his turn meet someone even stronger than he. Human life in common is only made possible when a majority come together which is stronger than any separate individual and which remains united against all separate individuals. The power of this community is then set up "right" in opposition to the power of the individual, which is condemned as "brute force." This replacement of the power of the individual by the power of a community constitutes the decisive step of civilization. The essence of it lies in the fact that the members of the community restrict themselves in their possibilities of satisfaction, whereas the individual knew no such restrictions. The first requisite of civilization, therefore, is that of justice—that is, the assurance that a law once made will not be broken in favour of an individual. This implies nothing as to the ethical value of such a law. The further course of cultural development seems to tend towards making the law no longer an expression of the will of a small community—a caste or a stratum of the population or a racial group—which, in its turn, behaves like a violent individual towards other, and perhaps more numerous, collections of people. The final outcome should be a rule of law to which all—except those who are not capable of entering a community—have contributed by a sacrifice of their instincts, and which leaves no one—again with the same exception—at the mercy of brute force.

The liberty of the individual is no gift of civilization. It was greatest before there was any civilization, though then, it is true, it had for the most part no value, since the individual was scarcely in a position to defend it. The development of civilization imposes restrictions on it, and justice demands that no one escape those restrictions. What makes itself felt in a human community as a desire for freedom may be their revolt against some existing injustice, and so may prove favourable to a further development of civilization; it may remain compatible with civilization. But it may also spring from the remains of their original personality, which is still untamed by civilization and may thus become the basis in them of hostility to civilization. The urge for freedom, therefore, is directed against particular forms and demands of civilization or against civilization altogether. It does not seem as though any influence could induce a man to change his nature into a termite's. No doubt he will always defend his claim to individual liberty against the will of the group. A good part of the struggles of mankind centre round the single task of finding an expedient accommodation—one, that is, that will bring happiness—between this claim of the individual and the cultural claims of the group; and one of the problems that touches the fate of humanity is whether such an accommodation can be reached by means of some particular form of civilization or whether this conflict is irreconcilable.

---------- **MOSES AND MONOTHEISM** ----------

1939

How is it possible that one single man can develop such extraordinary effectiveness, that he can create out of indifferent individuals and families *one* people, can stamp this people with its definite character and determine its fate for millennia to come? Is not such an assumption a retrogression to the manner of thinking that produced creation myths and

---

hero-worship, to times in which historical writing exhausted itself in narrating the dates and life-histories of certain individuals—sovereigns or conquerors? The inclination of modern times tends rather to trace back the events of human history to more hidden, general, and impersonal factors—the forcible influence of economic circumstances, changes in food supply, progress in the use of materials and tools, migrations caused by increase in population and change of climate. In these factors individuals play no other part than that of exponents or representatives of mass tendencies which must come to expression and which found that expression as it were by chance in such persons.

These are quite legitimate points of view, but they remind us of a significant discrepancy between the nature of our thinking-apparatus and the organization of the world which we are trying to apprehend. Our imperative need for cause and effect is satisfied when each process has one demonstrable cause. In reality, outside us this is hardly so; each event seems to be over-determined and turns out to be the effect of several converging causes. Intimidated by the countless complications of events, research takes the part of one chain of events against another, stipulates contrasts that do not exist and that are created merely through tearing apart more comprehensive relations.

If, therefore, the investigation of one particular case demonstrates the outstanding influence of a single human personality, our conscience need not reproach us that through accepting this conclusion we have dealt a blow at the doctrine of the significance of those general impersonal factors. In point of fact there is without doubt room for both. In the genesis of monotheism we cannot, it is true, point to any other external factor than those I have already mentioned: namely, that this development has to do with the establishing of closer connections among different nations and the existence of a great empire.

We will keep, therefore, a place for "the great man" in the chain, or rather in the network, of determining causes. It may not be quite useless, however, to ask under what condition we bestow this title of honour. We may be surprised to find that it is not so easy to answer this question. A first formulation which would define as great a human being specially endowed with qualities we value highly is obviously in all respects unsuitable. Beauty, for instance, and muscular strength, much as they may be envied, do not establish a claim to "greatness." There should perhaps be mental qualities present, psychical and intellectual distinction. In the latter respect we have misgivings: a man who has an outstanding knowledge in one particular field would not be called a great man without any further reason. We should certainly not apply the term to a master of chess or to a virtuoso on a musical instrument, and not necessarily to a distinguished artist or a man of science. In such a case we should be content to say he is a great writer, painter, mathematician, or physicist, a pioneer in this field or that, but we should pause before pronouncing him a great man. When we declare, for instance, Goethe, Leonardo da Vinci, and Beethoven to be great men, then something else must move us to do so beyond the admiration of their grandiose creations. If it were not for just such examples one might very well conceive the idea that the title "a great man" is reserved by preference for men of action—that is to say, conquerors, generals, and rulers—and was intended as a recognition of the greatness of their achievements and the strength of the influence that emanated from them. However, this, too, is unsatisfying, and is fully contradicted by our condemnation of so many worthless people of whom one cannot deny that they exercised a great influence on their own and later times. Nor can success be chosen as a distinguishing feature of greatness, if one thinks of the vast number of great men who, instead of being successful, perished after being dogged by misfortune.

We should therefore, tentatively, incline to the conclusion that it is hardly worth while to search for an unequivocal definition of the concept: "a great man." It seems to be a rather loosely used term, one bestowed without due consideration and given to the supernormal development of certain human qualities; in doing so we keep close to the original literal sense of the word "greatness." We may also remember that it is not so much the nature of the great man that arouses our interest as the question of what are the qualities by virtue of which he influences his contemporaries. I propose to shorten this investigation, however, since it threatens to lead us far from our goal.

Let us agree, therefore, that the great man influences his contemporaries in two ways: through his personality and through the idea for which he stands. This idea may lay stress on an old group of wishes in the masses, or point to a new aim for their wishes, or, again, lure the masses by other means. Sometimes—and this is surely the more primitive effect—the personality alone exerts its influence, and the idea plays a decidedly subordinate part. Why the great man should rise to significance at all we have no doubt whatever. We know that the great majority of people have a strong need for authority which they can admire, to which they can submit, and which dominates and sometimes even ill-treats them. We have learned from the psychology of the individual whence comes this need of the masses. It is the longing for the father that lives in each of us from his childhood days, for the same father whom the hero of legend boasts of having overcome. And now it begins to dawn on us that all the features with which we furnish the great man are traits of the father, that in this similarity lies the essence, which so far has eluded us, of the great man. The decisiveness of thought, the strength of will, the forcefulness of his deeds, belong to the picture of the father; above all other things, however, the self-reliance and independence of the great man, his divine conviction of doing the right thing, which may pass into ruthlessness. He must be admired, he may be trusted, but one cannot help also being afraid of him. We should have taken a cue from the word itself; who else but the father should in childhood have been the great man?

Comment

In one of his first forays into leadership and followership, *Group Psychology and the Analysis of the Ego*, Freud focused on groups or, more precisely, on what happens to individuals when they become members of groups. Freud came to three important conclusions. First, we change. That is, as individuals acting alone, we are one thing, whereas in groups, together with others, we are quite another. Second, leaders of groups and, by extension, of organizations, are of paramount importance. Literally, they are the governors, while the rest are the governed. Symbolically, they are the tie that binds one member of the group to all the other members of the group. As Freud wrote in *Group Psychology*, "an individual is a creature in a horde led by a chief." Third, Freud found that followers need and want leaders even more than leaders need and want followers. His insight is important, if only because while the longing to lead is easy enough to understand, the longing to follow is not. What Freud makes plain is that leadership and followership are arrangements from which both sides stand to benefit: "The leader of the group is still the dreaded primal father; the group still wishes to be governed by unrestricted force; it has an extreme passion for authority. . . ."

Group Psychology, which was published well before the rise of Hitler or even Stalin (who came to power roughly a decade before his German counterpart), was prescient. During the Nazi period, Germany, arguably the most cultured of all European countries, regressed to what Freud, rather like Hobbes, saw as the state of nature. More specifically, the German people reverted to what Freud termed a primal horde, led by a single leader who for all practical purposes was all-powerful.

Civilization and Its Discontents appeared about a decade after *Group Psychology*. By then Freud was more deeply entrenched in psychoanalytic theory. And by then he was more deeply enmeshed in heated debates over his various ideas, including the oedipal conflict, narcissism, transference, and the importance of the unconscious. *Civilization* is considered by literary critic Louis Menand to be in the pantheon of great literature, along with, for example, Plato's *Republic*, Milton's *Paradise Lost*, and Marx's *Capital*. On what grounds does Menand make so extravagant a claim? The book is not, he admitted, a work of art, nor is it philosophy. Rather, Menand termed it scientific speculation—albeit of the highest sort.

What discriminating readers have found so valuable in *Civilization and Its Discontents*, so original, is Freud's reversal of the widely accepted sequence of cause and effect. "Most people," Menand noted, "assume that individuals are shaped by the society in which they're raised. Freud thought that it was the other way around, that society . . . takes its imprint from individual psychology." This brings us back to the leader, to the father, to the all-powerful figure that we fear and love at the same time. According to Freud, it is he who triggers our guilt and depression (neurosis) because, as "civilized" people, we suppress the instinct or impulse to eliminate him, murder him, somehow kill him off. Instead, we turn these selfsame angers and anxieties inward, on ourselves.

The preceding selection from *Civilization* reflects Freud's preoccupation with the question of how, given the human condition, groups can be, and should be, organized. Here he dons the mantle of the political philosopher, evoking Hobbes in his view of the state of nature, but reaching a different conclusion altogether, one determined to avoid the tyranny that Hobbes thought necessary. In fact, Freud's description of the tension between the individual and the collective is more reminiscent of Locke than it is of anyone else: "A good part of the struggles of mankind centre round the single task of finding an expedient accommodation—one, that is, that will bring happiness—between this claim of the individual and the cultural claims of the group."

Given Freud's assumptions—first, that aggression is "an original, self-subsisting instinctual disposition in man," and second, that it constitutes the greatest impediment to civilization—his interest in "happiness" follows. Americans are familiar with the word *happiness* as a political construct. After all, the Declaration of Independence bestows on them rights that are "inalienable," including "life, liberty, and the pursuit of happiness." But what exactly did Freud mean by "happiness"? As the preceding quote would seem to suggest, to him it was no more than, though no less than, finding a balance between two competing claims: those of individuals on the one hand, and those of the groups of which they are members on the other. According to Freud, great leaders—defined in *Civilization* as "men of overwhelming force of mind or men in whom one of the human impulsions has found its strongest and purest, and therefore often its most one-sided, expression"—play a part in finding this balance. The problem is that such leaders are few and far between, which is why we are left in the main to fend for ourselves in this cold, hard, Hobbesian world, over which our earlier, more primitive selves continue to cast a shadow.

Finally, there is *Moses and Monotheism*, Freud's last major work, which he wrote as he was dying, an Austrian Jew who had only recently found harbor from Hitler in exile in England. This final book is not by any measure Freud's best. But it does return to some of his running themes, and it does display in one final burst his ongoing obsession with power and authority. By the time he wrote *Moses*, Freud and virtually every member of his family (to one degree or another) had been victimized by Hitler. Small wonder that his discussion of the great man begins with a question that reflects both his puzzlement and pain. "How is it possible that one single man can develop such extraordinary effectiveness?"

∾

MARY PARKER FOLLETT
1868–1933

JAMES MACGREGOR BURNS
1918–

Mary Parker Follett paved the way for the contemporary study of power, authority, and influence in business, in the private sector. James MacGregor Burns paved the way for the contemporary study of power, authority, and influence in politics, in the public sector. This is not to suggest that their work applies only to one sector or the other—not at all. Most of what Follett wrote could as well be assigned in schools of public administration; most of what Burns wrote can and has been studied by students of leadership in large corporations.

Both Follett and Burns had and continue to have many disciples, though Follett, being a woman, had to wait a half century or more before finally gaining the recognition that she deserved. And both Follett, in "The Essentials of Leadership," and Burns, in *Leadership*, deviated from what then as now was the prevailing norm: they took account not only of leaders, but also of followers. They understood, in a way that most people did not and do not, the importance of relations between leaders and led, and also among the led in their own right. To be sure, in both cases, leaders remained front and center. But in their work overall, Follett and Burns maintained a semblance of a balance between those who lead and their inevitable counterparts, those who follow.

MARY PARKER FOLLETT
–––––––– THE ESSENTIALS OF LEADERSHIP ––––––––
1933

But let us look further at the essentials of leadership. Of the greatest importance is the ability to grasp a total situation. The chief mistake in thinking of leadership as resting wholly on personality lies probably in the fact that the executive leader is not a leader of men only but of something we are learning to call the total situation. This includes facts, present and potential, aims and purposes and men. Out of a welter of facts, experience, desires, aims, the leader must find the unifying thread. He must see a whole, not a mere kaleidoscope of pieces. He must see the relation between all the different factors in a situation. The higher up you go, the more ability you have to have of this kind, because you have a wider range of facts from which to seize the relations. The foreman has a certain range—a comparatively small number of facts and small number of people. The head of a sub-department has a wider range; the head of a department a wider still, the general manager the widest of all. One of the principal functions of the general manager is to organize all the scattered forces of the business. The higher railway officials may not understand railway accounting, design of rolling stock, and assignment of rates as well as their expert assistants, but they know how to use their knowledge, how to relate it, how to make a total situation.

The leader then is one who can organise the experience of the group—whether it be the small group of the foreman, the larger group of the department, or the whole plant— . . . and thus get the full power of the group. The leader makes the team. This is pre-eminently the leadership quality—the ability to organise all the forces there are in an enterprise and make them serve a common purpose. Men with this ability create a group power rather than express a personal power. They penetrate to the subtlest connections of the forces at their command, and make all these forces available and most effectively available for the accomplishment of their purpose.

Some writers tell us that the leader should represent the accumulated knowledge and experience of his particular group, but I think he should go far beyond this. It is true that the able executive learns from everyone around him, but it is also true that he is far more than the depository where the wisdom of the group collects. When leadership rises to genius it has the power of transforming, of transforming experience into power. And that is what experience is for, to be made into power. The great leader creates as well as directs power. The essence of leadership is to create control, and that is what the world needs today, control of small situations or of our world situation.

I have said that the leader must understand the situation, must see it as a whole, must see the inter-relation of all the parts. He must do more than this. He must see the evolving situation, the developing situation. His wisdom, his judgment, is used, not on a situation that is stationary, but on one that is changing all the time. The ablest administrators do not merely draw logical conclusions from the array of facts of the past which their expert assistants bring to them, they have a vision of the future. To be sure, business estimates are always, or should be, based on the probable future conditions. Sales policy, for instance, is guided not only by past sales but by probable future sales. The leader, however, must see all the future trends and unite them. Business is always developing. Decisions have to anticipate the development. You remember how Alice in Wonderland had to run as fast as she could in order to stand still. That is a commonplace to every business man. And it is up to the general manager to see that his executives are running as fast as they can. Not, you understand, working as hard as they can—that is taken for granted—but anticipating as far as they can.

This insight into the future we usually call in business anticipating. But anticipating means more than forecasting or predicting. It means far more than meeting the next situation; it means making the next situation. If you will watch decisions, you will find that the highest grade decision does not have to do merely with the situation with which it is directly concerned. It is always the sign of the second-rate man when the decision merely meets the present situation. It is the left-over in a decision which gives it the greatest value. It is the carry-over in a decision which helps develop the situation in the way we wish it to be developed. In business we are always passing from one significant moment to another significant moment, and the leader's task is pre-eminently to understand the moment of passing. The leader sees one situation melting into another and has learned the mastery of that moment. We usually have the situation we make—no one sentence is more pregnant with meaning for business success. This is why the leader's task is so difficult, why the great leader requires the great qualities—the most delicate and sensitive perceptions, imagination and insight, and at the same time courage and faith. . . .

And now let me speak to you for a moment of something which seems to me of the utmost importance, but which has been far too little considered, and that is the part of the followers in the leadership situation. Their part is not merely to follow, they have a very active part to play and that is to keep the leader in control of a situation. Let us not think that we are either leaders or—nothing of much importance. As one of those led we have a part in leadership. In no aspect of our subject do we see a greater discrepancy between theory and practice than here. The definition given over and over again of the leader is one who can induce others to follow him. Or that meaning is taken for granted and the question is asked: "What is the technique by which a leader keeps his followers in line?" Some political scientists discuss why men obey or do not obey, why they tend to lead or to follow, as if leading and following were the essence of leadership. I think that following is a very small part of what the other members of a group have to do. I think that these authors are writing of theory, of words, of stereotypes of the past, that they are, at any rate, not noticing the changes that are going on in business thinking and business practice. If we want to treat these questions realistically, we shall watch what is actually happening, and what I see happening in some places is that the members of a group are not so much following a leader as helping to keep him in control of a situation.

How do we see this being done? For one thing, in looking at almost any business we see many suggestions coming up from below. We find sub-executives trying to get upper executives to install mechanical improvements, to try a new chemical process, to adopt a plan for increasing incentives for workers, and so on. The upper executives try to persuade the general manager and the general manager the board of directors. We have heard a good deal in the past about the consent of the governed; we have now in modern business much that might be called the consent of the governing, the suggestions coming from below and those at the top consenting. . . .

Leader and followers are both following the invisible leader—the common purpose. The best executives put this common purpose clearly before their group. While leadership depends on depth of conviction and the power coming therefrom, there must also be the ability to share that conviction with others, the ability to make purpose articulate. And then that common purpose becomes the leader. And I believe that we are coming more and more to act, whatever our theories, on our faith in the power of this invisible leader. Loyalty to the invisible leader gives us the strongest possible bond of union, establishes a sympathy which is not a sentimental but a dynamic sympathy.

Moreover, when both leader and followers are obeying the same demand, you have, instead of a passive, an active, self-willed obedience. The men on a fishing smack are all good fellows together, call each other by their first names, yet one is captain and the others obey him; but it is an intelligent, alert, self-willed obedience. . . .

Many are coming to think that the job of a man higher up is not to make decisions for his subordinates but to teach them how to handle their problems themselves, teach them how to make their own decisions. The best leader does not persuade men to follow his will. He shows them what it is necessary for them to do in order to meet their responsibility, a responsibility which has been explicitly defined to them. Such a leader is not one who wishes to do people's thinking for them, but one who trains them to think for themselves.

Indeed the best leaders try to train their followers themselves to become leaders. A second-rate executive will often try to suppress leadership because he fears it may rival his own. I have seen several instances of this. But the first-rate executive tries to develop leadership in those under him. He does not want men who are subservient to him, men who render him an unthinking obedience. While therefore there are still men who try to surround themselves with docile servants—you all know that type—the ablest men today have a larger aim, they wish to be leaders of leaders. This does not mean that they abandon one iota of power. But the great leader tries also to develop power wherever he can among those who work with him, and then he gathers all this power and uses it as the energizing force of a progressing enterprise.

JAMES MacGREGOR BURNS
---------- **LEADERSHIP** ----------
1978

Leadership is an aspect of power, but it is also a separate and vital process in itself.

Power over other persons, we have noted, is exercised when potential power wielders, motivated to achieve certain goals of their own, marshal in their power base resources (economic, military, institutional, or skill) that enable them to influence the behavior of respondents by activating motives of respondents relevant to those resources and to those goals. This is done in order to realize the purpose of the *power wielders, whether or not these are also the goals of the respondents.* Power wielders also exercise influence by mobilizing their own power base in such a way as to establish direct physical control over others' behavior, as in a war of conquest or through measures of harsh deprivation, but these are highly restricted exercises of power, dependent on certain times, cultures, and personalities, and they are often self-destructive and transitory.

Leadership over human beings is exercised when persons with certain motives and purposes mobilize, in competition or conflict with others, institutional, political, psychological, and other resources so as to arouse, engage, and satisfy the motives of followers. This is done in order to realize goals mutually held by both leaders and followers, as in Lenin's calls for peace, bread, and land. In brief, leaders with motive and power bases tap followers' motives in order to realize the purposes of both leaders and followers. Not only must motivation be relevant, as in power generally, but its purposes must be realized and satisfied. Leadership is exercised in a condition of *conflict* or *competition* in which leaders contend in appealing to the motive bases of potential followers. Naked power, on the other hand, admits of no competition or conflict—there is no engagement.

Leaders are a particular kind of power holder. Like power, leadership is relational, collective, and purposeful. Leadership shares with power the central function of achieving purpose. But the reach and domain of leadership are, in the short range at least, more limited than those of power. Leaders do not obliterate followers' motives though they may arouse certain motives and ignore others. They lead other creatures, not things (and lead animals only to the degree that they recognize animal motives—i.e., leading cattle to shelter rather than to slaughter). To control things—tools, mineral resources, money, energy—is an act of power, not leadership, for things have no motives. Power wielders may treat people as things. Leaders may not.

All leaders are actual or potential power holders, but not all power holders are leaders.

These definitions of power and of leadership differ from those that others have offered. Lasswell and Kaplan hold that power must be relevant to people's valued things; I hold that it must be relevant to the *power wielder's* valued things and may be relevant to the *recipient's* needs or values only as necessary to exploit them. Kenneth Janda defines power as "the ability to cause other persons to adjust their behavior in conformance with communicated behavior patterns." I agree, assuming that those behavior patterns aid the purpose of the power wielder. According to Andrew McFarland, "If the leader causes changes that he intended, he has exercised power; if the leader causes changes that he did not intend or want, he has exercised influence, but not power. . . ." I dispense with the concept of influence as unnecessary and unparsimonious. For me the leader is a very special, very circumscribed, but potentially the most effective of power holders, judged by the degree of intended "real change" finally achieved. Roderick Bell et al. contend that power is a relationship rather than an entity—an entity being something that "could be smelled and touched, or stored in a keg"; while I agree that power is a relationship, I contend that the relationship is one in which some entity—part of the "power base"—plays an indispensable part, whether that keg is a keg of beer, of dynamite, or of ink.

The crucial variable, again, is *purpose*. Some define leadership as leaders making followers do what *followers* would not otherwise do, or as leaders making followers do what the *leaders* want them to do; I define leadership as leaders inducing followers to act for certain goals that represent the values and the motivations—the wants and needs, the aspirations and expectations—*of both leaders and followers*. And the genius of leadership lies in the manner in which leaders see and act on their own and their followers' values and motivations.

Leadership, unlike naked power-wielding, is thus inseparable from followers' needs and goals. The essence of the leader-follower relation is the interaction of persons with different levels of motivations and of power potential, including skill, in pursuit of a common or at least joint purpose. That interaction, however, takes two fundamentally different forms. The first I will call transactional leadership (the nature of which will be developed in Part III). Such leadership occurs when one person takes the initiative in making contact with others for the purpose of an exchange of valued things. The exchange could be economic or political or psychological in nature: a swap of goods or of one good for money; a trading of votes between candidate and citizen or between legislators; hospitality to another person in exchange for willingness to listen to one's troubles. Each party to the bargain is conscious of the power resources and attitudes of the other. Each person recognizes the other as a *person*. Their purposes are related, at least to the extent that the purposes stand within the bargaining process and can be advanced by maintaining that process. But beyond this the relationship does not go. The bargainers have no enduring purpose that holds them together; hence they may go their separate ways. A leadership act took place, but it was not one that binds leader and follower together in a mutual and continuing pursuit of a higher purpose.

Contrast this with *transforming* leadership. Such leadership occurs when one or more persons *engage* with others in such a way that leaders and followers raise one another to higher levels of motivation and morality. (The nature of this motivation and this morality will be developed in Part II.) Their purposes, which might have started out as separate but related, as in the case of transactional leadership, become fused. Power bases are linked not as counterweights but as mutual support for common purpose. Various names are used for such leadership, some of them derisory: elevating, mobilizing, inspiring, exalting, uplifting, preaching, exhorting, evangelizing. The relationship can be moralistic, of course. But transforming leadership ultimately becomes *moral* in that it raises the level of human conduct and ethical aspiration of both leader and led, and thus it has a transforming effect on both. Perhaps the best modern example is Gandhi, who aroused and elevated the hopes and demands of millions of Indians and whose life and personality were enhanced in the process. Transcending leadership is dynamic leadership in the sense that the leaders throw themselves into a relationship with followers who will feel "elevated" by it and often become more active themselves, thereby creating new cadres of leaders. Transcending leadership is leadership *engagé*. Naked power-wielding can be neither transactional nor transforming; only leadership can be.

Leaders and followers may be inseparable in function, but they are not the same. The leader takes the initiative in making the leader-led connection; it is the leader who creates the links that allow communication and exchange to take place. An office seeker does this in accosting a voter on the street, but if the voter espies and accosts the politician, the voter is assuming a leadership function, at least for that brief moment. The leader is more skillful in evaluating followers' motives, anticipating their responses to an initiative, and estimating their power bases, than the reverse. Leaders continue to take the major part in maintaining and effectuating the relationship with followers and will have the major role in ultimately carrying out the combined purpose of leaders and followers. Finally, and most important by far, leaders address themselves to followers' wants, needs, and other motivations, as well as to their own, and thus they serve as an *independent force in changing the makeup of the followers' motive base through gratifying their motives.*

Certain forms of power and certain forms of leadership are near extremes on the power continuum. One is the kind of absolute power that, Lord Acton felt, "corrupts absolutely." It also coerces absolutely. The essence of this kind of power is the capacity of power wielders, given the necessary motivation, to override the motive and power bases of their targets. Such power objectifies its victims; it literally turns them into objects, like the inadvertent weapon tester in Mtésa's court. Such power wielders, as well, are objectified and dehumanized. Hitler, according to Richard Hughes, saw the universe as containing no persons other than himself, only "things." The ordinary citizen in Russia, says a Soviet linguist and dissident, does not identify with his government. "With us, it is there, like the wind, like a wall, like the sky. It is something permanent, unchangeable. So the individual acquiesces, does not dream of changing it—except a few, few people. . . ."

At the other extreme is leadership so sensitive to the motives of potential followers that the roles of leader and follower become virtually interdependent. Whether the leadership relationship is transactional or transforming, in it motives, values, and goals of leader and led have merged. . . .

More complex are relationships that lie between these poles of brute power and wholly reciprocal leadership-followership. Here empirical and theoretical questions still perplex both the analysts and the practitioners of power. One of these concerns the sheer measurement of power (or leadership). Traditionally we measure power resources by calculating each one and adding them up: constituency support plus access to leadership plus financial resources plus skill plus "popularity" plus access to information, etc., all in relation to the strength of opposing forces, similarly computed. But these calculations omit the vital factor of motivation and purpose and hence fall of their own weight. Another controversial measurement device is *reputation*. Researchers seek to learn from informed observers their estimates of the power or leadership role and resources of visible *community* leaders (projecting this into national arenas of power is a formidable task). Major questions arise as to the reliability of the estimates, the degree of agreement between interviewer and interviewee over their definition of power and leadership, the transferability of power from one area of decision-making to another. Another device for studying power and leadership is *linkage theory*, which requires elaborate mapping of communication and other interrelations among power holders in different spheres, such as the economic and the military. The difficulty here is that communication, which may expedite the processes of power and leadership, is not a substitute for them.

My own measurement of power and leadership is simpler in concept but no less demanding of analysis: *power and leadership are measured by the degree of production of intended effects*. This need not be a theoretical exercise. Indeed, in ordinary political life, the power resources and the motivations of presidents and prime ministers and political parties are measured by the extent to which presidential promises and party programs are carried out. Note that the variables are the double ones of *intent* (a function of motivation) and of capacity (a function of power base), but the test of the extent and quality of power and leadership is the degree of *actual accomplishment* of the promised change.

Other complexities in the study of power and leadership are equally serious. One is the extent to which power and leadership are exercised not by positive action but by *inaction* or *nondecision*. Another is that power and leadership are often exercised not directly on targets but indirectly, and perhaps through multiple channels, on multiple targets. We must ask not only whether P has the power to do X to R, but whether P can induce or force R to do Y to Z. The existence of power and leadership in the form of a stream of multiple direct and indirect forces operating over time must be seen as part of the broader sequences of historical causation. Finally, we must acknowledge the knotty problem of events of history that are beyond the control of identifiable persons capable of foreseeing developments and powerful enough to influence them and hence to be held accountable for them. We can only agree with C. Wright Mills that these are matters of fate rather than power or leadership.

We do well to approach these and other complexities of power and leadership with some humility as well as a measure of boldness. We can reject the "gee whiz" approach to power that often takes the form of the automatic presumption of "elite control" of communities, groups, institutions, entire nations. Certain concepts and techniques of the "elitist" school of power are indispensable in social and political analysis, but "elitism" is often used as a concept that *presupposes* the existence of the very degree and kind of power that is to be estimated and analyzed. Such "elite theorists" commit the gross error of equating power and leadership with the assumed power bases of preconceived leaders and power holders, without considering the crucial role of *motivations* of leaders and followers. Every good detective knows that one must look for the motive as well as the weapon.

Comment

Mary Parker Follett was the first in a series of pioneers in the study of leadership and management in large organizations, especially in American business. After her came Chester Barnard, who in 1938 published his influential book, *The Functions of the Executive*; then Philip Selznick, who in 1957 came out with his small, important volume, *Leadership in Administration*; and then Peter Drucker, who is widely considered the father of "modern management" and author of many books, including, for example, *The Effective Executive* (1966). While there were important differences among these four founders, together they prepared the soil for many thousands of scholars and students who have since gone on further to expand the now global study of leadership and management. In fact, the still burgeoning interest in leadership education and development drives the modern "leadership industry," that amorphous multi-million-dollar effort by leadership educators, trainers, coaches, and consultants to teach people how to lead and how to manage.

In her own time, Follett was widely admired, and she was successful. Moreover, in recent years, experts in the field such as Drucker,

Warren Bennis, and Rosabeth Moss Kanter have paid her homage. Drucker referred to her as "the prophet of management." Bennis described her as a "swashbuckling advance scout of management thinking." And Kanter wrote that Follett's work reminds us that there are "truths about human behavior that stand the test of time."

But for reasons that are not easily understood or widely agreed on, during the decades after her death, Follett was largely ignored and nearly forgotten. Bennis recalled that while he knew her name early in his career, in the 1950s and 1960s, at the time Follett was thought of as more of a "cult figure" than anything else. Drucker similarly remembered that in the early 1940s, when he tried to find out who mattered in management, no one "as much as mentioned Mary Parker Follett." Drucker claimed that her ideas were to blame for what in retrospect was a startling omission—they were, he thought, out of step with those that were then in fashion. Kanter's explanation, though, was different. She argued that Follett was dismissed for so long because of her gender. As Kanter put it, it is hard to "found or build a discipline without disciples." And it is hard to attract disciples "if one is very different from traditional authority figures."

In any event, Follett's work is now, finally, esteemed as it should be: considered simultaneously pathbreaking and cutting-edge. Flattened hierarchies, participative decision making, and employee empowerment—all ideas found in Follett's pioneering work, and all now in fashion. No wonder Follett is being hailed, and claimed, even by academics in areas other than her own. Feminist scholars such as Jane Mansbridge have come to consider her one of theirs. One of Follett's central tenets, Mansbridge wrote, "power-with" as opposed to power-over, is a "working part of feminist theory." And political theorists, Benjamin Barber among them, argue that those who are "concerned with democracy" must take into account Follett's work, in particular that on democracy in the workplace. In short, Follett's progressive views on leaders and, as significantly, on followers, who, she insisted, have "a very active part to play," are perfectly tuned to a world in which the dynamics of power, authority, and influence are more fluid than ever before.

Burns's career followed a different trajectory. By the time he wrote *Leadership*, he had long been among America's preeminent scholars and public intellectuals. Widely published and highly esteemed both in the academy and outside it, he was perhaps best known as an expert on the American presidency. In addition to his many books on the subject in general, Burns had written a two-volume biography of Franklin Delano Roosevelt that was awarded, among other honors, a Pulitzer Prize. In addition, Burns was an activist, president of any number of professional associations, candidate (unsuccessful) for a seat in the U.S. Congress, and gadfly within the academic establishment. He was especially tireless in his decades-long effort to legitimize Leadership Studies in the social sciences, to make the study of leadership and, by his clear implication, followership a discipline, or, at the least, a reasonably coherent, as well as respected, area of academic inquiry.

But the book that he titled simply *Leadership* was something else altogether. It transformed Burns into one of the types he described: an intellectual leader. Intellectual leaders, Burns wrote, "deal with both analytical and normative ideas and they bring both to bear on their environment." They are not "detached from their social milieus; typically they seek to change it." And so it was with Burns and his book—for *Leadership* was itself an agent of change. First, Burns did for students of political leadership what Follett ultimately did for students of corporate leadership: he demonstrated that it was a subject that could and should be taken seriously. This should have been unnecessary; twentieth-century historians and political scientists should have had the subject of leadership high on their academic agendas. But they did not. For a variety of reasons, among them that the study of leadership was not considered sufficiently scientific (as in social "science"), it was not—at least, not until Burns came along—thought by the academic establishment to be suitably serious. (Burns did create change, but it was more meager than he wanted and intended. In general, in the academy, the study of leadership is still somewhat suspect.)

The other major contribution of *Leadership* was, as suggested, substantive. Burns's two leadership types, transactional and transforming, made a big impression and had a big impact. Countless dissertations have been written on transactional leadership and/or transforming leadership. And transforming leadership came of itself to be considered the ideal, the paragon of leadership types. Transforming leadership was transcendent leadership—the type of leadership to which all leaders, and all followers, would seem to aspire.

This longing to be transforming returns us to what Follett (who also wrote about "the power of transforming") and Burns have in common. What they share perhaps more than anything else is a rather romantic notion of what great leadership can accomplish. Both suggest that, at its best, leadership is all-embracing, sweeping along anyone and everyone to take them, *with* their advice and consent, to a new and better place. As Burns writes of transforming leadership, it "ultimately becomes *moral* in that it raises the level of human conduct and ethical aspiration of both leader and led, and thus it has a transforming effect on both."

∽

STANLEY MILGRAM
1933–1984

HANNAH ARENDT
1906–1975

Yale University psychologist Stanley Milgram conducted the most famous (or, better, the most infamous) social science experiment of all time. The experiment was about followers—about obedience to authority. It was intended to shed light on why followers obeyed leaders who ordered them to do something that they would almost certainly not have done otherwise—inflict pain, obvious physical pain, on another human being. When Milgram was asked why he chose to conduct such an experiment, he said that it was the Holocaust, the murder by the Nazis of some 6 million Jews, that motivated him to investigate how ordinary people could act so "callously and inhumanely." Or, as he put it after the experiments were concluded, the question that had haunted him was, "Under what conditions could a person obey, when commanded, actions that went against his conscience?"

Milgram conducted his initial experiment in 1963. That same year, philosopher Hannah Arendt (to whom Milgram in the following text refers) published her classic volume on what was, in effect, the same subject. Arendt, already renowned for her work on, among other subjects, totalitarianism, was similarly moved by the horrors that had transpired in her native Germany during the Nazi period. Her book—*Eichmann in Jerusalem: A Report on the Banality of Evil*—was what its title suggested. It was an analysis of Adolf Eichmann, one of the few major Nazi perpetrators to come before the court years after the Nuremberg trials had ended, and certainly the most visible. Eichmann's justification for his part in the murderous process was what Arendt found so striking. Like other Nazi leaders who depicted themselves as ordinary people, as ordinary followers, he pleaded, "I was only following orders." The simplicity of his defense, its ubiquity and apparent accuracy led Arendt, rather like Milgram in *Obedience to Authority*, to conceive the inconceivable—that evil is banal.

STANLEY MILGRAM
-------- **OBEDIENCE TO AUTHORITY** --------
1974

Obedience is as basic an element in the structure of social life as one can point to. Some system of authority is a requirement of all communal living, and it is only the man dwelling in isolation who is not forced to respond, through defiance or submission, to the commands of others.

Obedience, as a determinant of behavior, is of particular relevance to our time. It has been reliably established that from 1933 to 1945 millions of innocent people were systematically slaughtered on command. Gas chambers were built, death camps were guarded, daily quotas of corpses were produced with the same efficiency as the manufacture of appliances. These inhumane policies may have originated in the mind of a single person, but they could only have been carried out on a massive scale if a very large number of people obeyed orders.

Obedience is the psychological mechanism that links individual action to political purpose. It is the dispositional cement that binds men to systems of authority. Facts of recent history and observation in daily life suggest that for many people obedience may be a deeply ingrained behavior tendency, indeed, a prepotent impulse overriding training in ethics, sympathy, and moral conduct. C. P. Snow (1961) points to its importance when he writes:

> When you think of the long and gloomy history of man, you will find more hideous crimes have been committed in the name of obedience than have ever been committed in the name of rebellion. If you doubt that, read William Shirer's *Rise and Fall of the Third Reich*. The German Officer Corps were brought up in the most rigorous code of obedience . . . in the name of obedience they were party to, and assisted in, the most wicked large scale actions in the history of the world. (p. 24)

The Nazi extermination of European Jews is the most extreme instance of abhorrent immoral acts carried out by thousands of people in the name of obedience. Yet in lesser degree this type of thing is constantly recurring: ordinary citizens are ordered to destroy other people, and they do so because they consider it their duty to obey orders. Thus, obedience to authority, long praised as a virtue, takes on a new aspect when it serves a malevolent cause; far from appearing as a virtue, it is transformed into a heinous sin. Or is it? . . .

The legal and philosophic aspects of obedience are of enormous import, but an empirically grounded scientist eventually comes to the point where he wishes to move from abstract discourse to the careful observation of concrete instances. In order to take a close look at the act of obeying, I set up a simple experiment at Yale University. Eventually, the experiment was to involve more than a thousand participants and would be repeated at several universities, but at the beginning, the conception was simple. A person comes to a psychological laboratory and is told to carry out a series of acts that come increasingly into conflict with conscience. The main question is how far the participant will comply with the experimenter's instructions before refusing to carry out the actions required of him.

But the reader needs to know a little more detail about the experiment. Two people come to a psychology laboratory to take part in a study of memory and learning. One of them is designated as a "teacher" and the other a "learner." The experimenter explains that the study is concerned with the effects of punishment on learning. The learner is conducted into a room, seated in a chair, his arms strapped to prevent excessive movement, and an electrode attached to his wrist. He is told that he is to learn a list of word pairs; whenever he makes an error, he will receive electric shocks of increasing intensity.

The real focus of the experiment is the teacher. After watching the learner being strapped into place, he is taken into the main experimental room and seated before an impressive shock generator. Its main feature is a horizontal line of thirty switches, ranging from 15 volts to 450 volts, in 15-volt increments. There are also verbal designations which range from SLIGHT SHOCK to DANGER—SEVERE SHOCK. The teacher is told that he is to administer the learning test to the man in the other room. When the learner responds correctly, the teacher moves on to the next item; when the other man gives an incorrect answer, the teacher is to give him an electric shock. He is to start at the lowest shock level (15 volts) and to increase the level each time the man makes an error, going through 30 volts, 45 volts, and so on.

The "teacher" is a genuinely naive subject who has come to the laboratory to participate in an experiment. The learner, or victim, is an actor who actually receives no shock at all. The point of the experiment is to see how far a person will proceed in a concrete and measurable situation in which he is ordered to inflict increasing pain on a protesting victim. At what point will the subject refuse to obey the experimenter?

Conflict arises when the man receiving the shock begins to indicate that he is experiencing discomfort. At 75 volts, the "learner" grunts. At 120 volts he complains verbally; at 150 he demands to be released from the experiment. His protests continue as the shocks escalate, growing increasingly vehement and emotional. At 285 volts his response can only be described as an agonized scream.

Observers of the experiment agree that its gripping quality is somewhat obscured in print. For the subject, the situation is not a game; conflict is intense and obvious. On one hand, the manifest suffering of the learner presses him to quit. On the other, the experimenter, a legitimate authority to whom the subject feels some commitment, enjoins him to continue. Each time the subject hesitates to administer shock, the experimenter orders him to continue. To extricate himself from the situation, the subject must make a clear break with authority. The aim of this investigation was to find when and how people would defy authority in the face of a clear moral imperative.

There are, of course, enormous differences between carrying out the orders of a commanding officer during times of war and carrying out the orders of an experimenter. Yet the essence of certain relationships remain, for one may ask in a general way: How does a man behave when he is told by a legitimate authority to act against a third individual? If anything, we may expect the experimenter's power to be considerably less than that of the general, since he has no power to enforce his imperatives, and participation in a psychological experiment scarcely evokes the sense of urgency and dedication engendered by participation in war. Despite these limitations, I thought it worthwhile to start careful observation of obedience even in this modest situation, in the hope that it would stimulate insights and yield general propositions applicable to a variety of circumstances.

A reader's initial reaction to the experiment may be to wonder why anyone in his right mind would administer even the first shocks. Would he not simply refuse and walk out of the laboratory? But the fact is that no one ever does. Since the subject has come to the laboratory to aid the experimenter, he is quite willing to start off with the procedure. There is nothing very extraordinary in this, particularly since the person who is to receive the shocks seems initially cooperative, if somewhat apprehensive. What is surprising is how far ordinary individuals will go in complying with the experimenter's instructions. Indeed, the results of the experiment are both surprising and dismaying. Despite the fact that many subjects experience stress, despite the fact that many protest to the experimenter, a substantial proportion continue to the last shock on the generator. Many subjects will obey the experimenter no matter how vehement the pleading of the person being shocked, no matter how painful the shocks seem to be, and no matter how much the victim pleads to be let out. This was seen time and again in our studies and has been observed in several universities where the experiment was repeated. It is the extreme willingness of adults to go to almost any lengths on the command of an authority that constitutes the chief finding of the study and the fact most urgently demanding explanation.

A commonly offered explanation is that those who shocked the victim at the most severe level were monsters, the sadistic fringe of society. But if one considers that almost two-thirds of the participants fall into the category of "obedient" subjects, and that they represented ordinary people drawn from working, managerial, and professional classes, the argument becomes very shaky. Indeed, it is highly reminiscent of the issue that arose in connection with Hannah Arendt's 1963 book, *Eichmann in Jerusalem*. Arendt contended that the prosecution's effort to depict Eichmann as a sadistic monster was fundamentally wrong, that he came closer to being an uninspired bureaucrat who simply sat at his desk and did his job. For asserting these views, Arendt became the object of considerable scorn, even calumny. Somehow, it was felt that the monstrous deeds carried out by Eichmann required a brutal, twisted, and sadistic personality, evil incarnate. After witnessing hundreds of ordinary people submit to the authority in our own experiments, I must conclude that Arendt's conception of the *banality of evil* comes closer to the truth than one might dare imagine. The ordinary person who shocked the victim did so out of a sense of obligation—a conception of his duties as a subject—and not from any peculiarly aggressive tendencies.

This is, perhaps, the most fundamental lesson of our study: ordinary people, simply doing their jobs, and without any particular hostility on their part, can become agents in a terrible destructive process. Moreover, even when the destructive effects of their work become patently clear, and they are asked to carry out actions incompatible with fundamental standards of morality, relatively few people have the resources needed to resist authority. A variety of inhibitions against disobeying authority come into play and successfully keep the person in his place.

Sitting back in one's armchair, it is easy to condemn the actions of the obedient subjects. But those who condemn the subjects measure them against the standard of their own ability to formulate high-minded moral prescriptions. That is hardly a fair standard. Many of the subjects, at the level of stated opinion, feel quite as strongly as any of us about the moral requirement of refraining from action against a helpless victim. They, too, in general terms know what ought to be done and can state their values when the occasion arises. This has little, if anything, to do with their actual behavior under the pressure of circumstances. . . .

The problem of obedience, therefore, is not wholly psychological. The form and shape of society and the way it is developing have much to do with it. There was a time, perhaps, when men were able to give a fully human response to any situation because they were fully absorbed in it as human beings. But as soon as there was a division of labor among men, things changed. Beyond a certain point, the breaking up of society into people carrying out narrow and very special jobs takes away from the human quality of work and life. A person does not get to see the whole situation but only a small part of it, and is thus unable to act without some kind of over-all direction. He yields to authority but in doing so is alienated from his own actions.

HANNAH ARENDT
EICHMANN IN JERUSALEM:
A REPORT ON THE BANALITY OF EVIL
1963

So Eichmann's opportunities for feeling like Pontius Pilate were many, and as the months and the years went by, he lost the need to feel anything at all. This was the way things were, this was the new law of the land, based on the Führer's order; whatever he did he did, as far as he could see, as a law-abiding citizen. He did his *duty*, as he told the police and the court over and over again; he not only obeyed *orders*, he also obeyed the *law*. Eichmann had a muddled inkling that this could be an important distinction, but neither the defense nor the judges ever took him up on it. The well-worn coins of "superior orders" versus "acts of state" were handed back and forth; they had governed the whole discussion of these matters during the Nuremberg Trials, for no other reason than that they gave the illusion that the altogether unprecedented could be judged according to precedents and the standards that went with them. Eichmann, with his rather modest mental gifts, was certainly the last man in the courtroom to be expected to challenge these notions and to strike out on his own. Since, in addition to performing what he conceived to be the duties of a law-abiding citizen, he had also acted upon orders—always so careful to be "covered"—he became completely muddled, and ended by stressing alternately the virtues and the vices of blind obedience, or the "obedience of corpses," *Kadavergehorsam*, as he himself called it. . . .

Doing his "duty" finally brought him into open conflict with orders from his superiors. During the last year of the war, more than two years after the Wannsee Conference, he experienced his last crisis of conscience. As the defeat approached, he was confronted by men from his own ranks who fought more and more insistently for exceptions and, eventually, for the cessation of the Final Solution. That was the moment when his caution broke down and he began, once more, taking initiative—for instance, he organized the foot marches of Jews from Budapest to the Austrian border after Allied bombing had knocked out the transportation system. It now was the fall of 1944, and Eichmann knew that Himmler had ordered the dismantling of the extermination facilities in Auschwitz and that the game was up. Around this time, Eichmann had one of his very few personal interviews with Himmler, in the course of which the latter allegedly shouted at him, "If up to now you have been busy liquidating Jews, you will from now on, since I order it, take good care of Jews, act as their nursemaid. I remind you that it was I—and neither Gruppenführer Müller nor you—who founded the R.S.H.A. in 1933; I am the one who gives orders here!" Sole witness to substantiate these words was the very dubious Mr. Kurt Becher; Eichmann denied that Himmler had shouted at him, but he did not deny that such an interview had taken place. Himmler cannot have spoken in precisely these words, he surely knew that the R.S.H.A. was founded in 1939, not in 1933, and not simply by himself but by Heydrich, with his endorsement. Still, something of the sort must have occurred, Himmler was then giving orders right and left that the Jews be treated well—they were his "soundest investment"—and it must have been a shattering experience for Eichmann. . . .

In Jerusalem, confronted with documentary proof of his extraordinary loyalty to Hitler and the Führer's order, Eichmann tried a number of times to explain that during the Third Reich "the Führer's words had the force of law" (*Führerworte haben Gesetzeskraft*), which meant, among other things, that if the order came directly from Hitler it did not have to be in writing. He tried to explain that this was why he had never asked for a written order from Hitler (no such document relating to the Final Solution has ever been found; probably it never existed), but had demanded to see a written order from Himmler. To be sure, this was a fantastic state of affairs, and whole libraries of very "learned" juridical comment have been written, all demonstrating that the Führer's *words*, his oral pronouncements, were the basic law of the land. Within this "legal" framework, every order contrary in letter or spirit to a word spoken by Hitler was, by definition, unlawful. Eichmann's position, therefore, showed a most unpleasant resemblance to that of the often-cited soldier who, acting in a normal legal framework, refuses to carry out orders that run counter to his ordinary experience of lawfulness and hence can be recognized by him as criminal. . . .

To be sure, it was not merely Eichmann's conviction that Himmler was now giving "criminal" orders that determined his actions. But the personal element undoubtedly involved was not fanaticism, it was his genuine, "boundless and immoderate admiration for Hitler" (as one of the defense witnesses called it)—for the man who had made it "from lance corporal to Chancellor of the Reich." It would be idle to try to figure out which was stronger in him, his admiration for Hitler or his determination to remain a law-abiding citizen of the Third Reich when Germany was already in ruins. Both motives came into play once more during the last days of the war, when he was in Berlin and saw with violent indignation how everybody around him was sensibly enough getting himself fixed up with forged papers before the arrival of the Russians or the Americans. A few weeks later, Eichmann, too, began to travel under an assumed name, but by then Hitler was dead, and the "law of the land" was no longer in existence, and he, as he pointed out, was no longer bound by his oath. For the oath taken by the members of the S.S. differed from the military oath sworn by the soldiers in that it bound them only to Hitler, not to Germany.

The case of the conscience of Adolf Eichmann, which is admittedly complicated but is by no means unique, is scarcely comparable to the case of the German generals, one of whom, when asked at Nuremberg, "How was it possible that all you honorable generals could continue to serve a murderer with such unquestioning loyalty?," replied that it was "not the task of a soldier to act as judge over his supreme commander. Let history do that or God in heaven." (Thus General Alfred Jodl, hanged at Nuremberg.) Eichmann, much less intelligent and without any education to speak of, at least dimly realized that it was not an order but a law which had turned them all into criminals. The distinction between an order and the Führer's word was that the latter's validity was not limited in time and space, which is the outstanding characteristic of the former. This is also the true reason why the Führer's order for the Final Solution was followed by a huge shower of regulations and directives, all drafted by expert lawyers and legal advisers, not by mere administrators; this order, in contrast to ordinary orders, was treated as a law. Needless to add, the resulting legal paraphernalia, far from being a mere symptom of German pedantry or thoroughness, served most effectively to give the whole business its outward appearance of legality.

And just as the law in civilized countries assumes that the voice of conscience tells everybody "Thou shalt not kill," even though man's natural desires and inclinations may at times be murderous, so the law of Hitler's land demanded that the voice of conscience tell everybody: "Thou shalt kill," although the organizers of the massacres knew full well that murder is against the normal desires and inclinations of most people. Evil in the Third Reich had lost the quality by which most people recognize it— the quality of temptation. Many Germans and many Nazis, probably an overwhelming majority of them, must have been tempted *not* to murder, *not* to rob, *not* to let their neighbors go off to their doom (for that the Jews were transported to their doom they knew, of course, even though many of them may not have known the gruesome details), and not to become accomplices in all these crimes by benefiting from them. But, God knows, they had learned how to resist temptation.

Comment

The selection from Milgram's book is included in this volume not on the grounds of its literary merit, nor because it, per se, constitutes an original contribution. Rather the original contribution was the experiment itself. The text is a classic, then, because Milgram describes in his own words his groundbreaking experiment, which changed forever our understanding of the relationship between superiors and subordinates.

Relationships between leaders and followers are generally seen from the perspective of the former, as opposed to the latter. We always were, and we remain, more attracted to and engaged by those who do have power, authority, and influence than by those who do not. But in the wake of World War II, Milgram came to see leadership and followership more clearly: as an exchange between at least two people, one who leads, or, at least, directs the action and, at a minimum, one other who follows or, to put it as he did, one person with authority and one without.

Milgram appreciated what up to then most historians had not: that the Holocaust was not Hitler's handiwork alone. Rather, it was the outcome of orders that were obeyed, more or less voluntarily, by hundreds of thousands of Germans who otherwise were ordinary.

Obedience is not by definition something to be abjured. To the contrary, some measure of obedience or at least compliance is necessary for the effective performance of nearly all groups and organizations, and for that matter of society as a whole. Moreover, there are circumstances—for example, in the heat of battle—when near-blind obedience is considered nearly essential. But as the Nazi regime receded into the past, the question of how one of the most highly educated and culturally sophisticated people in the world went along with (and then some) one of the worst cadres of leaders in human history became more compelling.

Crimes of obedience are a fact of life. Americans have been guilty of them, as have Germans and Japanese, Russians and Chinese, Rwandans and Argentines. Moreover, since Milgram, the ease and speed with which man's treatment of man can deteriorate has been replicated in the laboratory, most famously by Philip Zimbardo, whose Stanford prison experiments turned ordinary undergraduates into cruel overseers in just a few days. Additionally, by now, Milgram's experiment has been conducted in at least nine other countries, with findings that were substantially the same. And it was replicated some 40 years later, in 2008, in the United States, with similar results. So the question inevitably arises: what are the circumstances under which crimes of obedience are likely to be committed?

Hannah Arendt—widely considered one of the most influential of twentieth-century philosophers, and the author of a classic study of Nazism and Stalinism, *The Origins of Totalitarianism*—sought similarly to find an answer to this question. Her work on totalitarianism, published in 1951, was the necessary precursor to her work on Eichmann. While both were signal attempts to grasp the catastrophe that had engulfed Europe, and European Jews in particular, *Origins* did so through institutional analysis, while *Eichmann* did so through individual analysis. It was as if

Origins did not suffice to explain the inexplicable even to its own author. Thus, Arendt was driven to look further—to a single man, one of Hitler's top functionaries: Adolf Eichmann.

Origins set the stage for *Eichmann* in several ways, none more important than its references to the led as well as to the leader. Put another way, even in her earlier work, Arendt avoided the pitfall of being obsessed with Hitler. She understood better than most of her contemporaries that, as Margaret Canovan wrote, "only the selfless devotion given by those she calls 'the masses' made possible the totalitarian leaders' utter disregard for the lives and interests of their subjects." Arendt described these "masses" as being as rootless as they were ruthless, and as indispensable to the rise of the totalitarian state. But it was not until she arrived in Jerusalem in the early 1960s, and watched for months on end as Eichmann stood trial, that she began to formulate the idea for which she ultimately became best known.

When *Eichmann in Jerusalem* first came out, it created, as Milgram observed, a firestorm, among Jews and intellectuals in particular, both in Israel and in the United States. Two main charges were leveled against Arendt, both deadly serious. The first was that by criticizing Jewish community leaders in Nazi-occupied Europe for facilitating the deportations of their own people, she seemed to be blaming, if only in part, the victims. The second charge, which is of special interest here, was that she had the temerity to describe Eichmann as banal, as somehow like everyone else. (Recall that *Eichmann* appeared not long after the Second World War, so feelings remained raw and memories vivid. While this made it especially difficult for some in Arendt's audience to hear what she had to say, in fact, the debate over Arendt on Eichmann continues even now. Only recently was it suggested that her views on the banality of evil were colored by her close personal and professional connection to German philosopher Martin Heidegger. Heidegger, one of the most esteemed thinkers of the twentieth century, was also a dedicated Nazi.)

Arendt had concluded that Eichmann was not so much malevolent as he was callow. He was not so much an ideologue, a rabid anti-Semite, as he was without ideology altogether. And he was not in any apparent way extraordinary. On the contrary, he seemed to Arendt to be utterly ordinary. Eichmann as Arendt described him was "genuinely incapable of uttering a single sentence that was not a cliché." He was "full of empty talk," a bureaucrat whose "inability to speak was closely connected with an inability to *think*."

In Arendt's conception, Eichmann was the quintessential empty vessel. This makes a certain kind of sense: he did not ever, himself, so far as we know, kill another human being. Nor did he ever, personally, inflict physical harm. Rather, Eichmann was a cog—albeit a critical one—in the Nazi war machine. He was the "logistical wizard," who as much as anyone else was responsible for organizing the transports that moved hundreds of thousands of Jews out of sight and to their deaths. So far as Arendt was concerned, then, it was precisely his bureaucratic efficiency, his detachment from destruction and his distance from death that enabled his effectiveness at work. His inability, or, perhaps, his unwillingness, to stop and think led Arendt to conclude that Eichmann's trial was evidence of the "fearsome, word-and-thought-defying *banality of evil*."

Milgram found human nature to be pliable. Some situational variables incline us to obey orders, even when we think the orders wrong; other situational variables incline us to resist, even when to resist is to incur risk. Milgram also found that people do differ, one from another, in how they respond to orders from their superiors, especially if an order is contrary to conscience. It is, then, an amalgam of the individual and the situation that determines our response to authority, including obedience to authority when obedience is a crime.

Remarkably (or not), Arendt's conclusion was virtually the same. She came to the problem as a philosopher, not as a psychologist. So her explanation of what went hideously wrong in Nazi Germany is embedded in the work of Immanuel Kant, in particular in his conception of evil as necessarily involving intent. Still, Eichmann as Arendt depicted him was eerily similar to (most of) the men who were the subjects of Milgram's experiment. That is, Eichmann did not intend especially to do harm. Rather he was a conformist who adapted to an environment in which conformity was prized. This, then, is the point at which the two writers converge—the psychologist and the philosopher, Milgram and Arendt. Both concluded that the objects of their attention were not so different from you and me. They did as they were told—a response that is nothing if not familiar.

2

LITERATURE
AS
LEADERSHIP

True, This!—Beneath the rule
of men entirely great,
The pen is mightier than the sword.

—EDWARD BULWER-LYTTON

I T'S A REMARKABLE CONCEIT: the idea of changing the world simply by sitting and writing. But that's exactly what these eight men and four women who took pen to paper did—to right what they deeply felt was a wrong. Just as remarkable was their reward: they did what they set out to do. They changed the world.

Three of the women were pivotal in the fight for women's rights. In the eighteenth century, Wollstonecraft dared to suggest that women were "degraded by mistaken notions of female excellence." In the nineteenth century, Stanton dared to demand equity by equating the "Declaration of Sentiments" with the Declaration of Independence. And in the twentieth century, Friedan dared to urge women to "no longer ignore that voice" that said, "I want something more than my husband and my children and my home."

Four of the men were revolutionaries, insisting in their writings on no less than bringing down the old order. Paine was for upending the English in favor of the Americans; Marx and Engels were for upending the bourgeoisie in favor of the proletariat; and Fanon was for upending imperialists, colonialists, and other odious outsiders in favor of the righteous and rightful.

The rest were outliers: they wrote to campaign for causes that no one had previously championed, at least not successfully. Du Bois wanted to secure the best education available anywhere for the "talented tenth," Carson to sound the alert on the pollution of the planet, Alinsky to create change from the bottom up, Singer to advocate for nonhuman animals, and Kramer to provoke us to act on AIDS, a disease that then was still as mortifying to contract as it was likely to be lethal.

All of these writers—all of these *leaders*—did the nearly impossible. They wrote so well that we read them still. And they wrote so well that their literature was leadership.

~

MARY WOLLSTONECRAFT

1759–1797

Mary Wollstonecraft was first and foremost a figure of the Enlightenment, the product of a period during which absolute power was starting to slip away from those at the top and move toward those in the middle and even those at the bottom. Not by chance was Wollstonecraft's *A Vindication of the Rights of Women* published in 1792. This was the year during which the French National Convention abolished the monarchy. This was the year during which Thomas Paine wrote *The Rights of Man*. And this was the year during which there was a vigorous campaign for the abolition of slavery—in Britain.

Before being accepted as a writer, Wollstonecraft worked as a governess. But this was a governess who wrote in support of the French Revolution. And this was a governess who came to propagate fervently the radical idea that individual rights should be extended to include rights for women. In *A Vindication of the Rights of Women,* she addressed men, but only halfheartedly and secondarily. Her primary audience was her own kind, women, in high hopes of leading them to a new and better place.

A VINDICATION OF THE RIGHTS OF WOMEN

1792

INTRODUCTION

The conduct and manners of women, in fact, evidently prove that their minds are not in a healthy state; for, like the flowers which are planted in too rich a soil, strength and usefulness are sacrificed to beauty; and the flaunting leaves, after having pleased a fastidious eye, fade, disregarded on the stalk, long before the season when they ought to have arrived at maturity.—One cause of this barren blooming I attribute to a false system of education, gathered from the books written on this subject by men who, considering females rather as women than human creatures, have been more anxious to make them alluring mistresses than wives; and the understanding of the sex has been so bubbled by this specious homage, that the civilized women of the present century, with a few exceptions, are only anxious to inspire love, when they ought to cherish a nobler ambition, and by their abilities and virtues exact respect.

In a treatise, therefore, on female rights and manners, the works which have been particularly written for their improvement must not be overlooked; especially when it is asserted, in direct terms, that the minds of women are enfeebled by false refinement; that the books of instruction, written by men of genius, have had the same tendency as more frivolous productions; and that, in the true style of Mahometanism, they are only considered as females, and not as a part of the human species, when improvable reason is allowed to be the dignified distinction which raises men above the brute creation, and puts a natural sceptre in a feeble hand.

Yet, because I am a woman, I would not lead my readers to suppose that I mean violently to agitate the contested question respecting the equality or inferiority of the sex; but as the subject lies in my way, and I cannot pass it over without subjecting the main tendency of my reasoning to misconstruction, I shall stop a moment to deliver, in a few words, my opinion.—In the government of the physical world it is observable that the female, in general, [is] inferior to the male. The male pursues, the female yields—this is the law of nature; and it does not appear to be suspended or abrogated in favour of woman. This physical superiority cannot be denied—and it is a noble prerogative! But not content with this natural pre-eminence, men endeavour to sink us still lower, merely to render us alluring objects for a moment; and women, intoxicated by the adoration which men, under the influence of their senses, pay them, do not seek to obtain a durable interest in their hearts, or to become the friends of the fellow creatures who find amusement in their society.

I am aware of an obvious inference:—from every quarter have I heard exclamations against masculine women; but where are they to be found? If by this appellation men mean to inveigh against their ardour in hunting, shooting, and gaming, I shall most cordially join in the cry; but if it be against the imitation of manly virtues, or, more properly speaking, the attainment of those talents and virtues, the exercise of which ennobles the human character, and which raises females in the scale of animal being, when they are comprehensively termed mankind;—all those who view them with a philosophical eye must, I should think, wish with me, that they may every day grow more and more masculine.

This discussion naturally divides the subject. I shall first consider women in the grand light of human creatures, who, in common with men, are placed on this earth to unfold their faculties; and afterwards I shall more particularly point out their peculiar designation.

I wish also to steer clear of an error which many respectable writers have fallen into; for the instruction which has hither been addressed to women, has rather been applicable to *ladies*, if the little indirect advice, that is scattered through Sanford and Merton be excepted; but, addressing my sex in a firmer tone, I pay particular attention to those in the middle class, because they appear to be in the most natural state. Perhaps the seeds of false refinement, immorality, and vanity, have ever been shed by the great. Weak, artificial beings, raised above the common wants and affections of their race, in a premature unnatural manner, undermine the very foundation of virtue, and spread corruption through the whole mass of society! As a class of mankind they have the strongest claim to pity; the education of the rich tends to render them vain and helpless, and the unfolding mind is not strengthened by the practice of those duties which dignify the human character.—They only live to amuse themselves, and by the same law which in nature invariably produces certain effects, they soon only afford barren amusement.

But as I purpose taking a separate view of the different ranks of society, and of the moral character of women, in each, this hint is, for the present, sufficient; and I have only alluded to the subject, because it appears to me to be the very essence of an introduction to give a cursory account of the contents of the work it introduces.

My own sex, I hope, will excuse me, if I treat them like rational creatures, instead of flattering their *fascinating* graces, and viewing them as if they were in a state of perpetual childhood, unable to stand alone. I earnestly wish to point out in what true dignity and human happiness consists—I wish to persuade women to endeavour to acquire strength, both of mind and body, and to convince them that the soft phrases, susceptibility of heart, delicacy of sentiment, and refinement of taste, are almost synonymous with epithets of weakness, and that those beings who are only the objects of pity and that kind of love, which has been termed its sister, will soon become objects of contempt.

Comment

Mary Wollstonecraft's life was the stuff of legend. She was one of seven children parented by a father who was a violent alcoholic and an abused mother who suffered at her husband's hands. Wollstonecraft left home at 19 and supported herself in one or another of the few positions that were then available to what now would be considered middle-class women: successively as companion, teacher, and governess. Then she began, nearly out of nowhere, to write. In short order, Wollstonecraft's radical treatises won her a measure of fame, notoriety even, and she embarked on a life to match. She went to live for a few years in Paris, became romantically involved with an American businessman, and gave birth to an illegitimate daughter. Finally she returned to England; married an established political philosopher, William Godwin; and died just a few months later, shortly after giving birth to a second child, another daughter. This daughter, also named Mary, went on to marry the great poet Percy Bysshe Shelley and to write the most famous horror story of all time, *Frankenstein*.

More than most, Wollstonecraft's life is tied to her work. She learned from the earliest possible age the price that women paid for having to depend absolutely on their husbands; for presuming that they might rely on stereotypical, but transient, feminine felicities such as youth and beauty; and for allowing themselves to be kept in a condition, intellectually and economically, that was childlike. The amalgam of her own experience with the social and political ferment of the time transformed Wollstonecraft from what she had been into what she became: a famous crusader, fighting for women's rights.

To appreciate the degree of her daring, we need to go back in time to the world into which Mary Wollstonecraft was born, mid-eighteenth-century England. As Toni Bentley wrote, it was a world in which, if you happened to be a woman, and to be married, your property and your children belonged to your husband. Divorce was impossible, so if you had a horrid husband and dared to leave him, you had no choice but to desert your children in the process and become an outlaw. Marital rape was legal—although in 1782, a law was finally passed that required husbands who beat their wives to use a stick no wider than a thumb. For their part, women were expected at all times to acquiesce—and to please.

Wollstonecraft's message to women contained admonitions and exhortations. She cautioned, for example, against assuming that typically feminine ways and wiles would get women very far, or have an impact other than fleeting. "Soft phrases, susceptibility of heart, delicacy of sentiment, and refinement of taste, are almost synonymous with epithets of weakness," she warned. What, then, was to be done? What recourse did women have? On this Wollstoncraft was equally clear: if they could, they should get an education. (Her primary audience was women who had the benefit of being literate.)

Education was of the greatest importance to Wollstonecraft, both in her broader capacity as a liberal reformer and as a pioneering proponent of women's rights. Not only had she herself been a schoolmistress and governess, but the book that first established her as an author was titled *Thoughts on the Education of Daughters.* So she was persuaded of the importance of early learning for the sake of the individual, girls as well as boys, of course, and for society as a whole.

Wollstonecraft was not alone in this regard; in fact, she was in good company. As noted by Alan Richardson, "Other radical writers, most notably Thomas Paine, had also concluded that day schools funded by the state would best promote the spread of literacy, knowledge, and ultimately social and political equality." But Wollstonecraft's personal political agenda was more narrowly focused on the education of women and girls in particular. Going to school would make girls "free" and "independent." It would transform the lives even of women who confined themselves to the domestic sphere. And it would allow "the sexes to associate together in every pursuit."

Wollstonecraft is considered by some experts to be the greatest of polemical feminists. Ellen Moers wrote:

She wished to teach her whole sex not to grovel. From the observation of her own life, and that of her sisters, friends, pupils, and employers, from wide reading in the works of the *philosophes* to whose company she aspired, Wollstonecraft came to understand the social conditions governing the lives of all women and to denounce their institutionalized repression—a social fact that she was the first to grasp in its entirety, and that her writings did most to change.

What was most remarkable about Wollstonecraft was her utter fearlessness. She was as brave in her personal life as she was in her professional one. While she was derided by others—they called her a "hyena in petticoats"—she dared to tread where they did not. Additionally, she was always as stylish as she was serious. Listen again to the sound of her voice: "The conduct and manners of women, in fact, evidently prove that their minds are not in a healthy state; for, like the flowers which are planted in too rich a soil, strength and usefulness are sacrificed to beauty; and the flaunting leaves, after having pleased a fastidious eye, fade, disregarded on the stalk, long before the season when they ought to have arrived at maturity."

∾

THOMAS PAINE
1737–1809

He was born in England, and there his remains were ultimately returned. Nevertheless, Tom Paine was the fiercest of all defenders of American independence from the Crown, and the most ardently articulate.

His revolutionary tract, *Common Sense*, appeared in just the right place and at just the right time: in Philadelphia in January 1776. Most Americans were not yet persuaded that the fight for independence was worth the cost: their ties to England were close and long-standing, their future as a separate state was uncertain at best, and they did not hunger for war against His Majesty's troops. But Paine was without doubt. He was convinced of the correctness of his cause—a conviction that he conveyed in his passionate prose.

As I noted in the Introduction, *Common Sense* lit the fire that lit the revolution. It was a phenomenon: a half million copies were published in the first 12 months. Not for nothing did Benjamin Franklin declare the impact of *Common Sense* to be "prodigious." Not for nothing did Benjamin Rush recall that it "burst from the press with an effect which has rarely been produced . . . in any age or country." And not for nothing was John Adams envious, complaining to Jefferson that history would "ascribe the American Revolution to Thomas Paine."

What is recognized now was recognized then. *Common Sense* is great literature—and great leadership.

COMMON SENSE
1776

In the following pages I offer nothing more than simple facts, plain arguments, and common sense: and have no other preliminaries to settle with the reader, than that he will divest himself of prejudice and prepossession, and suffer his reason and his feelings to determine for themselves that he will put on, or rather that he will not put off, the true character of a man, and generously enlarge his views beyond the present day. . . .

I have heard it asserted by some, that as America has flourished under her former connection with Great Britain, the same connection is necessary towards her future happiness, and will always have the same effect. Nothing can be more fallacious than this kind of argument. We may as well assert that because a child has thrived upon milk, that it is never to have meat, or that the first twenty years of our lives is to become a precedent for the next twenty. But even this is admitting more than is true; for I answer roundly that America would have flourished as much, and probably much more, had no European power taken any notice of her. The commerce by which she hath enriched herself are the necessaries of life, and will always have a market while eating is the custom of Europe.

But she has protected us, say some. That she hath engrossed us is true, and defended the Continent at our expense as well as her own, is admitted; and she would have defended Turkey from the same motive, viz.— for the sake of trade and dominion.

Alas! we have been long led away by ancient prejudices and made large sacrifices to superstition. We have boasted the protection of Great Britain, without considering, that her motive was INTEREST not ATTACHMENT; and that she did not protect us from OUR ENEMIES on OUR ACCOUNT; but from HER ENEMIES on HER OWN ACCOUNT, from those who had no quarrel with us on any OTHER ACCOUNT, and who will always be our enemies on the SAME ACCOUNT. . . .

But Britain is the parent country, say some. Then the more shame upon her conduct. Even brutes do not devour their young, nor savages make war upon their families. Wherefore, the assertion, if true, turns to her reproach; but it happens not to be true, or only partly so, and the phrase PARENT OR MOTHER COUNTRY hath been jesuitically adopted by the King and his parasites, with a low papistical design of gaining an unfair bias on the credulous weakness of our minds. Europe, and not England, is the parent country of America. This new World hath been the asylum for the persecuted lovers of civil and religious liberty from EVERY PART of Europe. Hither have they fled, not from the tender embraces of the mother, but from the cruelty of the monster; and it is so far true of England, that the same tyranny which drove the first emigrants from home, pursues their descendants still. . . .

I challenge the warmest advocate for reconciliation to show a single advantage that this continent can reap by being connected with Great Britain. I repeat the challenge; not a single advantage is derived. Our corn will fetch its price in any market in Europe, and our imported goods must be paid for, buy them where we will.

But the injuries and disadvantages which we sustain by that connection, are without number; and our duty to mankind at large, as well as to ourselves, instruct us to renounce the alliance: because, any submission to, or dependence on, Great Britain, tends directly to involve this Continent in European wars and quarrels, and set us at variance with nations who would otherwise seek our friendship, and against whom we have neither anger nor complaint. As Europe is our market for trade, we ought to form no partial connection with any part of it. It is the true interest of America to steer clear of European contentions, which she never can do, while, by her dependence on Britain, she is made the makeweight in the scale of British politics.

Europe is too thickly planted with Kingdoms to be long at peace, and whenever a war breaks out between England and any foreign power, the trade of America goes to ruin, BECAUSE OF HER CONNECTION WITH BRITAIN. The next war may not turn out like the last, and should it not, the advocates for reconciliation now will be wishing for separation then, because neutrality in that case would be a safer convoy than a man of war. Every thing that is right or reasonable pleads for separation. The blood of the slain, the weeping voice of nature cries, 'TIS TIME TO PART. Even the distance at which the Almighty hath placed England and America is a strong and natural proof that the authority of the one over the other, was never the design of Heaven. The time likewise at which the Continent was discovered, adds weight to the argument, and the manner in which it was peopled, increases the force of it. The Reformation was preceded by the discovery of America: As if the Almighty graciously meant to open a sanctuary to the persecuted in future years, when home should afford neither friendship nor safety.

The authority of Great Britain over this continent, is a form of government, which sooner or later must have an end: And a serious mind can draw no true pleasure by looking forward, under the painful and positive conviction that what he calls "the present constitution" is merely temporary. As parents, we can have no joy, knowing that this government is not sufficiently lasting to ensure any thing which we may bequeath to posterity: And by a plain method of argument, as we are running the next generation into debt, we ought to do the work of it, otherwise we use them meanly and pitifully. In order to discover the line of our duty rightly, we should take our children in our hand, and fix our station a few years farther into life; that eminence will present a prospect which a few present fears and prejudices conceal from our sight.

Though I would carefully avoid giving unnecessary offence, yet I am inclined to believe, that all those who espouse the doctrine of reconciliation, may be included within the following descriptions. Interested men, who are not to be trusted, weak men who CANNOT see, prejudiced men who will not see, and a certain set of moderate men who think better of the European world than it deserves; and this last class, by an ill-judged deliberation, will be the cause of more calamities to this Continent than all the other three.

It is the good fortune of many to live distant from the scene of present sorrow; the evil is not sufficiently brought to their doors to make them feel the precariousness with which all American property is possessed. But let our imaginations transport us a few moments to Boston; that seat of wretchedness will teach us wisdom, and instruct us for ever to renounce a power in whom we can have no trust. The inhabitants of that unfortunate city who but a few months ago were in ease and affluence, have now no other alternative than to stay and starve, or turn out to beg. Endangered by the fire of their friends if they continue within the city and plundered by the soldiery if they leave it, in their present situation they are prisoners without the hope of redemption, and in a general attack for their relief they would be exposed to the fury of both armies.

Men of passive tempers look somewhat lightly over the offences of Great Britain, and, still hoping for the best, are apt to call out, "Come, come, we shall be friends again for all this." But examine the passions and feelings of mankind: bring the doctrine of reconciliation to the touchstone of nature, and then tell me whether you can hereafter love, honour, and faithfully serve the power that hath carried fire and sword into your land? If you cannot do all these, then are you only deceiving yourselves, and by your delay bringing ruin upon posterity. Your future connection with Britain, whom you can neither love nor honour, will be forced and unnatural, and being formed only on the plan of present convenience, will in a little time fall into a relapse more wretched than the first. But if you say, you can still pass the violations over, then I ask, hath your house been burnt? Hath your property been destroyed before your face? Are your wife and children destitute of a bed to lie on, or bread to live on? Have you lost a parent or a child by their hands, and yourself the ruined and wretched survivor? If you have not, then are you not a judge of those who have. But if you have, and can still shake hands with the murderers, then are you unworthy the name of husband, father, friend or lover, and whatever may be your rank or title in life, you have the heart of a coward, and the spirit of a sycophant.

This is not inflaming or exaggerating matters, but trying them by those feelings and affections which nature justifies, and without which, we should be incapable of discharging the social duties of life, or enjoying the felicities of it. I mean not to exhibit horror for the purpose of provoking revenge, but to awaken us from fatal and unmanly slumbers, that we may pursue determinately some fixed object. It is not in the power of Britain or of Europe to conquer America, if she do not conquer herself by *delay* and *timidity*. The present winter is worth an age if rightly employed, but if lost or neglected, the whole continent will partake of the misfortune; and there is no punishment which that man will not deserve, be he who, or what, or where he will, that may be the means of sacrificing a season so precious and useful.

It is repugnant to reason, to the universal order of things to all examples from former ages, to suppose, that this continent can longer remain subject to any external power. The most sanguine in Britain does not think so. The utmost stretch of human wisdom cannot, at this time, compass a plan short of separation, which can promise the continent even a year's security. Reconciliation is *now* a falacious dream. Nature hath deserted the connexion, and Art cannot supply her place. For, as Milton wisely expresses, "never can true reconcilement grow where wounds of deadly hate have pierced so deep."

Every quiet method for peace hath been ineffectual. Our prayers have been rejected with disdain; and only tended to convince us, that nothing flatters vanity, or confirms obstinacy in Kings more than repeated petitioning—and nothing hath contributed more than that very measure to make the Kings of Europe absolute: Witness Denmark and Sweden. Wherefore, since nothing but blows will do, for God's sake, let us come to a final separation, and not leave the next generation to be cutting throats, under the violated unmeaning names of parent and child.

To say, they will never attempt it again is idle and visionary, we thought so at the repeal of the stamp act, yet a year or two undeceived us; as well may we suppose that nations, which have been once defeated, will never renew the quarrel.

As to government matters, it is not in the power of Britain to do this continent justice: The business of it will soon be too weighty, and intricate, to be managed with any tolerable degree of convenience, by a power, so distant from us, and so very ignorant of us; for if they cannot conquer us, they cannot govern us. To be always running three or four thousand miles with a tale or a petition, waiting four or five months for an answer, which when obtained requires five or six more to explain it in, will in a few years be looked upon as folly and childishness—There was a time when it was proper, and there is a proper time for it to cease. . . .

O ye that love mankind! Ye that dare oppose, not only the tyranny, but the tyrant, stand forth! Every spot of the old world is overrun with oppression. Freedom hath been hunted round the globe. Asia, and Africa, have long expelled her.—Europe regards her like a stranger, and England hath given her warning to depart. O! receive the fugitive, and prepare in time an asylum for mankind.

Comment

Thomas Paine is the exception, not the rule—a writer who led brilliantly or, if you will, a leader who wrote brilliantly. As Thomas Jefferson, himself no slouch with a pen, said of his compatriot, "No writer has exceeded Paine in ease and familiarity of style, in perspicuity of expression, happiness of elucidation, and in simple and unassuming language."

Paine was a radical—which is precisely why he used language that was easy to access. His intention was to make the strongest possible case to the widest possible audience. Not that Paine's simple prose was in the least simple-minded. As Edward Larkin pointed out, Paine was well versed in the classical tradition, and he was sophisticated in his rhetoric and argumentation. But he insisted that the truth was simple rather than complex, and by doing so he first manipulated and finally enfranchised his huge popular audience. What Paine ultimately managed was the literary equivalent of a neat trick: he reached the people without reaching down.

Paine was, curiously, the most unlikely of great writers, as well as the most unlikely of American revolutionists. Born in England, he was schooled formally only to the age of 12. For the next quarter century, until he was 37, when he set sail for America, his life was, as Hobbes might have put it, nasty and brutish. He suffered the slings and arrows of failure, grief (a wife and child died in childbirth), and impoverishment, and when he arrived in Philadelphia in 1774, he was so sickened by typhus that when he left the ship, he had to be carried.

What, then, when he arrived in America, did he have to recommend him? How did he get from here to there, from inconspicuous penury to fame if not fortune in less than two years? Clearly the man was a genius at invoking the power of language. In addition, he had a letter to recommend him from Benjamin Franklin, whom he knew, though only slightly. Most important, he was fiercely determined to do what he did best: brandish his pen on behalf of his cause. A few years earlier, he had written a pamphlet—this one titled "The Case of the Officers of Excise"—which, like its legendary successor, spoke truth to power. So for all the misery and chaos in his life, Paine did have purpose, and he did have passion. Though he himself was without power, authority, or influence, he had the temerity to stand up to, and inveigh against, those more richly endowed.

In America, the man met the moment. Not long after his arrival in the new world, Paine's prose was pulling in readers, great numbers of readers who, not knowing where to turn, turned to him, of all people, for leadership. Paine titled his book, his pamphlet really, *Common Sense* for good reason: he made everything seem so entirely obvious, so altogether logical. Paine told of two steps. First, out with the old. Cut the cord to the English king, not only because the Crown constrained and corrupted, but also because, "There is something very absurd in supposing a continent to be perpetually governed by an island." Then go on—go on to build the new. Paine painted a picture of promise. In time, he wrote, a land as "happily situated" as America would become "an asylum for mankind."

Paine's seeds were planted in fertile soil. The colonists were becoming increasingly restive. Protests against England, against one or another real or imagined slight by the Crown, were growing in number. Individual colonists were growing more confident and becoming better able to govern themselves. And, finally, there was among the colonies a growing sense of community and connectedness. In September 1774, delegates from all 13 colonies except Georgia met in Philadelphia at the First Continental Congress. Over the next two years, the colonies' sense of themselves as being collaborative and independent increased, and their sense of self as separate and dependent decreased. So when Paine's cry for freedom was sounded, it was heard loudly and clearly all up and down America's eastern seaboard. He had struck not only a chord, but a nerve.

Notwithstanding his key role at a watershed moment in history, Paine's life was full of tribulation at the end, as it had been at the beginning. Shunned by many of his American contemporaries, in part for his views on religion (years later, Theodore Roosevelt called him a "filthy little atheist"), he returned to England, where he crafted another equally powerful revolutionary document, *Rights of Man*. But the government would have none of it. The king's prime minister, William Pitt, brought a charge of seditious writings against Paine, whereupon Paine fled to France. He lived there for a decade, only to end up arrested and imprisoned, again for his sharp tongue and corrosive quill. Finally he returned to America, but times had changed and so had the land he had long ago loved. Having radicalized revolutionaries in three different countries on two different continents, Paine died in New York, nearly alone, partly of drink.

~

ELIZABETH CADY STANTON
1815–1902

The history of political thought is one of contagion. In ways that are hard to see close up but easy to see from a distance, ideas that are powerful enough to resonate in one place tend to resonate at the same time in another. This held true long before globalization in its most recent incarnation, and long before the advent of technologies that made it obvious how information and ideas were disseminated.

It was no accident, no mere coincidence, that though France and America were an ocean apart at a time when being an ocean apart was huge, revolutions broke out in both countries at almost the same time. Similarly, it was no accident, no mere coincidence, that Elizabeth Cady Stanton's *Declaration of Sentiments* was published in the same year, 1848, as Karl Marx and Friedrich Engels's *The Communist Manifesto*. Both the *Declaration* and the *Manifesto* urged the overthrow of nearly everything that was old: the old political and economic order, and the old social order as well.

The *Declaration of Sentiments* was issued at the now-legendary Seneca Falls Convention, where some 300 people, most but not all of them women, gathered in the summer of 1848 to declare that the patterns of the past would no longer do. They demanded change—the kind of change that would prevent men from dominating women, both in the public realm and in the private one. Their *Declaration* mirrored the Declaration of Independence, which was, of course, deliberate. Like the Founding Fathers, these women, these Founding Mothers, declared that *their* time for life, liberty, and the pursuit of happiness was now.

---------- DECLARATION OF SENTIMENTS ----------
1848

When, in the course of human events, it becomes necessary for one portion of the family of man to assume among the people of the earth a position different from that which they have hitherto occupied, but one to which the laws of nature and of nature's God entitle them, a decent respect to the opinions of mankind requires that they should declare the causes that impel them to such a course.

We hold these truths to be self-evident: that all men and women are created equal; that they are endowed by their Creator with certain inalienable rights; that among these are life, liberty, and the pursuit of happiness; that to secure these rights governments are instituted, deriving their just powers from the consent of the governed. Whenever any form of Government becomes destructive of these ends, it is the right of those who suffer from it to refuse allegiance to it, and to insist upon the institution of a new government, laying its foundation on such principles, and organizing its powers in such form as to them shall seem most likely to effect their safety and happiness. Prudence, indeed, will dictate that governments long established should not be changed for light and transient causes; and accordingly, all experience hath shown that mankind are more disposed to suffer, while evils are sufferable, than to right themselves by abolishing the forms to which they are accustomed. But when a long train of abuses and usurpations, pursuing invariably the same object, evinces a design to reduce them under absolute despotism, it is their duty to throw off such government, and to provide new guards for their future security. Such has been the patient sufferance of the women under this government, and such is now the necessity which constrains them to demand the equal station to which they are entitled.

The history of mankind is a history of repeated injuries and usurpations on the part of man toward woman, having in direct object the establishment of an absolute tyranny over her. To prove this, let facts be submitted to a candid world.

He has never permitted her to exercise her inalienable right to the elective franchise.

He has compelled her to submit to laws, in the formation of which she had no voice.

He has withheld from her rights which are given to the most ignorant and degraded men—both natives and foreigners.

Having deprived her of this first right of a citizen, the elective franchise, thereby leaving her without representation in the halls of legislation, he has oppressed her on all sides.

He has made her, if married, in the eye of the law, civilly dead.

He has taken from her all right in property, even to the wages she earns.

He has made her, morally, an irresponsible being, as she can commit many crimes with impunity, provided they be done in the presence of her husband. In the covenant of marriage, she is compelled to promise obedience to her husband, he becoming, to all intents and purposes, her master—the law giving him power to deprive her of her liberty, and to administer chastisement.

He has so framed the laws of divorce, as to what shall be the proper causes of divorce; in case of separation, to whom the guardianship of the children shall be given; as to be wholly regardless of the happiness of women—the law, in all cases, going upon the false supposition of the supremacy of man, and giving all power into his hands.

After depriving her of all rights as a married woman, if single and the owner of property, he has taxed her to support a government which recognizes her only when her property can be made profitable to it.

He has monopolized nearly all the profitable employments, and from those she is permitted to follow, she receives but a scanty remuneration.

He closes against her all the avenues to wealth and distinction, which he considers most honorable to himself. As a teacher of theology, medicine, or law, she is not known.

He has denied her the facilities for obtaining a thorough education—all colleges being closed against her.

He allows her in Church as well as State, but a subordinate position, claiming Apostolic authority for her exclusion from the ministry, and, with some exceptions, from any public participation in the affairs of the Church.

He has created a false public sentiment, by giving to the world a different code of morals for men and women, by which moral delinquencies which exclude women from society, are not only tolerated but deemed of little account in man.

He has usurped the prerogative of Jehovah himself, claiming it as his right to assign for her a sphere of action, when that belongs to her conscience and her God.

He has endeavored, in every way that he could to destroy her confidence in her own powers, to lessen her self-respect, and to make her willing to lead a dependent and abject life.

Now, in view of this entire disfranchisement of one-half the people of this country, their social and religious degradation—in view of the unjust laws above mentioned, and because women do feel themselves aggrieved, oppressed, and fraudulently deprived of their most sacred rights, we insist that they have immediate admission to all the rights and privileges which belong to them as citizens of these United States.

In entering upon the great work before us, we anticipate no small amount of misconception, misrepresentation, and ridicule; but we shall use every instrumentality within our power to effect our object. We shall employ agents, circulate tracts, petition the State and national Legislatures, and endeavor to enlist the pulpit and the press in our behalf. We hope this Convention will be followed by a series of Conventions, embracing every part of the country. . . .

Whereas, the great precept of nature is conceded to be, "that man shall pursue his own true and substantial happiness," Blackstone, in his Commentaries, remarks, that this law of Nature being coeval with mankind, and dictated by God himself, is of course superior in obligation to any other. It is binding over all the globe, in all countries, and at all times; no human laws are of any validity if contrary to this, and such of them as are valid, derive all their force, and all their validity, and all their authority, mediately and immediately, from this original; Therefore,

Resolved, That such laws as conflict, in any way, with the true and substantial happiness of woman, are contrary to the great precept of nature, and of no validity; for this is "superior in obligation to any other."

Resolved, That all laws which prevent woman from occupying such a station in society as her conscience shall dictate, or which place her in a position inferior to that of man, are contrary to the great precept of nature, and therefore of no force or authority.

Resolved, That woman is man's equal—was intended to be so by the Creator, and the highest good of the race demands that she should be recognized as such.

Resolved, That the women of this country ought to be enlightened in regard to the laws under which they live, that they may no longer publish their degradation, by declaring themselves satisfied with their present position, nor their ignorance, by asserting that they have all the rights they want.

Resolved, That inasmuch as man, while claiming for himself intellectual superiority, does accord to woman moral superiority, it is pre-eminently his duty to encourage her to speak, and teach, as she has an opportunity, in all religious assemblies.

Resolved, That the same amount of virtue, delicacy, and refinement of behavior, that is required of woman in the social state, should also be required of man, and the same transgressions should be visited with equal severity on both man and woman.

Resolved, That the objection of indelicacy and impropriety, which is so often brought against woman when she addresses a public audience, comes with a very ill grace from those who encourage, by their attendance, her appearance on the stage, in the concert, or in the feats of the circus.

Resolved, That woman has too long rested satisfied in the circumscribed limits which corrupt customs and a perverted application of the Scriptures have marked out for her, and that it is time she should move in the enlarged sphere which her great Creator has assigned her.

Resolved, That it is the duty of the women of this country to secure to themselves their sacred right to the elective franchise.

Resolved, That the equality of human rights results necessarily from the fact of the identity of the race in capabilities and responsibilities.

Resolved, therefore, That, being invested by the Creator with the same capabilities, and the same consciousness of responsibility for their exercise, it is demonstrably the right and duty of woman, equally with man, to promote every righteous cause, by every righteous means; and especially in regard to the great subjects of morals and religion, it is self-evidently her right to participate with her brother in teaching them, both in private and in public, by writing and by speaking, by any instrumentalities proper to be used, and in any assemblies proper to be held; and this being a self-evident truth, growing out of the divinely implanted principles of human nature, any custom or authority adverse to it, whether modern or wearing the hoary sanction of antiquity, is to be regarded as self-evident falsehood, and at war with the interests of mankind. . . .

Resolved, That the speedy success of our cause depends upon the zealous and untiring efforts of both men and women, for the overthrow of the monopoly of the pulpit, and for the securing to woman an equal participation with men in the various trades, professions and commerce.

Comment

The fight for women's rights seems somehow to be endless. More than a half century before Elizabeth Cady Stanton called a convention at Seneca Falls, Mary Wollstonecraft had written *A Vindication of the Rights of Women*, which, like its fabled successor, did no more than, though no less than, demand some semblance of equity between the sexes. To be sure, the *Declaration* is a more advanced document, more sophisticated and precise. Stanton, for example, spoke of specifics, of education, property, and jobs. But the theme was essentially the same: that men controlled women in ways that were outrageous and egregious, and that it was high time for men's dominance and women's deference finally to end.

To look at the trajectory of the women's movement from one angle is to see it as only an issue of gender, of women demanding equity with men. But to look at it from another angle is to see the women's movement as part of a larger struggle—for human rights generally. This was obviously the case with Stanton, and also with her close collaborator, Susan B. Anthony: their activism on behalf of women was closely connected to their activism on behalf of slaves.

During the first half of the nineteenth century, the American anti-slavery and women's movements were entwined, as was evidenced most famously by the Grimke sisters, Sarah and Angelina, who first and foremost were abolitionists. Only after being attacked for being "public performers" and for speaking to groups that extended to men did the sisters conclude that they no longer had a choice. They had to fight for women's rights, if only to protect their ability to promote their primary passion, the abolition of slavery. It was a time of heated public debate, in which feminists and feminism could flourish. It was also a time in which leaders of the women's movement, including Stanton and Anthony, belonged simultaneously to the American Anti-Slavery Society.

Though Elizabeth Cady Stanton was not alone in crafting the document that became the *Declaration*, she was the driving force behind it. And what a force of nature she was! She had seven children, lived to 87 in nearly perfect health, was famously large and sensuous, and was as learned as she was clever and witty. Moreover, she combined her fierce intellect with a flair for political organization that enabled her, far better than even her stellar contemporaries, to translate anger into action. As Ellen Carol DuBois wrote, "It fell to Elizabeth Stanton, a militant feminist who understood the importance of political organization for reformers, to recognize that feminism, like abolition, had to become a political movement to 'give reality' to its principles. This was the basis on which she demanded women's suffrage." In fact, the first in her long list of grievances against men was that women were being denied their "inalienable right to the elective franchise."

The two-day meeting that constituted the Seneca Falls Convention launched the organized movement for women's rights in the United States and, along with it, Stanton's career as an activist and public intellectual. Though the idea of the women's rights convention was Lucretia Mott's as well as Stanton's, it was the latter who was the leader. It was she who suggested that the Declaration of Independence be used as a model for the manifesto. It was she who assembled the list of grievances that was grist for the mill for decades to come. And it was she who thought to focus on the vote, which, as DuBois further observed, "distinguished Seneca Falls from the women's rights activity that had preceded it."

This is not to say that Stanton was a paragon of virtue. In fact, in her new biography of Stanton, Lori Ginzberg argues that Stanton was an abolitionist more out of convenience than out of conviction, and that she was an elitist if not also a racist. Still, she was a pioneer, a pathbreaker. Her decision to model the *Declaration of Sentiments* on the Declaration of Independence was of utmost importance. Not only did this new version of the old document provide women with a newfound sense of confidence (at first they felt "as hopeless as if they had been suddenly asked to construct a steam engine"), but it lent the campaign for women's rights legitimacy and respectability. Moreover, as Sue Davis has pointed out, "the connection with the fight for independence from England emphasized the liberal nature of women's rights reform and minimized its most far-reaching implications insofar as it established that women were only seeking the rights for which men had fought." In other words, by lashing their document so closely to the original one, Stanton and the women at Seneca Falls presented themselves as doing nothing more radical than acting in accordance with the passions and purposes of the American Revolution. They also provided men with an apparently simple solution: acknowledge that our rights are the same as yours and change the laws accordingly.

But if the similarities between the two declarations were of the utmost importance, so were the differences. Following Stanton's lead, the women at Seneca Falls were wordsmiths of immediacy and even intimacy. They wrote of marriage and divorce. They wrote of being obliged by law to obey their husbands. They wrote of having to leave their children in the hands of men, "wholly regardless of the happiness of women." And they wrote of having their confidence destroyed and their self-respect diminished, and of oppression as a way of life. Stanton and her band of sisters wed the public sphere to the private one. They declared that the two were as inseparable as they were inviolable, and they demanded in no uncertain terms that women receive the "equal station to which they are entitled."

~

KARL MARX
1818–1883

FRIEDRICH ENGELS
1820–1895

It could reasonably be argued that no other piece of political prose ever had the impact of Karl Marx and Friedrich Engels's small, slender volume, *The Communist Manifesto*. Consider this: during the second half of the twentieth century, Communists were in control of fully one-third of the world's population, and Communist governments held sway over wide swaths of Europe and Asia, of South and Central America, and of Africa.

This brings us to the question of historical causation: what role, if any, did Marx and Engels play in creating the kind of communism that came to pass years after they themselves had passed? The communism to which I refer implies crimes of various kinds, from minor to major, and repression by regimes that were as malevolent as they were controlling. To be clear, no one has argued that Marx and Engels deliberately drafted a document disposed to despots. But questions remain. For at least since Lenin drew on *The Communist Manifesto* as the theory on which to build communist practice—most importantly in the Soviet Union and China, under Stalin and Mao Zedong, respectively, but also in smaller countries such as Cambodia under Pol Pot—these governments have been relentlessly ruthless, to the point of killing many millions of their own.

Given this subsequent history, and given the complexities of the argument, it is important to go back to the beginning, to when *The Communist Manifesto* was originally penned and published. The year was 1848, and the place was Western Europe. It was a time of change: increasing international commerce, improved communications, a growing middle class (the bourgeoisie), and pervasive political ferment. It was a moment that seemed to some, Marx and Engels among them, ripe for revolution.

Of course they could not know then what we know now—that the future of capitalism would turn out to be long and largely healthy. Their failures as prognosticators did not, however, preclude genius of another sort. For *The Communist Manifesto* is a masterpiece of the leadership literature. Marx and Engels's ultimate exhortation—"WORKERS OF THE WORLD, UNITE!"—reverberated worldwide in the nineteenth and twentieth centuries, and it does still, in the twenty-first.

THE COMMUNIST MANIFESTO
1848

A spectre is haunting Europe—the spectre of Communism. All the powers of old Europe have entered into a holy alliance to exorcize this spectre: Pope and Tsar, Metternich and Guizot, French radicals and German police spies.

Where is the party in opposition that has not been decried as communistic by its opponents in power? Where the opposition that has not hurled back the branding reproach of Communism, against the more advanced opposition parties, as well as against its reactionary adversaries?

Two things result from this fact:

1. Communism is already acknowledged by all European powers to be itself a power.

2. It is high time that Communists should openly, in the face of the whole world, publish their views, their aims, their tendencies, and meet this nursery tale of the Spectre of Communism with a manifesto of the party itself.

To this end, Communists of various nationalities have assembled in London, and sketched the following manifesto, to be published in the English, French, German, Italian, Flemish and Danish languages.

I. Bourgeois and Proletarians

The history of all hitherto existing society is the history of class struggles.

Freeman and slave, patrician and plebeian, lord and serf, guild-master and journeyman, in a word, oppressor and oppressed, stood in constant opposition to one another, carried on an uninterrupted, now hidden, now open fight, a fight that each time ended, either in a revolutionary reconstitution of society at large, or in the common ruin of the contending classes.

In the earlier epochs of history, we find almost every where a complicated arrangement of society into various orders, a manifold gradation of social rank. In ancient Rome we have patricians, knights, plebeians, slaves; in the Middle Ages, feudal lords, vassals, guild-masters, journeymen, apprentices, serfs; in almost all of these classes, again, subordinate gradations.

The modern bourgeois society that has sprouted from the ruins of feudal society has not done away with class antagonisms. It has but established new classes, new conditions of oppression, new forms of struggle in place of the old ones.

Our epoch, the epoch of the bourgeoisie, possesses, however, this distinctive feature: It has simplified the class antagonisms. Society as a whole is more and more splitting up into two great hostile camps, into two great classes directly facing each other: bourgeoisie and proletariat. . . .

The bourgeoisie, historically, has played a most revolutionary part.

The bourgeoisie, wherever it has got the upper hand, has put an end to all feudal, patriarchal, idyllic relations. It has pitilessly torn asunder the motley feudal ties that bound man to his "natural superiors," and has left remaining no other nexus between man and man than naked self-interest, than callous "cash payment." It has drowned the most heavenly ecstasies of religious fervour, of chivalrous enthusiasm, of philistine sentimentalism, in the icy water of egotistical calculation. It has resolved personal worth into exchange value, and in place of the numberless indefeasible chartered freedoms, has set up that single, unconscionable freedom—free trade. In one word, for exploitation, veiled by religious and political illusions, it has substituted naked, shameless, direct, brutal exploitation.

The bourgeoisie has stripped of its halo every occupation hitherto honoured and looked up to with reverent awe. It has converted the physician, the lawyer, the priest, the poet, the man of science, into its paid wage labourers.

The bourgeoisie has torn away from the family its sentimental veil, and has reduced the family relation to a mere money relation.

The bourgeoisie has disclosed how it came to pass that the brutal display of vigour in the Middle Ages, which reactionists so much admire, found its fitting compliment in the most slothful indolence. It has been the first to show what man's activity can bring about. It has accomplished wonders far surpassing Egyptian pyramids, Roman aqueducts, Gothic cathedrals; it has conducted expeditions that put in the shade all former exoduses of nations and crusades.

The bourgeoisie cannot exist without constantly revolutionizing the instruments of production, and thereby the relations of production, and with them the whole relations of society. Conservation of the old modes of production in unaltered form was, on the contrary, the first condition of existence for all earlier industrial classes. Constant revolutionizing of production, uninterrupted disturbance of all social conditions, everlasting uncertainty and agitation distinguish the bourgeois epoch from all earlier ones. All fixed, fast-frozen relations, with their train of ancient and venerable prejudices and opinions, are swept away, all new-formed ones become antiquated before they can ossify. All that is solid melts into air, all that is holy is profaned. . . .

II. Proletarians and Communists

In what relation do the Communists stand to the proletarians as a whole?

The Communists do not form a separate party opposed to other working-class parties.

They have no interests separate and apart from those of the proletariat as a whole.

They do not set up any sectarian principles of their own, by which to shape and mould the proletarian movement.

The Communists are distinguished from the other working-class parties by this only:

1. In the national struggles of the proletarians of the different countries, they point out and bring to the front the common interests of the entire proletariat, independently of all nationality.

2. In the various stages of development which the struggle of the working class against the bourgeoisie has to pass through, they always and everywhere represent the movement as a whole.

The Communists, therefore, are on the one hand, practically, the most advanced and resolute section of the working-class parties of every country, that section which pushes forward all others; on the other hand, theoretically, they have over the great mass of the proletariat the advantage of clearly understanding the line of march, the conditions, and the ultimate general results of the proletarian movement.

The immediate aim of the Communists is the same as that of all the other proletarian parties: formation of the proletariat into a class, overthrow of the bourgeois supremacy, conquest of political power by the proletariat.

The theoretical conclusions of the Communists are in no way based on ideas or principles that have been invented, or discovered, by this or that would-be universal reformer.

They merely express, in general terms, actual relations springing from an existing class struggle, from a historical movement going on under our very eyes. The abolition of existing property relations is not at all a distinctive feature of communism.

IV. Position of the Communists in Relation to the Various Existing Opposition Parties

Section II has made clear the relations of the Communists to the existing working-class parties, such as the Chartists in England and the agrarian reformers in America.

The Communists fight for the attainment of the immediate aims, for the enforcement of the momentary interests of the working-class; but in the movement of the present they also represent and take care of the future of that movement. In France the Communists ally themselves with the Social-Democrats, against the conservative and radical bourgeoisie, reserving, however, the right to take up a critical position in regard to phrases and illusions traditionally handed down from the great Revolution.

In Switzerland they support the Radicals, without losing sight of the fact that this party consists of antagonistic elements, partly of democratic socialists, in the French sense, partly of radical bourgeois.

In Poland they support the party that insists on an agrarian revolution as the prime condition for national emancipation, that party which fomented the insurrection of Cracow in 1846.

In Germany they fight with the bourgeoisie whenever it acts in a revolutionary way, against the absolute monarchy, the feudal squirearchy, and the petty bourgeoisie.

But they never cease, for a single instant, to instill into the working class the clearest possible recognition of the hostile antagonism between bourgeoisie and proletariat, in order that the German workers may straightway use, as so many weapons against the bourgeoisie, the social and political conditions that the bourgeoisie must necessarily introduce along with its supremacy, and in order that, after the fall of the reactionary classes in Germany, the fight against the bourgeoisie itself may immediately begin.

The Communists turn their attention chiefly to Germany, because that country is on the eve of a bourgeois revolution that is bound to be carried out under more advanced conditions of European civilization, and with a much more developed proletariat, than that of England was in the seventeenth, and of France in the eighteenth century, and because the bourgeois revolution in Germany will be but the prelude to an immediately following proletarian revolution.

In short, the Communists everywhere support every revolutionary movement against the existing social and political order of things.

In all these movements they bring to the front, as the leading question in each, the property question, no matter what its degree of development at the time.

Finally, they labour everywhere for the union and agreement of the democratic parties of all countries.

The Communists disdain to conceal their views and aims. They openly declare that their ends can be attained only by the forcible overthrow of all existing conditions. Let the ruling classes tremble at a communistic revolution. The proletarians have nothing to lose but their chains. They have a world to win.

WORKING MEN OF ALL COUNTRIES, UNITE!

Comment

For a change, consider *The Communist Manifesto* not as a political treatise intended to incite a revolution, but as a work of literature. It is best, then, to begin at the beginning, with the first line: "A spectre is haunting Europe—the spectre of Communism." How can we *not* be drawn in? How can we *not* be drawn into a scene in which someone is being threatened and someone is doing the threatening, in which the odor of danger is no less powerful for being vague and in the distance, and in which the outcome, though still unknown, seems nevertheless predetermined?

The Communist Manifesto has had so great a historical impact that it is underappreciated as a work of literature. An exception to this general rule is British historian Eric Hobsbawm, whose introduction to the book is an appreciation in full of its nearly perfect prose and concise construction. Hobsbawm writes:

> The new reader can hardly fail to be swept away by the passionate conviction, the concentrated brevity, the intellectual and stylistic force, of this astonishing pamphlet. It is written, as though in a single creative burst, in lapidary sentences almost naturally transforming themselves into the memorable aphorisms which have become

known far beyond the world of political debate. . . . Whatever else it is, *The Communist Manifesto* as political rhetoric has an almost biblical force. In short, it is impossible to deny its compelling power as literature.

Who can say where literature ends and politics begins? Who can say how much of the *Manifesto's* power derives from its language as opposed to its content? To be sure, they go hand in hand, in this case being equally persuasive as explicators for why the book has been so extraordinarily effective as an agent of change. Which brings us to intent—to what exactly Karl Marx, who was educated in law and philosophy, and Friedrich Engels, who was trained as a merchant and inclined to activism, anticipated accomplishing when they made their case against the existing order and for one altogether new.

The two men began their collaboration in 1844, brought together by a shared disgust with what was and by similarly shared notions of what could be. The word *communism* was new. It had come into use only a few years earlier, a radical offshoot of the republicanism that followed the French Revolution. From the start, communism was seen as a political movement, and one with enormous economic implications. It was, if you will, the opposite of liberalism: whereas John Locke believed, as did other members of the British and American Enlightenment, that the right to own property was a virtue, Marx and Engels believed that property was a vice. In fact, according to them, private property had to be eliminated, lest ownership perpetuate the inequities that they determined to obliterate.

By the mid-1840s, political unrest was increasing, exacerbated by a growing population that far exceeded opportunities for employment. So when Marx met Engels, in the spring of 1847, they joined a revolutionary secret society, the League of Communists (based in Paris), and together promised to provide it with a policy document. It was a turning point. From that point on, they, like the league they joined, were committed to the overthrow of the bourgeoisie and to the establishment of a new, classless society.

Two further points: first, the extreme equity advocated by Marx and Engels was then, as it is now, utopian. There have been nearly no societies or systems in which everyone was equal and stayed equal, with the same power and privileges as everyone else. While the intentions of utopians are noble, groups and organizations virtually always stratify over time, with some members at the top and others in the middle or at the bottom.

Second, *The Communist Manifesto* declared the instrument of revolution to be the proletariat, which raises these questions: who exactly was this proletariat, and how could men as clever as Marx and Engels imagine that he could, and would, overturn the existing order? As Gareth Stedman Jones has made clear, in the 1840s, the word *proletariat* was associated in Germany and France not with the working class, but rather with those who had only casual employment or even no employment, and therefore with misery, poverty, and crime. Because people (men) like these lacked even a small stake in the existing system, Marx and Engels imagined them as being not only able to challenge the status quo, but ready and willing to do so as well.

But the proletariat as painted in the *Manifesto*—who clearly was a city, not a country, dweller—never did play much of a role in the advent of communism. Not only did it take another 70 years for Lenin and his comrades finally to create a communist state, but in 1917 (the year of the revolution), Russia was still backward, an agrarian land that did not at all resemble the *Manifesto*'s urban landscape. Moreover, the same was true of China, another huge, largely rural land in which Communists were installed, this time by Mao in 1949.

So the *Manifesto* was slow to find its audience, and when it finally did, events unfolded in ways that Marx and Engels did not anticipate. Moreover, now that the Berlin Wall is down, and the Soviet Union is no more, and China has modernized, one could consider the *Manifesto* obsolete. But it is not. While it failed utterly in its immediate intention, it was in ways prophetic. For all its flaws, and for all that has happened since, *The Communist Manifesto* resonates still as a visionary work. Its spare, unsparing prose imagines a world that is better than the one they had then and, in some ways, better than the one we have now.

∾

W. E. B. DU BOIS
1868–1963

W. E. B. Du Bois was a polymath. Best known for being a civil rights activist and, later in his long life, a Pan-Africanist, this first-ever African American to receive a doctorate from Harvard University (in 1895) was, simultaneously, a scholar and educator; a writer as reporter, poet, and novelist; an editor; a musicologist; a dramaturge and impresario; and a public intellectual. During the first half of the twentieth century and then some, he was a magnet—and a catalyst. Intent on creating change, Du Bois was determined either to end racism or, if he could not, to quit his country for another, a continent away.

The astonishing accomplishments of Du Bois, who was described by historian Manning Marable as "the central architect for the modern social protest movement for freedom in the United States," must be considered in context. Some of his most significant work was done during a time in which blacks were still being lynched and disenfranchised, and in which racism generally remained as personally palatable as it was politically entrenched. Times changed, of course, and so did Du Bois. He veered between advocating integration and separation, with his thrusting and parrying depending on both his own intellectual development and the temper of the times.

"The Talented Tenth" must be read, then, in the context of Du Bois's early life as an educator and activist. It was written in 1903, when he held out hope, as he did not later in his life, that such a thing as a liberal education, for leaders in particular, could and would end such a thing as racism.

---------- **THE TALENTED TENTH** ----------
1903

The Negro race, like all races, is going to be saved by its exceptional men. The problem of education, then, among Negroes must first of all deal with the Talented Tenth; it is the problem of developing the Best of this race that they may guide the Mass away from the contamination and death of the Worst, in their own and other races. Now the training of men is a difficult and intricate task. Its technique is a matter for educational experts, but its object is for the vision of seers. If we make money the object of man-training, we shall develop money-makers but not necessarily men; if we make technical skill the object of education, we may possess artisans but not, in nature, men. Men we shall have only as we make manhood the object of the work of the schools—intelligence, broad sympathy, knowledge of the world that was and is, and of the relation of men to it—this is the curriculum of that Higher Education which must underlie true life. On this foundation we may build bread winning, skill of hand and quickness of brain, with never a fear lest the child and man mistake the means of living for the object of life.

If this be true—and who can deny it—three tasks lay before me; first to show from the past that the Talented Tenth as they have risen among American Negroes have been worthy of leadership; secondly, to show how these men may be educated and developed; and thirdly, to show their relation to the Negro problem.

You misjudge us because you do not know us. From the very first it has been the educated and intelligent of the Negro people that have led and elevated the mass, and the sole obstacles that nullified and retarded their efforts were slavery and race prejudice; for what is slavery but the legalized survival of the unfit and the nullification of the work of natural internal leadership? Negro leadership, therefore, sought from the first to rid the race of this awful incubus that it might make way for natural selection and the survival of the fittest. . . .

Can the masses of the Negro people be in any possible way more quickly raised than by the effort and example of this aristocracy of talent and character? Was there ever a nation on God's fair earth civilized from the bottom upward? Never; it is, ever was and ever will be from the top downward that culture filters. The Talented Tenth rises and pulls all that are worth the saving up to their vantage ground. This is the history of human progress; and the two historic mistakes which have hindered that progress were the thinking first that no more could ever rise save the few already risen; or second, that it would better the unrisen to pull the risen down.

How then shall the leaders of a struggling people be trained and the hands of the risen few strengthened? There can be but one answer: The best and most capable of their youth must be schooled in the colleges and universities of the land. We will not quarrel as to just what the university of the Negro should teach or how it should teach it—I willingly admit that each soul and each race-soul needs its own peculiar curriculum. But this is true: A university is a human invention for the transmission of knowledge and culture from generation to generation, through the training of quick minds and pure hearts, and for this work no other human invention will suffice, not even trade and industrial schools.

All men cannot go to college but some men must; every isolated group or nation must have its yeast, must have for the talented few centers of training where men are not so mystified and befuddled by the hard and necessary toil of earning a living, as to have no aims higher than their bellies, and no God greater than Gold. This is true training. . . .

To furnish five millions ignorant people with teachers of their own race and blood, in one generation, was not only a very difficult undertaking, but a very important one, in that it placed before the eyes of almost every Negro child an attainable ideal. It brought the masses of the blacks in contact with modern civilization, made black men the leaders of their communities and trainers of the new generation. In this work college-bred Negroes were first teachers, and then teachers of teachers. And here it is that the broad culture of college work has been of peculiar value. Knowledge of life and its wider meaning, has been the point of the Negro's deepest ignorance, and the sending out of teachers whose training has not been simply for bread winning, but also for human culture, has been of inestimable value in the training of these men. . . .

Men of America, the problem is plain before you. Here is a race transplanted through the criminal foolishness of your fathers. Whether you like it or not the millions are here, and here they will remain. If you do not lift them up, they will pull you down. Education and work are the levers to uplift a people. Work alone will not do it unless inspired by the right ideals and guided by intelligence. Education must not simply teach work—it must teach Life. The Talented Tenth of the Negro race must be made leaders of thought and missionaries of culture among their people. No others can do this work and Negro colleges must train men for it. The Negro race, like all other races, is going to be saved by its exceptional men.

Comment

"The Talented Tenth" was one of several essays published under the title *The Negro Problem*. The collection concerned the still wretched conditions of African Americans, five decades after the publication of Harriet Beecher Stowe's groundbreaking *Uncle Tom's Cabin*, and four decades after slavery was abolished. The most famous contributor was Booker T. Washington, considered the successor to the recently deceased preeminent African American Frederick Douglass. The second best known was W. E. B. Du Bois, who, even before he was 40, was thought of as America's leading black intellectual.

The two men came down on different sides of a question without an obvious answer: how should the oppressed respond to their oppressors? Then as now, Washington was considered the conciliator, loath to recommend anything to blacks that would arouse the ire of whites. Du Bois, in contrast, was already an activist: ready, willing, and able to push, sometimes hard, for black progress.

Under the rubric of *The Negro Problem*, the differences between the two men were genteel—they focused on what, given the circumstances, constituted a good education. Washington proposed an industrial or vocational education, one that would train people in a trade and would be open to all African Americans. He believed that equity would be gained gradually, through economic self-sufficiency. Du Bois set his sights higher. He insisted that nothing but the best would do, at least for the best and brightest African Americans, who he maintained should be educated exactly like the best and brightest white Americans. His idea was to develop an elite cadre of black Americans—a "talented tenth"—by providing them with a liberal arts education second to none.

It was not that Du Bois opposed Washington's option of an industrial education. But Du Bois was more ambitious, imagining a select curriculum for a select few. More precisely, he thought that the way to raise his race was by providing young (black) leaders with the best education, a traditional liberal arts education, the kind from which he himself had benefited. "How then shall the leaders of a struggling people be trained and the hands of the risen few strengthened?" he asked. "There can be but one answer: The best and most capable of their youth must be schooled in the colleges and universities of the land. . . . No other human invention will suffice."

In "The Talented Tenth," Du Bois follows in the footsteps of long-ago predecessors such as Plato, who similarly proposed extraordinary education for extraordinary men, and Thomas Carlyle, who similarly conceived of leaders as saviors. Du Bois envisioned a racial vanguard—an elite cadre of black leaders who were refined as well as informed, and who would, in the words of Derrick Alridge, "pull the black masses up the ladder of civilization and progress."

"The Talented Tenth" was the work of still rather a young man, too young to have grown cynical. But by the 1930s, Du Bois was less sanguine. He had come to conclude that the talented tenth were no better than their white counterparts, using their excellent educations for their own benefit rather than for the benefit of others. By the 1940s, his disillusionment was complete. As he said at the time, "In my youth and idealism, I did not realize that selfishness is even more natural than sacrifice."

And so Du Bois put his money on the many: the "talented tenth" became the "guiding hundredth." As he envisioned it, the guiding hundredth would constitute a kind of "group leadership" that would have "a clear vision of present world conditions and dangers" and "conduct American Negroes to alliance with culture groups in Europe, America, Asia and Africa."

In retrospect, it seems clear that even early on, beneath the veneer of Du Bois the educator was Du Bois the activist, and even Du Bois the revolutionary. Ostensibly, "The Talented Tenth" is about pedagogy. But, perhaps inevitably, the author's anger, and even rage, is evident. To wit: "Men of [white] America, the problem is plain before you. Here is a race transplanted through the criminal foolishness of your fathers. Whether you like it or not the millions are here, and here they will remain. If you do not lift them up, they will pull you down."

Small wonder, then, that the more disappointed Du Bois became, the more he became disenchanted. Small wonder, then, that as an old man, he went into exile, to live in Ghana. He died there at 95, in Accra, not America.

~

FRANTZ FANON

1925–1961

He died young, at age 36. But during his short life, he wrote one book, maybe two—*Black Skin, White Masks* (1952) and *The Wretched of the Earth* (1961)—that will endure as long as there are oppressors on the one side and oppressed on the other.

Frantz Fanon was born in Martinique, educated in France, and buried in Algeria. He studied philosophy, trained as a psychiatrist, and toward the end of his life became an activist, a militant political activist. He was what the French call *un homme engagé*, a man who was entirely engaged, in life and in work, practicing what he preached on three continents.

Like other great leaders, literary and otherwise, the man met the moment. Fanon came of age at the end of the Second World War, and at the start of the long, bloody demise of European colonialism. He was obsessed with the colonial experience, which was the lens through which he viewed the world, a world of black and white, both literally and figuratively. By the time he wrote *The Wretched of the Earth*, his view was simple and Manichaean: masters and slaves, colonizers and colonized, bourgeoisie and workers, whites and blacks, the former free, the latter in chains, not necessarily physically, but certainly psychologically. Fanon's mission in life was to end the inequity, to once and for all, by using force if necessary, bring down those with power, authority, and influence in favor of those without.

-------- **THE WRETCHED OF THE EARTH** --------

1961

ON VIOLENCE

National liberation, national reawakening, restoration of the nation to the people or Commonwealth, whatever the name used, whatever the latest

---

expression, decolonization is always a violent event. At whatever level we study it—individual encounters, a change of name for a sports club, the guest list at a cocktail party, members of a police force or the board of directors of a state or private bank—decolonization is quite simply the substitution of one "species" of mankind by another. The substitution is unconditional, absolute, total, and seamless. We could go on to portray the rise of a new nation, the establishment of a new state, its diplomatic relations and its economic and political orientation. But instead we have decided to describe the kind of tabula rasa which from the outset defines any decolonization. What is singularly important is that it starts from the very first day with the basic claims of the colonized. In actual fact, proof of success lies in a social fabric that has been changed inside out. This change is extraordinarily important because it is desired, clamored for, and demanded. The need for this change exists in a raw, repressed, and reckless state in the lives and consciousness of colonized men and women. But the eventuality of such a change is also experienced as a terrifying future in the consciousness of another "species" of men and women: the *colons*, the colonists.

Decolonization, which sets out to change the order of the world, is clearly an agenda for total disorder. But it cannot be accomplished by the wave of a magic wand, a natural cataclysm, or a gentleman's agreement. Decolonization, we know, is an historical process: In other words, it can only be understood, it can only find its significance and become self coherent insofar as we can discern the history-making movement which gives it form and substance. Decolonization is the encounter between two congenitally antagonistic forces that in fact owe their singularity to the kind of reification secreted and nurtured by the colonial situation. Their first confrontation was colored by violence and their cohabitation—or rather the exploitation of the colonized by the colonizer—continued at the point of the bayonet and under cannon fire. . . .

[This explains why] decolonization reeks of red-hot cannonballs and bloody knives. For the last can be the first only after a murderous and decisive confrontation between the two protagonists. This determination to have the last move up to the front, to have them clamber up (too quickly, say some) the famous echelons of an organized society, can only succeed by resorting to every means, including, of course, violence.

You do not disorganize a society, however primitive it may be, with such an agenda if you are not determined from the very start to smash every obstacle encountered. The colonized, who have made up their mind to make such an agenda into a driving force, have been prepared for violence from time immemorial. As soon as they are born it is obvious to them that their cramped world, riddled with taboos, can only be challenged by out and out violence. . . .

Conclusion

Now, comrades, now is the time to decide to change sides. We must shake off the great mantle of night which has enveloped us, and reach for the light. The new day which is dawning must find us determined, enlightened and resolute.

We must abandon our dreams and say farewell to our old beliefs and former friendships. Let us not lose time in useless laments or sickening mimicry. Let us leave this Europe which never stops talking of man yet massacres him at every one of its street corners, at every corner of the world.

For centuries Europe has brought the progress of other men to a halt and enslaved them for its own purposes and glory; for centuries it has stifled virtually the whole of humanity in the name of a so-called "spiritual adventure." Look at it now teetering between atomic destruction and spiritual disintegration. . . .

Today we are witnessing a stasis of Europe. Comrades, let us flee this stagnation where dialectics has gradually turned into a logic of the status quo. Let us reexamine the question of man. Let us reexamine the question of cerebral reality, the brain mass of humanity in its entirety whose affinities must be increased, whose connections must be diversified and whose communications must be humanized again.

Come brothers, we have far too much work on our hands to revel in outmoded games. Europe has done what it had to do and all things considered, it has done a good job; let us stop accusing it, but let us say to it firmly it must stop putting on such a show. We no longer have reason to fear it, let us stop then envying it.

The Third World is today facing Europe as one colossal mass whose project must be to try and solve the problems this Europe was incapable of finding the answers to.

But what matters now is not a question of profitability, not a question of increased productivity, not a question of production rates. No, it is not a question of back to nature. It is the very basic question of not dragging man in directions which mutilate him, of not imposing on his brain tempos that rapidly obliterate and unhinge it. The notion of catching up must not be used as a pretext to brutalize man, to tear him from himself and his inner consciousness, to break him, to kill him.

No, we do not want to catch up with anyone. But what we want is to walk in the company of man, every man, night and day, for all times. It is not a question of stringing the caravan out where groups are spaced so far apart they cannot see the one in front, and men who no longer recognize each other, meet less and less and talk to each other less and less.

The Third World must start over a new history of man which takes account of not only the occasional prodigious theses maintained by Europe but also its crimes, the most heinous of which have been committed at the very heart of man, the pathological dismembering of his functions and the erosion of his unity, and in the context of the community, the fracture, the stratification and the bloody tensions fed by class, and finally, on the immense scale of humanity, the racial hatred, slavery, exploitation and, above all, the bloodless genocide whereby one and a half billion men have been written off.

So comrades, let us not pay tribute to Europe by creating states, institutions, and societies that draw their inspiration from it.

Humanity expects other things from us than this grotesque and generally obscene emulation.

If we want to transform Africa into a new Europe, America into a new Europe, then let us entrust the destinies of our countries to the Europeans. They will do a better job than the best of us.

But if we want humanity to take one step forward, if we want to take it to another level than the one where Europe has placed it, then we must innovate, we must be pioneers.

If we want to respond to the expectations of our peoples, we must look elsewhere besides Europe.

Moreover, if we want to respond to the expectations of the Europeans we must not send them back a reflection, however ideal, of their society and their thought that periodically sickens even them.

For Europe, for ourselves and for humanity, comrades, we must make a new start, develop a new way of thinking, and endeavor to create a new man.

Comment

The Wretched of the Earth is perhaps the most militant of the classic revolutionary texts. Fanon's argument is nothing if not clear: to create the new order, the old order, dictated by Europe, must be "smashed." How? Through the use of violence—the circumstances dictated the choice.

Fanon's unambiguous defense of violence to eliminate inequity explains his influence on political leaders such as Cuba's Che Guevara, who drew on extreme theory to justify extreme practice. It similarly explains his influence on intellectual leaders such as Jean-Paul Sartre, who came to believe that Fanon had "shown the way as spokesman" for anticolonialism. But the main reason that Fanon was so powerful a presence then, and endures even now, in the postcolonial era is the acuity of his analysis. As David Macey pointed out, it was only after his death that Fanon was adopted as Third World champion of the "wretched of the earth," only after his death that he (among others) inspired the black power movement in the United States (among black intellectuals), and only after his death that his writings were integrated into college curriculums. (American students regularly read Fanon in courses on inequality, identity, and racial and sexual politics.) His ability to transcend time and space, to move, as writers of classics invariably do, from the particular to the universal, is the consequence both of his view on what to do and of his view on why.

Fanon applied his psychiatry to his politics—a mix that made him a most unusual agent of change. (Fanon also did pioneering work as a physician. During his tenure at a psychiatric facility in Algeria, he developed a new method of treatment, "socio-therapy," that placed patients in the context of their cultures.) Though he claimed later in his life to have abandoned psychiatry in favor of politics, what Fanon really did was to merge the two: he tied the trials and tribulations of individuals to the trials and tribulations of the society within which they were embedded. As Hussein Abdilahi Bulhan observed, so far as Fanon was concerned, "if therapy aims at restoring integrity of mind and body, then the colonial order undermined that integrity in the first place and did not permit its restoration in the second place."

Bulhan's book, *Frantz Fanon and the Psychology of Oppression*, put Fanon in the vanguard of the study of the self in political life. Fanon viewed "violence" as a physical blow—and as a psychological one. His view of oppressors (his reference point was primarily, but not exclusively, white European colonialists) was that they not only occupied other people's lands and expropriated their labors, but sought also to "advance ever deeper and place [themselves] in the very center of the dominated," to reside "not only *without*, but also *within*." Therefore, unless the battle was joined on two fronts simultaneously, the physical and the psychological, the cycle of domination was certain to continue. It was a catch-22 in which the only way out, the only way for the oppressed to regain their dignity and self-respect, was to use force, to become, if only for a time, the oppressor. In Bulhan's words, Fanon concluded, "The oppressed who are dehumanized by the violence of the oppressor . . . regain their identity, reclaim their history, reconstitute their bonding, and forge their future through violence."

Fanon led an extraordinary life. He fled his homeland, Martinique, at age 18 to fight with the French in the Second World War. After the war he moved to Lyon, where he studied literature and philosophy and wrote three plays. Finally, he turned to medicine, qualified as a psychiatrist and, in 1953, moved to Algeria, where he secured an appointment at a psychiatric hospital. Though *Black Skin, White Masks* was written during the end of his time in France, it was in Algeria that he came of political age. Soon after the start of the Algerian revolution (1954), he quit his psychiatric work to become a man of action, a full-time revolutionary who dedicated himself to the cause of colonized people in Algeria and, later, in other countries in Africa as well.

Before he died young of leukemia, Fanon put his life on the line to fight a system that he experienced as being as entrenched as it was egregious. It was his pen, though, particularly *The Wretched of the Earth*, that put him in the vanguard of the postcolonial movement. While his work seems now in some ways dated—after all, European colonialism is of the past, not the present, and a black man was elected president of the United

States—it is not. For so long as the divides between haves on the one hand and have-nots on the other persist, Fanon will pertain.

~

RACHEL CARSON
1907–1964

She was angry. Rachel Carson was angry at all the soiling and spoiling: of the air and water and God's green earth. To this anger she harnessed her formidable powers—two in particular.

First, in writing *Silent Spring*, she exploited her expertise. This was no mealymouthed, ladylike lady, shedding wasted tears over the loss of what once had been. No, this woman was an anomaly, especially in the 1950s and 1960s, a highly trained scientist (marine biologist) who marshaled her great knowledge on behalf of her great cause, the environment. Second, Carson wielded her pen with the power and passion of a poet. Her gorgeous yet harrowing descriptions of what was lost already and her vivid, frightening depictions of the continuing destruction of the natural world because of our fecklessness and recklessness were impossible to resist, or to deny.

Some would argue that the modern environmental movement began in the 1890s with the founding of the Sierra Club by John Muir. But most people credit *Silent Spring* with jump-starting the now worldwide effort to save the planet from decay and destruction. The change she created was not revolutionary—it was too slow to be so considered. But it was, and is even now, evolutionary. Since Carson, there has been a shift from nearly complete carelessness to at least a heightened awareness of how, unchecked, we bite the hand that, literally, feeds us.

Carson's book begins with a "fable"—a beautifully crafted nightmare scenario describing the demise of life as we know it—that ends with an admonition. The fearful silence she imagined was not the result of "witchcraft" or of "enemy action." Rather, "the people had done it themselves."

———— SILENT SPRING ————
1962

1. A FABLE FOR TOMORROW

There was once a town in the heart of America where all life seemed to live in harmony with its surroundings. The town lay in the midst of a checkerboard of prosperous farms, with fields of grain and hillsides of orchards where, in spring, white clouds of bloom drifted above the green fields. In autumn, oak and maple and birch set up a blaze of color that flamed and flickered across a backdrop of pines. Then foxes barked in the hills and deer silently crossed the fields, half hidden in the mists of the fall mornings.

Along the roads, laurel, viburnum and alder, great ferns and wildflowers delighted the traveler's eye through much of the year. Even in winter the roadsides were places of beauty, where countless birds came to feed on the berries and on the seed heads of the dried weeds rising above the snow. The countryside was, in fact, famous for the abundance and variety of its bird life, and when the flood of migrants was pouring through in spring and fall people traveled from great distances to observe them. Others came to fish the streams, which flowed clear and cold out of the hills and contained shady pools where trout lay. So it had been from the days many years ago when the first settlers raised their houses, sank their wells, and built their barns.

Then a strange blight crept over the area and everything began to change. Some evil spell had settled on the community: mysterious maladies swept the flocks of chickens; the cattle and sheep sickened and died. Everywhere was a shadow of death. The farmers spoke of much illness among their families. In the town the doctors had become more and more puzzled by new kinds of sickness appearing among their patients. There had been several sudden and unexplained deaths, not only among adults but even among children, who would be stricken suddenly while at play and die within a few hours.

There was a strange stillness. The birds, for example—where had they gone? Many people spoke of them, puzzled and disturbed. The feeding stations in the backyards were deserted. The few birds seen anywhere were moribund; they trembled violently and could not fly. It was a spring without voices. On the mornings that had once throbbed with the dawn chorus of robins, catbirds, doves, jays, wrens, and scores of other bird voices there was now no sound; only silence lay over the fields and woods and marsh.

On the farms the hens brooded, but no chicks hatched. The farmers complained that they were unable to raise any pigs—the litters were small and the young survived only a few days. The apple trees were coming into bloom but no bees droned among the blossoms, so there was no pollination and there would be no fruit.

The roadsides, once so attractive, were now lined with browned and withered vegetation as though swept by fire. These, too, were silent, deserted by all living things. Even the streams were now lifeless. Anglers no longer visited them, for all the fish had died.

In the gutters under the eaves and between the shingles of the roofs, a white granular powder still showed a few patches; some weeks before it had fallen like snow upon the roofs and the lawns, the fields and streams.

No witchcraft, no enemy action had silenced the rebirth of new life in this stricken world. The people had done it themselves.

This town does not actually exist, but it might easily have a thousand counterparts in America or elsewhere in the world. I know of no community that has experienced all the misfortunes I describe. Yet every one of these disasters has actually happened somewhere, and many real communities have already suffered a substantial number of them. A grim specter has crept upon us almost unnoticed, and this imagined tragedy may easily become a stark reality we all shall know.

What has already silenced the voices of spring in countless towns in America? This book is an attempt to explain.

2. THE OBLIGATION TO ENDURE

The history of life on earth has been a history of interaction between living things and their surroundings. To a large extent, the physical form and the habits of the earth's vegetation and its animal life have been molded by the environment. Considering the whole span of earthly time, the opposite effect, in which life actually modifies its surroundings, has been relatively slight. Only within the moment of time represented by the present century has one species—man—acquired significant power to alter the nature of his world.

During the past quarter century this power has not only increased to one of disturbing magnitude but it has changed in character. The most alarming of all man's assaults upon the environment is the contamination of air, earth, rivers, and sea with dangerous and even lethal materials. This pollution is for the most part irrecoverable; the chain of evil it initiates not only in the world that must support life but in living tissues is for the most part irreversible. In this now universal contamination of the environment, chemicals are the sinister and little-recognized partners of radiation in changing the very nature of the world—the very nature of its life. Strontium 90, released through nuclear explosions into the air, comes to earth in rain or drifts down as fallout, lodges in soil, enters into the grass or corn or wheat grown there, and in time takes up its abode in the bones of a human being, there to remain until his death. Similarly, chemicals sprayed on croplands or forests or gardens lie long in soil, entering into living organisms, passing from one to another in a chain of poisoning and death. Or they pass mysteriously by underground streams until they emerge and, through the alchemy of air and sunlight, combine into new forms that kill vegetation, sicken cattle, and work unknown harm on those who drink from once pure wells. As Albert Schweitzer has said, "Man can hardly even recognize the devils of his own creation."

It took hundreds of millions of years to produce the life that now inhabits the earth—eons of time in which that developing and evolving and diversifying life reached a state of adjustment and balance with its surroundings. The environment, rigorously shaping and directing the life it supported, contained elements that were hostile as well as supporting. Certain rocks gave out dangerous radiation; even within the light of the sun, from which all life draws its energy, there were short-wave radiations with power to injure. Given time—time not in years but in millennia—life adjusts, and a balance has been reached. For time is the essential ingredient; but in the modern world there is no time.

The rapidity of change and the speed with which new situations are created follow the impetuous and heedless pace of man rather than the deliberate pace of nature. Radiation is no longer merely the background radiation of rocks, the bombardment of cosmic rays, the ultraviolet of the sun that have existed before there was any life on earth; radiation is now the unnatural creation of man's tampering with the atom. The chemicals to which life is asked to make its adjustment are no longer merely the calcium and silica and copper and all the rest of the minerals washed out of the rocks and carried in rivers to the sea; they are the synthetic creations of man's inventive mind, brewed in his laboratories, and having no counterparts in nature.

To adjust to these chemicals would require time on the scale that is nature's; it would require not merely the years of a man's life but the life of generations. And even this, were it by some miracle possible, would be futile, for the new chemicals come from our laboratories in an endless stream; almost five hundred annually find their way into actual use in the United States alone. The figure is staggering and its implications are not easily grasped—500 new chemicals to which the bodies of men and animals are required somehow to adapt each year, chemicals totally outside the limits of biologic experience.

Among them are many that are used in man's war against nature. Since the mid-1940's over 200 basic chemicals have been created for use in killing insects, weeds, rodents, and other organisms described in the modern vernacular as "pests"; and they are sold under several thousand different brand names.

These sprays, dusts, and aerosols are now applied almost universally to farms, gardens, forests, and homes—nonselective chemicals that have the power to kill every insect, the "good" and the "bad," to still the song of birds and the leaping of fish in the streams, to coat the leaves with a deadly film, and to linger on in soil—all this though the intended target may be only a few weeds or insects. Can anyone believe it is possible to lay down such a barrage of poisons on the surface of the earth without making it unfit for all life? They should not be called "insecticides," but "biocides."

The whole process of spraying seems caught up in an endless spiral. Since DDT was released for civilian use, a process of escalation has been going on in which ever more toxic materials must be found. This has happened because insects, in a triumphant vindication of Darwin's principle of the survival of the fittest, have evolved super races immune to the particular insecticide used, hence a deadlier one has always to be developed—and then a deadlier one than that. It has happened also because, for reasons to be described later, destructive insects often undergo a "flareback," or resurgence, after spraying, in numbers greater than before. Thus the chemical war is never won, and all life is caught in its violent crossfire.

Along with the possibility of the extinction of mankind by nuclear war, the central problem of our age has therefore become the contamination of man's total environment with such substances of incredible potential for harm—substances that accumulate in the tissues of plants and animals and even penetrate the germ cells to shatter or alter the very material of heredity upon which the shape of the future depends.

Some would-be architects of our future look toward a time when it will be possible to alter the human germ plasm by design. But we may easily be doing so now by inadvertence, for many chemicals, like radiation, bring about gene mutations. It is ironic to think that man might determine his own future by something so seemingly trivial as the choice of an insect spray.

All this has been risked—for what? Future historians may well be amazed by our distorted sense of proportion. How could intelligent beings seek to control a few unwanted species by a method that contaminated the entire environment and brought the threat of disease and death even to their own kind? Yet this is precisely what we have done. We have done it, moreover, for reasons that collapse the moment we examine them. We are told that the enormous and expanding use of pesticides is necessary to maintain farm production. Yet is our real problem not one of *overproduction*? Our farms, despite measures to remove acreages from production and to pay farmers *not* to produce, have yielded such a staggering excess of crops that the American taxpayer in 1962 is paying out more than one billion dollars a year as the total carrying cost of the surplus-food storage program. And is the situation helped when one branch of the Agriculture Department tries to reduce production while another states, as it did in 1958, "It is believed generally that reduction of crop acreages under provisions of the Soil Bank will stimulate interest in use of chemicals to obtain maximum production on the land retained in crops."

All this is not to say there is no insect problem and no need of control. I am saying, rather, that control must be geared to realities, not to mythical situations, and that the methods employed must be such that they do not destroy us along with the insects. . . There is still very limited awareness of the nature of the threat. This is an era of specialists, each of whom sees his own problem and is unaware of or intolerant of the larger frame into which it fits. It is also an era dominated by industry, in which the right to make a dollar at whatever cost is seldom challenged. When the public protests, confronted with some obvious evidence of damaging results of pesticide applications, it is fed little tranquilizing pills of half truth. We urgently need an end to these false assurances, to the sugar coating of unpalatable facts. It is the public that is being asked to assume the risks that the insect controllers calculate. The public must decide whether it wishes to continue on the present road, and it can do so only when in full possession of the facts. In the words of Jean Rostand, "The obligation to endure gives us the right to know."

Comment

What does it take to write a book that is, in itself, an act of leadership? No one disputes or denies that *Silent Spring* was just that: a "galvanic jolt," as preeminent biologist Edward O. Wilson put it, "to public consciousness." What, though, are the elements that constitute this alchemy? How was it that Carson was able in a single volume to change our attitude and even our behavior toward the planet we inhabit?

Timing is important, very important. Had Carson's book appeared just a few years earlier, it would not have had the same great impact. The 1950s were a decade during which Americans conformed, in large part because they believed, and wanted to believe, that what they were told, by their government in particular, was right and good and true. It was the postwar period, Dwight David Eisenhower was president, and the so-called Eisenhower generation was not in the least inclined to question public policy, including the increasing use of new classes of insecticides, herbicides, and fungicides to eliminate pests. Mark Lytle points out the connection between the chemical weapons developed to fight communists and the chemical weapons developed to fight pests. This led to "close ties between chemical company executives and the government officials who supported each other's interests with enthusiasm." As a result, without any perceptible dissent, chemicals such as DDT were freely applied in the war "against the hordes of insects within our borders." Lytle further notes that during this period—which, not incidentally, coincided with the height of the Cold War—the "reality that all-out war on insects might be dangerous and that some insects might be beneficial or even essential to life" escaped nearly everyone.

But by the early 1960s, America's transformation had begun. *Silent Spring* was published in 1962. Even by then there was a growing realization that science could be perilous as well as promising, that the U.S. government was not perfect and, most important, that times were changing. Martin Luther King's breakthrough "Letter from Birmingham Jail" came out in 1963, and Betty Friedan's seminal book, *The Feminine Mystique*, was published the same year. In other words, within a period of approximately 12 months, no fewer than three different manifestos appeared, each of which started a sociopolitical movement of major significance and continuing consequence. It was a watershed moment, when, as *Silent Spring* in time testified, people without obvious sources of power, authority, or influence created change by taking matters into their own hands.

What is so striking about the so-called rights movements of the 1960s and 1970s—including, but by no means limited to, the antiwar movement, the civil rights movement, the women's movement, and the environmental movement—is that followers finally came into their own. For this is not only a story about a few key actors such as Carson, King, and Friedan; it is also a story about ordinary people priming themselves to act, to become far more engaged and involved than they had ever been before.

Carson herself was less a firebrand than a missionary. She was a born writer who wrote from an early age, a loner who longed to connect and did so through her prose. Before *Silent Spring*, she had, for example, written *The Sea Around Us*, a brilliant appreciation of water worlds that won the National Book Award and was a bestseller as well. Still, Carson's final book—her testament, if you will—was different. Written when she was gravely ill, *Silent Spring* is full of urgency and anger and the sense that time was running out, both for her and for the flora and fauna that she had loved all her life.

Silent Spring is both science and literature. On the one hand, it is a litany of facts and figures and lines like these: The organic chemist "may work with hydrocarbon molecules consisting of many carbon atoms, arranged in rings or chains, with side chains or branches, holding to themselves with chemical bonds not merely simple atoms of hydrogen or chlorine but also a wide variety of chemical groups." And on the other hand, it is an accumulation of imaginings and images intended to invoke the treasure of nature and the sense of imminent loss: "Over increasingly large areas of the United States, spring now comes unheralded by the return of the birds, and the early mornings are strangely silent where once they were filled with the beauty of bird song." How to argue? How to argue with a crusader who drew on her formidable powers as researcher and writer to see so clearly and caution so carefully?

But many did take issue with Carson. *Silent Spring* caused a furor; furious readers took issue with its author and sought to discredit her. But by then she was well defended. Before she died, she knew that *Silent Spring* had been translated into 20 different languages; had testified before a concerned Congress; was vindicated by a fickle media; and was given succor by growing numbers of strong supporters. Covered with honors and garlanded with praise, Carson knew full well what she was—a pathbreaking woman whose pen was mightier than any sword.

~

BETTY FRIEDAN
1921–2006

Why must a movement—in this case, the women's movement—have so many incarnations? Why does it not suffice to muster energies once or twice, not to speak of thrice? Must the same battles be fought over and over and over again?

Perhaps the best way to think about this is that women such as Mary Wollstonecraft, Elizabeth Cady Stanton, and Betty Friedan did not fight the same battles. Instead, they fought the same *war*—the same overarching and ongoing struggle for equity with men. The battles and the skirmishes, though, were different because the times were different, each with its own angry indignations, righteous grievances, and assertive assaults on the status quo.

Arguably Betty Friedan faced the most daunting task of all. At least it can be said of a fighting feminist such as Stanton that her targets were large and glaringly obvious. In the mid-nineteenth century, the inequities were so numerous, various, and onerous that they were easy to take on—rather like shooting fish in a barrel. For Friedan, however, who appeared on the scene a century later, the circumstances were different. By the time she wrote *The Feminine Mystique*, which is widely considered the bible of the modern feminist movement, women had nothing much left to gripe about—or so it seemed. After all, the middle- and upper-class white women who made up Friedan's main constituency had time and money as well as the vote. So what exactly was the problem? Precisely because it was covert as opposed to overt, because it was vague and ill defined rather than blatantly apparent, Friedan called it "the problem that has no name."

THE FEMININE MYSTIQUE
1963

THE PROBLEM THAT HAS NO NAME

The problem lay buried, unspoken, for many years in the minds of American women. It was a strange stirring, a sense of dissatisfaction, a yearning that women suffered in the middle of the twentieth century in the United States. Each suburban wife struggled with it alone. As she made the beds, shopped for groceries, matched slipcover material, ate peanut butter sandwiches with her children, chauffeured Cub Scouts and Brownies, lay beside her husband at night—she was afraid to ask even of herself the silent question—"Is this all?"

For over fifteen years there was no word of this yearning in the millions of words written about women, for women, in all the columns, books and articles by experts telling women their role was to seek fulfillment as wives and mothers. Over and over women heard in voices of tradition and of Freudian sophistication that they could desire—no greater destiny than to glory in their own femininity. Experts told them how to catch a man and keep him, how to breastfeed children and handle their toilet training, how to cope with sibling rivalry and adolescent rebellion; how to buy a dishwasher, bake bread, cook gourmet snails, and build a swimming pool with their own hands; how to dress, look, and act more feminine and make marriage more exciting; how to keep their husbands from dying young and their sons from growing into delinquents. They were taught to pity the neurotic, unfeminine, unhappy women who wanted to be poets or physicists or presidents. They learned that truly feminine women do not want careers, higher education, political rights— the independence and the opportunities that the old-fashioned feminists fought for. Some women, in their forties and fifties, still remembered painfully giving up those dreams, but most of the younger women no longer even thought about them. A thousand expert voices applauded their femininity, their adjustment, their new maturity. All they had to do was devote their lives from earliest girlhood to finding a husband and bearing children. . . .

If I am right, the problem that has no name stirring in the minds of so many American women today is not a matter of loss of femininity or too much education, or the demands of domesticity. It is far more important than anyone recognizes. It is the key to these other new and old problems which have been torturing women and their husbands and children, and puzzling their doctors and educators for years. It may well be the key to our future as a nation and a culture. We can no longer ignore that voice within women that says: "I want something more than my husband and my children and my home."

Comment

Betty Friedan was a force of nature—a lifelong rabble-rouser. From an early age, she deviated from what was considered conventional, willingly and even eagerly taking on those who had more power and authority than she. Her extensive writings and political engagements were, moreover, of a piece, intended to upend what was and supplant it with what ought to be or, at least, with what she thought ought to be.

Born in the American heartland, in Peoria, Illinois, she found her voice in the east, at Smith College, where she was a star. Friedan was editor in chief of the leading campus newspaper and the most visible and vocal of students on the left. Embroiled in controversy at nearly every turn, she graduated from Smith at the top of her class, primed for political action, particularly on behalf of women and workers.

For the rest of her life, while her career veered, the course she charted in college did not. Her first job was in labor journalism. It allowed her to hone her talents as an activist and author and to focus her prodigious energy on groups that included Jews and African Americans as well as women and workers. "In fundamental ways," wrote Friedan biographer Daniel Horowitz, "Friedan's association with the labor movement gave her a thorough education in issues concerning women's work and sexual discrimination."

During the 1950s, Friedan married, had children, and moved to New York City. But if her circumstances changed, she did not, or at least not much. She remained politically engaged and became editor of the local newspaper, transforming it in short order from chatty to confrontational. After another move, this one to a small town outside New York City, her attention shifted away from working-class women and toward women who, like she, were middle-class, and who, also like she, lived a comfortable life in a comfortable suburb, but who nevertheless somehow were dissatisfied.

Along with her foray into more conventional journalism, targeted particularly at "the modern American housewife," her experience in and exposure to suburbia provided perfect preparation for *The Feminine Mystique*. The book was as thoroughly researched as it was carefully crafted—and it appeared at just the right time. Women, especially educated women, were ready to hear what Friedan had to say: get a job, get a job outside the home, and get a job that pays you for your work. These women were similarly open to Friedan's not infrequent sexual references, implicit and explicit, and ready to respond to a discussion of gender that was more sophisticated and informed than the pap and palaver that were their usual diet.

But there was more: Friedan's book came out in 1963. It was the year that Martin Luther King, Jr., penned his "Letter from Birmingham Jail";

the year that President John F. Kennedy was shot; a year that preceded, but not by much, the social and political unrest unleashed by the war in Vietnam. In other words, *The Feminine Mystique* appeared at—and contributed to—a watershed moment in American history.

That Friedan had hit a nerve was apparent almost immediately. As Christina Hoff Sommers put it, "Her essential point was both down-to-earth and true: Postwar America had taken the ideal of femininity to absurd extremes," with women being encouraged to be childlike, passive, dependent, and "fluffy." (Shades of Wollstonecraft!) But *The Feminine Mystique* was not without its critics, in part because Friedan herself was nothing if not combative. Most of the fuss and furor were over her apparent denigration of the domestic sphere, in particular of women who chose, freely and gladly, to tend to home and hearth. While Friedan later regretted her apparent antipathy toward stay-at-home mothers, the debate did not die. In fact, it lingers even now, nearly 50 years later.

Friedan continued to be politically active to the end of her life and to write books, all of which were respectfully received. But *The Feminine Mystique* was her signal contribution—her act of leadership. As noted in her obituary in the *New York Times*, the book "ignited the contemporary women's movement in 1963 and as a result permanently transformed the social fabric of the United States and countries around the world." Not incidentally, *The Feminine Mystique* still carries a punch. In her introduction to a 2001 edition of the book, Anna Quindlen wrote, "Four decades later, millions of individual transformations later, there is still so much to learn from this book about how sex and home and work and norms are used to twist the lives of women into weird and unnatural shapes."

Friedan herself—never inclined to hide her light under a bushel—was conscious of her contribution. On the twentieth anniversary of the publication of *The Feminine Mystique*, she wrote: "I am still awed by the revolution that book helped spark. It's a mystery to me that I was able to put it together, at the time it was needed, and that women, and men, even now stop me on the street, and remember where they were when they read it."

~

SAUL ALINSKY

1909–1972

In the beginning of Saul Alinsky's second book, *Rules for Radicals*, there's a quote by Thomas Paine: "Let them call me a rebel and welcome. I feel no concern from it; but I should suffer the misery of devils, were I to make a whore of my soul." Alinsky not only admired Paine, but followed in his tracks.

"What is a radical?" Alinsky asks in his first book, *Reveille for Radicals*. Then he proceeds to answer his own question. "The American radical," Alinsky writes, "fights privilege and power, whether it be inherited or acquired . . . whether it be political or financial or organized creed. He curses a caste system, aware that it exists despite all patriotic denials." Put directly, according to Alinsky, radicals dedicate their lives to fighting for those who have little or nothing, if necessary at the expense of those who have more.

Alinsky is the father of—the patron saint of—community organizing. But, although he believed with all his heart in the power of the people, in power exercised from the bottom up, he did not dispense with leaders. He called them "organizers" and considered them critical—which is why he made a point of putting on paper their "ideal elements."

-------- RULES FOR RADICALS --------
1971

The qualities we were trying to develop in organizers in the years of attempting to train them included some qualities that in all probability cannot be taught. They either had them, or could get them only through a miracle from above or below. Other qualities they might have as potentials that could be developed. Sometimes the development of one quality triggered off unsuspected others. I learned to check against the list and spot the negatives; and if it was impossible to develop that quality, at least

I could be aware and on guard to try to diminish its negative effect upon the work.

Here is the list of the ideal elements of an organizer—the items one looks for in identifying potential organizers and in appraising the future possibilities of new organizers, and the pivot points of any kind of educational curricula for organizers. Certainly it is an idealized list—I doubt that such qualities, in such intensity, ever come together in one man or woman; yet the best of organizers should have them all, to a strong extent, and any organizer needs at least a degree of each.

Curiosity. What makes an organizer organize? He is driven by a compulsive curiosity that knows no limits. Warning clichés such as "curiosity killed a cat" are meaningless to him, for life is for him a search for a pattern, for similarities in seeming differences, for differences in seeming similarities, for an order in the chaos about us, for a meaning to the life around him and its relationship to his own life—and the search never ends. He goes forth with the question as his mark, and suspects that there are no answers, only further questions. The organizer becomes a carrier of the contagion of curiosity, for a people asking "why" are beginning to rebel. The questioning of the hitherto accepted ways and values is the reformation stage that precedes and is so essential to the revolution.

Here, I couldn't disagree more with Freud. In a letter to Marie Bonaparte, he said, "the moment a man questions the meaning and value of life, he is sick." If there is, somewhere, an answer about life, I suspect that the key to it is finding the core question.

Actually, Socrates was an organizer. The function of an organizer is to raise questions that agitate, that break through the accepted pattern. Socrates, with his goal of "know thyself," was raising the internal questions within the individual that are so essential for the revolution which is external to the individual. So Socrates was carrying out the first stage of making revolutionaries. If he had been permitted to continue raising questions about the meaning of life, to examine life and refuse the conventional values, the internal revolution would soon have moved out into the political arena. Those who tried him and sentenced him to death knew what they were doing.

Irreverence. Curiosity and irreverence go together. Curiosity cannot exist without the other. Curiosity asks, "Is this true?" Just because this has always been the way, is this the best or right way of life, the best or right religion, political or economic value, morality? To the questioner nothing is sacred. He detests dogma, defies any finite definition of morality, rebels against any repression of a free, open search for ideas no matter where they may lead. He is challenging, insulting, agitating, discrediting. He stirs unrest. As with all life, this is a paradox, for his irreverence is rooted in a deep reverence for the enigma of life, and an incessant search for its meaning. It could be argued that reverence for others, for their freedom from injustice, poverty, ignorance, exploitation, discrimination, disease, war, hate, and fear, is not a necessary quality in a successful organizer. All I can say is that such reverence is a quality I would have to see in anyone I would undertake to teach.

Imagination. Imagination is the inevitable partner of irreverence and curiosity. How can one be curious without being imaginative?

According to Webster's Unabridged, imagination is the "mental synthesis of new ideas from elements experienced separately . . . The broader meaning . . . starts with the notion of mental imaging of things suggested but not previously experienced, and thence expands . . . to the idea of mental creation and poetic idealization [creative imagination] . . ." To the organizer, imagination is not only all this but something deeper. It is the dynamism that starts and sustains him in his whole life of action as an organizer. It ignites and feeds the force that drives him to organize for change.

There was a time when I believed that the basic quality that an organizer needed was a deep sense of anger against injustice and that this was the prime motivation that kept him going. I now know that it is something else: this abnormal imagination that sweeps him into a close identification with mankind and projects him into its plight. He suffers with them and becomes angry at the injustice and begins to organize the rebellion. Clarence Darrow put it on more of a self-interest basis: "I had a vivid imagination. Not only could I put myself in the other person's place, but I could not avoid doing so. My sympathies always went out to the weak, the suffering, and the poor. Realizing their sorrows I tried to relieve them in order that I myself might be relieved."

Imagination is not only the fuel for the force that keeps organizers organizing, it is also the basis for effective tactics and action. The organizer knows that the real action is in the reaction of the opposition. To realistically appraise and anticipate the probable reactions of the enemy, he must be able to identify with them, too, in his imagination, and foresee their reactions to his actions.

A sense of humor. Back to Webster's Unabridged: humor is defined as "The mental faculty of discovering, expressing, or appreciating ludicrous or absurdly incongruous elements in ideas, situations, happenings, or acts . . ." or "A changing and uncertain state of mind . . ."

The organizer, searching with a free and open mind void of certainty, hating dogma, finds laughter not just a way to maintain his sanity but also a key to understanding life. Essentially, life is a tragedy; and the converse of tragedy is comedy. One can change a few lines in any Greek tragedy and it becomes a comedy, and vice versa. Knowing that contradictions are the signposts of progress he is ever on the alert for contradictions. A sense of humor helps him identify and make sense out of them.

Humor is essential to a successful tactician, for the most potent weapons known to mankind are satire and ridicule.

A sense of humor enables him to maintain his perspective and see himself for what he really is: a bit of dust that burns for a fleeting second. A sense of humor is incompatible with the complete acceptance of any dogma, any religious, political or economic prescription for salvation. It synthesizes with curiosity, irreverence, and imagination. The organizer has a personal identity of his own that cannot be lost by absorption or acceptance of any kind of group discipline or organization. I now begin to understand what I stated somewhat intuitively in *Reveille for Radicals* almost twenty years ago, that "the organizer in order to be part of all can be part of none."

A bit of a blurred vision of a better world. Much of an organizer's daily work is detail repetitive and deadly in its monotony. In the totality of things he is engaged in one small bit. It is as though as an artist he is painting a tiny leaf. It is inevitable that sooner or later he will react with "What am I doing spending my whole life just painting one little leaf? The hell with it, I quit." What keeps him going is a blurred vision of a great mural where other artists—organizers—are painting their bits, and each piece is essential to the total.

An organized personality. The organizer must be well organized himself so he can be comfortable in a disorganized situation, rational in a sea of irrationalities. It is vital that he be able to accept and work with irrationalities for the purpose of change.

With very rare exceptions, the right things are done for the wrong reasons. It is futile to demand that men do the right thing for the right reason—this is a fight with a windmill. The organizer should know and accept that the right reason is only introduced as a moral rationalization after the right end has been achieved, although it may have been achieved for the wrong reason—therefore he should search for and use the wrong reasons to achieve the right goals. He should be able, with skill and calculation, to use irrationality in his attempts to progress toward a rational world. . . .

An organizer must become sensitive to everything that is happening around him. He is always learning, and every incident teaches him something. He notices that when a bus has only a few empty seats, the crowd trying to get on will push and shove; if there are many empty seats the crowd will be courteous and considerate; and he muses that in a world of opportunities for all there would be a change in human behavior for the good. In his constant examination of life and of himself he finds himself becoming more and more of an organized personality.

A well-integrated political schizoid. The organizer must become schizoid, politically, in order not to slip into becoming a true believer. Before men can act an issue must be polarized. Men will act when they are convinced that their cause is 100 per cent on the side of the angels and that the opposition are 100 per cent on the side of the devil. He knows that there can be no action until issues are polarized to this degree. I have already discussed an example in the Declaration of Independence—the Bill of Particulars that conspicuously omitted all the advantages the colonies had gained from the British and cited only the disadvantages.

What I am saying is that the organizer must be able to split himself into two parts—one part in the arena of action where he polarizes the issue to 100 to nothing, and helps to lead his forces into conflict, while the other part knows that when the time comes for negotiations that it really is only a 10 per cent difference—and yet both parts have to live comfortably with each other. Only a well-organized person can split and yet stay together. But this is what the organizer must do.

Ego. Throughout these desired qualities is interwoven a strong ego, one we might describe as monumental in terms of solidity. Here we are using the word *ego* as discussed in the previous chapter, clearly differentiated from egotism. Ego is unreserved confidence in one's ability to do what he believes must be done. An organizer must accept, without fear or worry, that the odds are always against him. Having this kind of ego, he is a doer and does. The thought of copping out never stays with him for more than a fleeting moment; life is action.

A free and open mind, and political relativity. The organizer in his way of life, with his curiosity, irreverence, imagination, sense of humor, distrust of dogma, his self-organization, his understanding of the irrationality of much of human behavior, becomes a flexible personality, not a rigid structure that breaks when something unexpected happens. Having his own identity, he has no need for the security of an ideology or a panacea. He knows that life is a quest for uncertainty; that the only certain fact of life is uncertainty; and he can live with it. He knows that all values are relative, in a world of political relativity. Because of these qualities he is unlikely to disintegrate into cynicism and disillusionment, for he does not depend on illusion.

Finally, the organizer is constantly creating the new out of the old. He knows that all new ideas arise from conflict; that every time man has had a new idea it has been a challenge to the sacred ideas of the past and the present and inevitably a conflict has raged. Curiosity, irreverence, imagination, sense of humor, a free and open mind, an acceptance of the relativity of values and of the uncertainty of life, all inevitably fuse into the kind of person whose greatest joy is creation. He conceives of creation as the very essence of the meaning of life. In his constant striving for the new, he finds that he cannot endure what is repetitive and unchanging. For him hell would be doing the same thing over and over again.

This is the basic difference between the leader and the organizer. The leader goes on to build power to fulfill his desires, to hold and wield the power for purposes both social and personal. He wants power himself. The organizer finds his goal in creation of power for others to use.

Comment

Saul Alinsky was the subject of Hillary Clinton's senior honors thesis at Wellesley College. And when Barack Obama took a job in Chicago working as a community organizer for all of $13,000 a year, he was hired by Alinsky's disciples. Though his name is not well known, Alinsky's considerable influence continues, especially on the young liberal-left activists that he once would have mentored, and now on activists more generally, including some on the right who are content to employ his means to their ends without necessarily being aware of who Alinsky was.

His skills were honed in the American union movement. Nevertheless, Alinsky decided early on that his talents lay elsewhere. He became an independent agent, a lone operator and organizer, Chicago-based, who early in his career was able almost single-handedly to forge an unlikely coalition consisting of merchants, union leaders, local churches, and stockyard workers (resembling those immortalized by Upton Sinclair in *The Jungle*). Drawing on tactics and strategies available even to those without power, authority, or influence, such as boycotts and sitdowns, he enabled his followers to wring concessions from City Hall and to transform part of Chicago into a model community for the working class.

The work was not easy. Alinsky spent time in prison and depended on the kindness of strangers while carrying a card that read, "Have trouble, will travel." But his accomplishments were real. Not only was he able more often than not to create the changes that he intended, but he left a legacy through his literature. While physically unprepossessing—he was described by a contemporary as a "tall, grey-haired, squarely-built, bespectacled, and conservatively dressed man who looks less like a practicing revolutionary than a bemused professor of philosophy"—he was a firebrand. Alinsky was a potentially incendiary figure, about whom it was "impossible to be neutral."

For all his rebelliousness and contrariness, Alinsky was first and foremost a patriot. He idealized the United States, which explains to some extent his anger and disappointment when the United States fell short. "America was a land green, fresh, and young," he wrote. "It was a land rich not only in natural beauty, but richer yet in a vision of a noble life which pervaded the earth and the heavens." His problem, then, was not with what was originally imagined and intended, but with what had happened since. He was enchanted by the American dream—and disenchanted by what he perceived to be the distortion thereof.

Though Alinsky was loath to use the word—in the preceding excerpt, he went so far as to distinguish between "leaders" and "organizers"—organizers *were* leaders. He claimed that the difference was that leaders want power for themselves, whereas organizers create "power for others to use." Still, Alinsky's organizers were trained in nothing if not to lead, trained to get others to do what they could not or would not have been able to do for themselves. As Alinsky himself attested, interventions of this sort were essential. "The building of many mass power organizations . . . cannot come without many organizers."

The task, then, was first to recruit good organizers—leaders—and then to train them. Training was considered critical, which is why Alinsky started a school. It provided a full-time, 15-month program, and it drew students ranging from "middle-class women activists to Catholic priests and Protestant ministers of all denominations, from militant Indians to Chicanos to Puerto Ricans to blacks from all parts of the black power spectrum, from Panthers to radical philosophers, from a variety of campus activists, S.D.S. and others, to a priest who was joining a revolutionary party in South America."

Alinsky described the curriculum in some detail: conferences on organizational problems, analyses of power patterns, and lessons on everything from communication to negotiation. But in the end he relied on some of the old verities. As he himself came to conclude, the qualities he sought to develop in his organizers were "present in any free, creative person."

~

PETER SINGER

1946–

The animal rights movement is of relatively recent vintage and, on the face of it, implausible. How did this particular rights revolution come to pass? How did the well-being of nonhuman animals come to be a collective concern when previously, with few exceptions, they were thought to be property or worse, treated with impunity and even cruelty?

The animal rights movement was one of several social movements that emerged in the 1960s and 1970s, all of which resembled one another in that those *without* power, authority, or influence had the temerity to take on those *with*. However, the movement for animal rights is different in one obvious, all-important way: animals cannot speak for themselves or fight on their own behalf. Necessarily, nonhuman animals depend on human animals to represent them.

This is the task that Australian-born philosopher Peter Singer took on, single-handedly. Specifically, he wrote a book, *Animal Liberation*, that changed the way we think and, more important, the way we *feel* about animals and the lives they live. Singer's personal passion in tandem with his professional persuasiveness made it impossible for people simply to ignore what he had to say. He provided animal rights activists with intellectual legitimacy—thereby transforming his cause into a movement.

ANIMAL LIBERATION

1975

PREFACE TO THE 1975 EDITION

This book is about the tyranny of human over nonhuman animals. This tyranny has caused and today is still causing an amount of pain and

Reprinted by permission of Peter Singer.

suffering that can only be compared with that which resulted from the centuries of tyranny by white humans over black humans. The struggle against this tyranny is a struggle as important as any of the moral and social issues that have been fought over in recent years.

Most readers will take what they have just read to be a wild exaggeration. Five years ago I myself would have laughed at the statements I have now written in complete seriousness. Five years ago I did not know what I know today. If you read this book carefully, paying special attention to the second and third chapters, you will then know as much of what I know about the oppression of animals as it is possible to get into a book of reasonable length. Then you will be able to judge if my opening paragraph is a wild exaggeration or a sober estimate of a situation largely unknown to the general public. So I do not ask you to believe my opening paragraph now. All I ask is that you reserve your judgment until you have read the book.

Soon after I began work on this book my wife and I were invited to tea—we were living in England at the time—by a lady who had heard that I was planning to write about animals. She herself was very interested in animals, she said, and she had a friend who had already written a book about animals and would be so keen to meet us.

When we arrived our hostess's friend was already there, and she certainly was keen to talk about animals. "I do love animals," she began. "I have a dog and two cats, and do you know they get on together wonderfully well. Do you know Mrs. Scott? She runs a little hospital for sick pets . . ." and she was off. She paused while refreshments were served, took a ham sandwich, and then asked us what pets we had.

We told her we didn't own any pets. She looked a little surprised, and took a bite of her sandwich. Our hostess, who had now finished serving the sandwiches, joined us and took up the conversation: "But you *are* interested in animals, aren't you, Mr. Singer?"

We tried to explain that we were interested in the prevention of suffering and misery; that we were opposed to arbitrary discrimination; that we thought it wrong to inflict needless suffering on another being, even if that being were not a member of our own species; and that we believed animals were ruthlessly and cruelly exploited by humans, and we wanted this changed. Otherwise, we said, we were not especially "interested in" animals. Neither of us had ever been inordinately fond of dogs, cats or horses in the way that many people are. We didn't "love" animals. We simply wanted them treated as independent sentient beings that they are, and not as a means to human ends—as the pig whose flesh was now in our hostess's sandwiches had been treated.

This book is not about pets. It is not likely to be comfortable reading for those who think that love for animals involves no more than stroking a cat or feeding birds in the garden. It is intended rather for people who are concerned about ending oppression and exploitation wherever they occur, and in seeing that the basic moral principle of equal consideration of interests is not arbitrarily restricted to members of our own species. The assumption that in order to be interested in such matters one must be an "animal-lover" is itself an indication of the absence of the slightest inkling that the moral standards that we apply among human beings might extend to other animals. No one, except a racist concerned to smear his opponents as "nigger-lovers," would suggest that in order to be concerned about equality for mistreated racial minorities you have to love those minorities, or regard them as cute and cuddly. So why make this assumption about people who work for improvements in the conditions of animals?

The portrayal of those who protest against cruelty to animals as sentimental, emotional "animal-lovers" has had the effect of excluding the entire issue of our treatment of nonhumans from serious political and moral discussion. It is easy to see why we do this. If we did give the issue serious consideration, if, for instance, we looked closely at the conditions in which animals live in the modern "factory farms" that produce our meat, we might be made uncomfortable about ham sandwiches, roast beef, fried chicken, and all those other items in our diet that we prefer not to think of as dead animals.

This book makes no sentimental appeals for sympathy toward "cute" animals. I am no more outraged by the slaughter of horses or dogs for meat than I am by the slaughter of pigs for this purpose. When the United States Defense Department finds that its use of beagles to test lethal gases has evoked a howl of protest and offers to use rats instead, I am not appeased.

This book is an attempt to think through, carefully and consistently, the question of how we ought to treat nonhuman animals. In the process it exposes the prejudices that lie behind our present attitudes and behavior. In the chapters that describe what these attitudes mean in practical terms—how animals suffer from the tyranny of human beings—there are passages that will arouse some emotions. These will, I hope, be emotions of anger and outrage, coupled with a determination to do something about the practices described. Nowhere in this book, however, do I appeal to the reader's emotions where they cannot be supported by reason. When there are unpleasant things to be described it would be dishonest to try to describe them in some neutral way that hid their real unpleasantness. You cannot write objectively about the experiments of the Nazi concentration camp "doctor" on those they considered "sub-human" without stirring emotions; and the same is true of a description of some of the experiments performed today on nonhumans in laboratories in America, Britain, and elsewhere. The ultimate justification for opposition to both these kinds of experiments, though, is not emotional. It is an appeal to basic moral principles which we all accept, and the application of these principles to the victims of both kinds of experiment is demanded by reason, not emotion.

The title of this book has a serious point behind it. A liberation movement is a demand for an end to prejudice and discrimination based on an arbitrary characteristic like race or sex. The classic instance is the Black Liberation movement. The immediate appeal of this movement, and its initial, if limited, success, made it a model for other oppressed groups. We soon became familiar with Gay Liberation and movements on behalf of American Indians and Spanish-speaking Americans. When a majority group—women—began their campaign some thought we had come to the end of the road. Discrimination on the basis of sex, it was said, was the last form of discrimination to be universally accepted and practiced without secrecy or pretense, even in those liberal circles that have long prided themselves on their freedom from prejudice against racial minorities.

We should always be wary of talking of "the last remaining form of discrimination." If we have learned anything from the liberation movements we should have learned how difficult it is to be aware of latent prejudices in our attitudes to particular groups until these prejudices are forcefully pointed out to us.

A liberation movement demands an expansion of our moral horizons. Practices that were previously regarded as natural and inevitable come to be seen as the result of an unjustifiable prejudice. Who can say with any confidence that none of his or her attitudes and practices can legitimately be questioned? If we wish to avoid being numbered among the oppressors, we must be prepared to rethink all our attitudes to other groups, including the most fundamental of them. We need to consider our attitudes from the point of view of those who suffer by them, and by the practices that follow from them. If we can make this unaccustomed mental switch we may discover a pattern in our attitudes and practices that operates so as consistently to benefit the same group—usually the group to which we ourselves belong—at the expense of another group. So we come to see that there is a case for a new liberation movement.

The aim of this book is to lead you to make this mental switch in your attitudes and practices toward a very large group of beings: members of species other than our own. I believe that our present attitudes to these beings are based on a long history of prejudice and arbitrary discrimination. I argue that there can be no reason—except the selfish desire to preserve the privileges of the exploiting group—for refusing to extend the basic principle of equality of consideration to members of other species. I ask you to recognize that your attitudes to members of other species are a form of prejudice no less objectionable than prejudice about a person's race or sex. . . .

CHAPTER 1
ALL ANIMALS ARE EQUAL . . .

or why the ethical principle on which human equality rests requires us to extend equal consideration to animals too

"Animal Liberation" may sound more like a parody of other liberation movements than a serious objective. The idea of "The Rights of Animals" actually was once used to parody the case for women's rights. When Mary Wollstonecraft, a forerunner of today's feminists, published her *Vindication of the Rights of Woman* in 1792, her views were widely regarded as absurd, and before long an anonymous publication appeared entitled *A Vindication of the Rights of Brutes*. The author of this satirical work (now known to have been Thomas Taylor, a distinguished Cambridge philosopher) tried to refute Mary Wollstonecraft's arguments by showing that they could be carried one stage further. If the argument for equality was sound when applied to women, why should it not be applied to dogs, cats, and horses? The reasoning seemed to hold for these "brutes" too; yet to hold that brutes had rights was manifestly absurd. Therefore the reasoning by which this conclusion had been reached must be unsound, and if unsound when applied to brutes, it must also be unsound when applied to women, since the very same arguments had been used in each case.

In order to explain the basis of the case for the equality of animals, it will be helpful to start with an examination of the case for the equality of women. Let us assume that we wish to defend the case for women's rights against the attack by Thomas Taylor. How should we reply?

One way in which we might address this is by saying that the case for equality between men and women cannot validly be extended to nonhuman animals. Women have a right to vote, for instance, because they are just as capable of making rational decisions about the future as men are; dogs, on the other hand, are incapable of understanding the significance of voting, so they cannot have the right to vote. There are many other obvious ways in which men and women resemble each other closely, while humans and animals differ greatly. So, it might be said, men and women are similar beings and should have similar rights, while humans and non-humans are different and should not have equal rights.

The reasoning behind this reply to Taylor's analogy is correct but it does not go far enough. There are obviously important differences between humans and animals, and these differences must give rise to some differences in the rights that each have. Recognizing this evident fact, however, is no barrier to the case for extending the basic principle of equality to nonhuman animals. The differences that exist between men and women are equally undeniable, and the supporters of Women's Liberation are aware that these differences may give rise to different rights. Many feminists hold that women have the right to an abortion on request. It does not follow that since these same feminists are campaigning for equality between men and women they must support the right of men to have abortions too. Since a man cannot have an abortion, it is meaningless to talk of his right to have one. Since dogs can't vote, it is meaningless to talk of their right to vote. There is no reason why either Women's Liberation or Animal Liberation should get involved in such nonsense. The extension of the basic principle of equality from one group to another does not imply that we must treat both groups in exactly the same way, or grant exactly the same rights to both groups. Whether we should do so will depend on the nature of the members of the two groups. The basic principle of equality does not require equal or identical *treatment*; it requires equal consideration. Equal consideration for different beings may lead to different treatment and different rights. . . .

Jeremy Bentham, the founder of the reforming utilitarian school of moral philosophy, incorporated the essential basis of moral equality into his system of ethics by means of the formula: "Each to count for one and none for more than one." In other words, the interests of every being affected by an action are to be taken into account and given the same weight as the like interests of any other being. A later utilitarian, Henry Sidgwick, put the point in this way: "The good of any one individual is of no more importance, from the point of view (if I may say so) of the Universe, than the good of any other." More recently the leading figures in contemporary moral philosophy have shown a great deal of agreement in specifying as a fundamental presupposition of their moral theories some similar requirement that works to give everyone's interests equal consideration—although these writers generally cannot agree on how this requirement is best formulated.

It is an implication of this principle of equality that our concern for others and our readiness to consider their interests ought not to depend on what they are like or on what abilities they may possess. Precisely what our concern or consideration requires us to do may vary according to the characteristics of those affected by what we do: concern for the well-being of children growing up in America would require that we teach them to read; concern for the well-being of pigs may require no more than that we leave them with other pigs in a place where there is adequate food and room to run freely. But the basic element—the taking into account of the interests of the being, whatever those interests may be—must, according to the principle of equality, be extended to all beings, black or white, masculine or feminine, human or nonhuman. . . .

It is on this basis that the case against racism and the case against sexism must both ultimately rest; and it is in accordance with this principle that the attitude that we may call "speciesism," by analogy with racism, must also be condemned. Speciesism—the word is not an attractive one, but I can think of no better term—is a prejudice or attitude of bias in favor of the interests of members of one's own species and against those of members of other species. It should be obvious that the fundamental objections to racism and sexism made by Thomas Jefferson and Sojourner Truth apply equally to speciesism. If possessing a higher degree of intelligence does not entitle one human to use another for his or her own ends, how can it entitle humans to exploit nonhumans for the same purpose?

Many philosophers and other writers have proposed the principle of equal consideration of interests, in some form or other, as a basic moral principle; but not many of them have recognized that this principle applies to members of other species as well as to our own. Jeremy Bentham was one of the few who did realize this. In a forward-looking passage written at a time when black slaves had been freed by the French but in the British dominions were still being treated in the way we now treat animals, Bentham wrote:

> The day *may* come when the rest of the animal creation may acquire those rights which never could have been with-holden from them but by the hand of tyranny. The French have already discovered that the blackness of the skin is no reason why a human being should be abandoned without redress to the caprice of a tormentor. It may one day come to be recognized that the number of the legs, the villosity of the skin, or the termination of the *os sacrum* are reasons equally insufficient for abandoning a sensitive being to the same fate. What else is it that should trace the insuperable line? Is it the faculty of reason, or perhaps the faculty of discourse? But a full-grown horse or dog is beyond comparison a more rational, as well as a more conversable animal, than an infant of a day or a week or even a month, old. But suppose they were otherwise, what would it avail? The question is not, Can they *reason?* nor Can they *talk?* but, Can they *suffer?*

In this passage Bentham points to the capacity for suffering as the vital characteristic that gives a being the right to equal consideration. The capacity for suffering—or more strictly, for suffering and/or enjoyment or happiness—is not just another characteristic like the capacity for language or higher mathematics. Bentham is not saying that those who try to mark "the insuperable line" that determines whether the interests of a being should be considered happen to have chosen the wrong characteristic. By saying that we must consider the interests of all beings with the capacity for suffering or enjoyment Bentham does not arbitrarily exclude from consideration any interests at all—as those who draw the line with reference to the possession of reason or language do. The capacity for suffering and enjoyment is *a prerequisite for having interests at all*, a condition that must be satisfied before we can speak of interests in a meaningful way. It would be nonsense to say that it was not in the interests of a stone to be kicked along the road by a schoolboy. A stone does not have interests because it cannot suffer. Nothing that we can do to it could possibly make any difference to its welfare. The capacity for suffering and enjoyment is, however, not only necessary, but also sufficient for us to say that a being has interests—at an absolute minimum, an interest in not suffering. A mouse, for example, does have an interest in not being kicked along the road, because it will suffer if it is.

Although Bentham speaks of "rights" in the passage I have quoted, the argument is really about equality rather than about rights. Indeed, in a different passage, Bentham famously described "natural rights" as "nonsense" and "natural and imprescriptable rights" as "nonsense upon stilts." He talked of moral rights as a shorthand way of referring to protections that people and animals morally ought to have; but the real weight of the moral argument does not rest on the assertion of the existence of the right, for this in turn has to be justified on the basis of the possibilities for suffering and happiness. In this way we can argue for equality for animals without getting embroiled in philosophical controversies about the ultimate nature of rights. . . .

If a being suffers there can be no moral justification for refusing to take that suffering into consideration. No matter what the nature of the being, the principle of equality requires that its suffering be counted equally with the like suffering—insofar as rough comparisons can be made—of any other being. If a being is not capable of suffering, or of experiencing enjoyment or happiness, there is nothing to be taken into account. So the limit of sentience (using the term as a convenient if not strictly accurate shorthand for the capacity to suffer and/or experience enjoyment) is the only defensible boundary of concern for the interests of others. To mark this boundary by some other characteristic like intelligence or rationality would be to mark it in an arbitrary manner. Why not choose some other characteristic, like skin color?

Racists violate the principle of equality by giving greater weight to the interests of members of their own race when there is a clash between their interests and the interests of those of another race. Sexists violate the principle of equality by favoring the interests of their own sex. Similarly, speciesists allow the interests of their own species to override the greater interests of members of other species. The pattern is identical in each case.

Comment

Peter Singer was not the first to fight for this cause. In seventeenth-century England, laws were passed to protect animals against cruel practices, including pulling wool off sheep and attaching plows to horses' tails. In eighteenth-century France, the philosopher Jean-Jacques Rousseau argued similar to Bentham that although animals were not rational, they were sentient, and so should be shielded by natural law. And in mid-twentieth-century Germany, it was the Nazis who, ironically, passed the most comprehensive set of animal protection laws in Europe. But it was not until the end of the twentieth century that animal rights caught on. Only in the recent past have animals come to be seen—by large numbers of people in large numbers of places, as opposed only to a few here and there—as having a claim to protection.

It is widely agreed among animal rights activists that Singer's book is the bible. *Animal Liberation* is the founding philosophical document for those who now consider animal rights to be even remotely comparable to human rights.

This is not to say that among animal rights activists there is agreement on all the specifics—there is not. In particular, there is strong disagreement on how animals should be used, if at all. To take the most obvious example, at the one end are those who will not eat meat, who believe that animals should not be used for food (or, for that matter, for anything other than companionship). At the other end are those who do eat meat and do wear leather, but who believe strongly that as long as they live, animals have the right to a good life. Still, by and large the animal rights movement has been smart enough, strategic enough, to overcome differences like these. The great growth of the movement is attributable, in fact, to its being more inclusive than exclusive.

Singer has had a distinguished career as a philosopher. But it is his impact outside the academy that distinguishes him from his peers. He is among a small number of philosophers who are involved in practical ethics—in applying the rigors of the discipline to the demands of public policy—and who have succeeded in making a major difference. Dale Jamieson notes that Singer's conception of practical ethics led him not only to write *Animal Liberation*, but also "to march, demonstrate, and sit in a cage in a city square to publicize the plight of battery hens." Singer was further enjoined from criticizing a circus, arrested for trying to photograph sows confined on a farm belonging to an Australian prime minister, and defeated as the Green Party candidate in Australian federal elections.

Singer has his critics, of course, among them other philosophers. Not only does he touch on third-rail issues (including, in addition to animal liberation, abortion, euthanasia, and infanticide), but his rhetoric seems sometimes, to some anyway, unnecessarily inflammatory. Here is how Jamieson puts the problem: Singer thinks that "you are more likely to do something wrong by killing a healthy pig rather than your severely handicapped infant; and if you are choosing between an early abortion and killing an adult cow, you should probably have the abortion." Small wonder that the agricultural lobby, the scientific establishment, and the pro-life enthusiasts are among those who take strong exception to Singer. Small wonder that his attempt to level the playing field—between human rights on the one hand and animal rights on the other—has bred uncertainty and even hostility. An Australian edition of *Time* framed the question this way: is Singer "saintly or satanic"?

All the sound and fury do not, though, do justice to the complexity of Singer's argument. *Animal Liberation* is grounded in utilitarianism. It expands on Jeremy Bentham's original formulation to become all-inclusive: every animal should count for one, and none should count for more than one. Singer's position would seem easy enough to defend, for what he is railing against is, simply, discrimination. But, the discrimination that he determined to take on is "speciesism"—bias against a particular creature only on the grounds of its being a certain species.

Singer remains controversial even now, decades after the publication of *Animal Liberation*. Notwithstanding, his influence is as great as ever. Along with other leading animal rights activists such as Ingrid Newkirk and Alex Pacheco, who in 1980 cofounded People for the Ethical Treatment of Animals (PETA), and researchers such as legendary primatologists Jane Goodall and Dian Fossey, Singer changed our collective conception of what it means to be humane.

Among the changes, animal rights are now considered a legitimate area of intellectual inquiry. Courses on animal rights are offered in colleges and universities across the United States and Europe, and animal rights law is taught in more than 100 American law schools. In addition, food companies all over the world have made modifications, such as pledging to use only eggs from cage-free hens; a statute was passed in California (in 2008) that phases out some of the most restrictive confinements used by factory farms; and in Spain a parliamentary committee recommended that certain rights be extended to great apes. As Singer himself put it in 2003, "The most obvious difference between the current debate over the moral status of animals and that of thirty years ago is that in the early 1970s, to an extent barely credible today, scarcely any one thought that the treatment of individual animals raised an ethical issue worth taking seriously."

∾

LARRY KRAMER

1935–

His is not a household name—far from it. Why is that? Why is Larry Kramer, who is among the most effective political leaders in recent American history, so unfamiliar a figure?

The answer seems clear: it's not about the leader but about the led. For while homosexuals are far more empowered now than they were just a few decades ago, they remain on the margins, outside mainstream American society. Gay men and lesbian women continue to be among the most embattled of Americans, fighting for rights that others take for granted, such as the right to marry.

Still, homosexuals feel far freer than before to stake their claims, in numbers and with a sense of entitlement that until recently was unimaginable. The fight for gay and lesbian rights should, like every other similar struggle, be considered in context, which in the United States was hard on the heels of African Americans and women beginning to demand (once again) what they considered to be rightfully theirs. In fact, the event that is often said to have sparked the gay liberation movement took place during the heady days of the late 1960s—in June 1969, to be exact—when a brawl broke out between the New York City police and the patrons of Stonewall Inn, a downtown bar known for its gay clientele.

But at a certain point, the fight fought by gay men in particular became something different altogether: it became desperate. For by the early 1980s, they faced a crisis, a health crisis that amounted to a death sentence. It was this threat—the threat of AIDS—that Larry Kramer took on head on. He was a fearless, furious, and ferocious advocate who, when AIDS struck with a vengeance, did more for those afflicted with the disease than did anyone else.

1,112 AND COUNTING
1983

If this article doesn't scare the shit out of you, we're in real trouble. If this article doesn't rouse you to anger, fury, rage, and action, gay men may have no future on this earth. Our continued existence depends on just how angry you can get.

I am writing this as Larry Kramer, and I am speaking for myself, and my views are not to be attributed to Gay Men's Health Crisis,

I repeat: Our continued existence as gay men upon the face of this earth is at stake. Unless we fight for our lives, we shall die. In all the history

From Larry Kramer, *Reports from the holocaust: The Making of an AIDS Activist.* New York: St. Martin's, 1989, pp. 33–47. Reprinted by permission of Larry Kramer.

of homosexuality we have never before been so close to death and extinction. Many of us are dying or already dead.

Before I tell you what we must do, let me tell you what is happening to us.

There are now 1,112 cases of serious Acquired Immune Deficiency Syndrome. When we first became worried, there were only 41. In only twenty-eight days, from January 13th to February 9th [1983], there were 164 new cases—and 73 more dead. The total death tally is now 418. Twenty percent of all cases were registered this January alone. There have been 195 dead in New York City from among 526 victims. Of all serious AIDS cases, 47.3 percent are in the New York metropolitan area.

These are the serious cases of AIDS, which means Kaposi's sarcoma, *Pneumocystis carinii* pneumonia, and other deadly infections. These numbers do not include the thousands of us walking around with what is also being called AIDS: various forms of swollen lymph glands and fatigues that doctors don't know what to label or what they might portend.

The rise in these numbers is terrifying. Whatever is spreading is now spreading faster as more and more people come down with AIDS.

And, for the first time in this epidemic, leading doctors and researchers are finally admitting they don't know what's going on. I find this terrifying too—as terrifying as the alarming rise in numbers. For the first time, doctors are saying out loud and up front, "I don't know."

For two years they weren't talking like this. For two years we've heard a different theory every few weeks. We grasped at the straws of possible cause: promiscuity, poppers, back rooms, the baths, rimming, fisting, anal intercourse, urine, semen, shit, saliva, sweat, blood, blacks, a single virus, a new virus, repeated exposure to a virus, amoebas carrying a virus, drugs, Haiti, voodoo, Flagyl, constant bouts of amebiasis, hepatitis A and B, syphilis, gonorrhea.

I have talked with the leading doctors treating us. One said to me, "If I knew in 1981 what I know now, I would never have become involved with this disease." Another said, "The thing that upsets me the most in all of this is that at any given moment one of my patients is in the hospital and something is going on with him that I don't understand. And it's destroying me because there's some craziness going on in him that's destroying him." A third said to me, "I'm very depressed. A doctor's job is to make patients well. And I can't. Too many of my patients die."

After almost two years of an epidemic, there still are no answers. After almost two years of an epidemic, the cause of AIDS remains unknown. After almost two years of an epidemic, there is no cure.

Hospitals are now so filled with AIDS patients that there is often a waiting period of up to a month before admission, no matter how sick you are. And, once in, patients are now more and more being treated like lepers as hospital staffs become increasingly worried that AIDS is infectious.

Suicides are now being reported of men who would rather die than face such medical uncertainty, such uncertain therapies, such hospital treatment, and the appalling statistic that 86 percent of all serious AIDS cases die after three years' time.

If all of this had been happening to any other community for two long years, there would have been, long ago, such an outcry from that community and all its members that the government of this city and this country would not know what had hit them.

Why isn't every gay man in this city so scared shitless that he is screaming for action? Does every gay man in New York *want* to die?

Let's talk about a few things specifically.

- Let's talk about which gay men get AIDS.
  No matter what you've heard, there is no single profile for all AIDS victims. There are drug users and non-drug users. There are the truly promiscuous and the almost monogamous. There are reported cases of single-contact infection.

  All it seems to take is the one wrong fuck. That's not promiscuity—that's bad luck.

- Let's talk about AIDS happening in straight people.
  We have been hearing from the beginning of this epidemic that it was only a question of time before the straight community came down with AIDS, and that when that happened AIDS would suddenly be high on all agendas for funding and research and then we would finally be looked after and all would then be well.

I myself thought, when AIDS occurred in the first baby, that would be the breakthrough point. It was. For one day the media paid an enormous amount of attention. And that was it, kids.

There have been no confirmed cases of AIDS in straight, white, non-intravenous-drug-using, middle-class Americans. The only confirmed straights struck down by AIDS are members of groups just as disenfranchised as gay men: intravenous drug users, Haitians, eleven hemophiliacs (up from eight), black and Hispanic babies, and wives or partners of IV drug users and bisexual men.

If there have been—and there may have been—any cases in straight, white, non-intravenous-drug-using, middle-class Americans, the Centers for Disease Control isn't telling anyone about them. When pressed, the CDC says there are "a number of cases that don't fall into any of the other categories." The CDC says it's impossible to fully investigate most of these "other category" cases; most of them are dead. The CDC also tends not to believe living, white, middle-class male victims when they say they're straight, or female victims when they say their husbands are straight and don't take drugs.

Why isn't AIDS happening to more straights? Maybe it's because gay men don't have sex with them.

Of all serious AIDS cases, 72.4 percent are in gay and bisexual men.

- Let's talk about "surveillance."
The Centers for Disease Control is charged by our government to fully monitor all epidemics and unusual diseases.

To learn something from an epidemic, you have to keep records and statistics. Statistics come from interviewing victims and getting as much information from them as you can. Before they die. To get the best information, you have to ask the right questions.

There have been so many AIDS victims that the CDC is no longer able to get to them fast enough. It has given up. (The CDC also had been using a questionnaire that was fairly insensitive to the lives of gay men, and thus the data collected from its early study of us have been disputed by gay epidemiologists. The National Institutes of Health is also fielding a very naïve questionnaire.)

Important, vital case histories are now being lost because of this cessation of CDC interviewing. This is a woeful waste with as terrifying implications for us as the alarming rise in case numbers and doctors finally admitting they don't know what's going on. As each man dies, as one or both sets of men who had interacted with each other come down with AIDS, yet more information that might reveal patterns of transmissibility is not being monitored and collected and studied. We are being denied perhaps the easiest and fastest research tool available at this moment.

It will require at least $200,000 to prepare a new questionnaire to study the next important question that must be answered: *How* is AIDS being transmitted? (In which bodily fluids, by which sexual behaviors, in what social environments?)

For months the CDC has been asked to begin such preparations for continued surveillance. The CDC is stretched to its limits and is dreadfully underfunded for what it's being asked, in all areas, to do. . . .

I am sick of our electing officials who in no way represent us. I am sick of our stupidity in believing candidates who promise us everything for our support and promptly forget us and insult us after we have given them our votes. [Mayor Ed] Koch is the prime example, but not the only one. [Senator] Daniel Patrick Moynihan isn't looking very good at this moment, either. Moynihan was requested by gay leaders to publicly ask Margaret Heckler at her confirmation hearing for Secretary of Health and Human Services if she could be fair to gays in view of her voting record of definite anti-gay bias. (Among other horrors, she voted to retain the sodomy law in Washington, D.C., at Jerry Falwell's request.) Moynihan refused to ask this question, as he has refused to meet with us about AIDS, despite our repeated requests. Margaret Heckler will have important jurisdiction over the CDC, over the NIH, over the Public Health Service, over the Food and Drug Administration—indeed, over all areas of AIDS concerns. Thank you, Daniel Patrick Moynihan. I am sick of our not realizing we have enough votes to defeat these people, and I am sick of our not electing our own openly gay officials in the first place. Moynihan doesn't even have an openly gay person on his staff, and he represents the city with the largest gay population in America.

I am sick of closeted gay doctors who won't come out to help us fight to rectify any of what I'm writing about. Doctors—the very letters "M.D."—have enormous clout, particularly when they fight in groups. Can you imagine what gay doctors could accomplish, banded together in a network, petitioning local and federal governments, straight colleagues, and the American Medical Association? I am sick of the passivity or nonparticipation or halfhearted protestation of all the gay medical associations (American Physicians for Human Rights, Bay Area Physicians for Human Rights, Gay Psychiatrists of New York, etc., etc.), and particularly our own New York Physicians for Human Rights, a group of 175 of our gay doctors who have, as a group, done *nothing*. You can count on one hand the number of our doctors who have really worked for *us*.

I am sick of the *Advocate*, one of this country's largest gay publications, which has yet to quite acknowledge that there's anything going on. That newspaper's recent AIDS issue was so innocuous you'd have thought all we were going through was little worse than a rage of the latest designer flu. And their own associate editor, Brent Harris, died from AIDS. Figure that one out.

With the exception of the *New York Native* and a few, very few, other gay publications, the gay press has been useless. If we can't get our own papers and magazines to tell us what's really happening to us, and this negligence is added to the negligent non-interest of the straight press (*The New York Times* took a leisurely year and a half between its major pieces, and the *Village Voice* took a year and a half to write anything at all), how are we going to get the word around that we're dying? Gay men in smaller towns and cities everywhere must be educated, too. Has the *Times* or the *Advocate* told you that twenty-nine cases have been reported from Paris?

I am sick of gay men who won't support gay charities. Go give your bucks to straight charities, fellows, while we die. Gay Men's Health Crisis is going crazy trying to accomplish everything it does—printing and distributing hundreds of thousands of educational items, taking care of several hundred AIDS victims (some of them straight) in and out of hospitals, arranging community forums and speakers all over this country, getting media attention, fighting bad hospital care, on and on and on, fighting for you and us in two thousand ways, *and* trying to sell 17,600 Circus tickets, too. Is the Red Cross doing this for you? Is the American Cancer Society?

Your college alumni fund? The United Jewish Appeal? Catholic Charities? The United Way? The Lenox Hill Neighborhood Association, or any of the other fancy straight charities for which faggots put on black ties and dance at the Plaza? The National Gay Task Force—our only hope for national leadership, with its new and splendid leader, Virginia Apuzzo—which is spending more and more time fighting for the AIDS issue, is broke. Senior Action in a Gay Environment and Gay Men's Health Crisis are, within a few months, going to be without office space they can afford, and thus will be out on the street. The St. Mark's Clinic, held together by some of the few devoted gay doctors in this city who aren't interested in becoming rich, lives in constant terror of even higher rent and eviction. This community is desperate for the services these organizations are providing for it. And these organizations are all desperate for money, which is certainly not coming from straight people or President Reagan or Mayor Koch. (If every gay man within a 250-mile radius of Manhattan isn't in Madison Square Garden on the night of April 30th to help Gay Men's Health Crisis make enough money to get through the next horrible year of fighting against AIDS, I shall lose all hope that we have any future whatsoever.)

I am sick of closeted gays. It's 1983 already, guys, when are you going to come out? By 1984 you could be dead. Every gay man who is unable to come forward now and fight to save his own life is truly helping to kill the rest of us. There is only one thing that's going to save some of us, and this is *numbers* and pressure and our being perceived as united and a threat. As more and more of my friends die, I have less and less sympathy for men who are afraid their mommies will find out or afraid their bosses will find out or afraid their fellow doctors or professional associates will find out. Unless we can generate, visibly, numbers, masses, we are going to die.

I am sick of everyone in this community who tells me to stop creating a panic. How many of us have to die before *you* get scared off your ass and into action? Aren't 195 dead New Yorkers enough? Every straight person who is knowledgeable about the AIDS epidemic can't understand why gay men aren't marching on the White House. Over and over again I hear from them, "Why aren't you guys doing anything?" Every politician I have spoken to has said to me confidentially, "You guys aren't making enough noise. Bureaucracy only responds to pressure."

I am sick of people who say "it's no worse than statistics for smokers and lung cancer" or "considering how many homosexuals there are in the United States, AIDS is really statistically affecting only a very few." That would wash if there weren't 164 cases in twenty-eight days. That would wash if case numbers hadn't jumped from 41 to 1,112 in eighteen months. That would wash if cases in one city—New York—hadn't jumped to cases in fifteen countries and thirty-five states (up from thirty-four last week). That would wash if cases weren't coming in at more than four a day nationally and over two a day locally. That would wash if the mortality rate didn't start at 38 percent the first year of diagnosis and climb to a grotesque 86 percent after three years. Get your stupid heads out of the sand, you turkeys!

I am sick of guys who moan that giving up careless sex until this blows over is worse than death. How can they value life so little and cocks and asses so much? Come with me, guys, while I visit a few of our friends in Intensive Care at NYU. Notice the looks in their eyes, guys. They'd give up sex forever if you could promise them life.

I am sick of guys who think that all being gay means is sex in the first place. I am sick of guys who can only think with their cocks.

I am sick of "men" who say, "We've got to keep quiet or *they* will do such and such." *They* usually means the straight majority, the "Moral" Majority, or similarly perceived representatives of *them*. Okay, you "men"—be my guests: You can march off now to the gas chambers; just get right in line.

We shall always have enemies. Nothing we can ever do will remove them. Southern newspapers and Jerry Falwell's publications are already printing editorials proclaiming AIDS as God's deserved punishment on homosexuals. So what? Nasty words make poor little sissy pansy wilt and die?

And I am very sick and saddened by every gay man who does not get behind this issue totally and with commitment—to fight for his life.

Comment

When Larry Kramer wrote "1,112 and Counting," AIDS was unfamiliar. Almost none of the afflicted knew yet what exactly the disease was. Almost none of the afflicted were disposed yet to admit to the problem and cry for help. And almost none of the afflicted were willing yet to face the fact that AIDS could, and in the early days especially often did, kill.

Larry Kramer, though, was different. He was freely and openly gay. And he was unapologetically angry and ready to do battle—with straight people for their hostility and intolerance, with closeted gays for being too timorous, and with gay men for leading lives that he judged empty and hedonistic. Kramer was by trade a writer, and by the late 1970s he had wed his pen to his passion. He wrote a novel, *Faggots*, about gay men and the lives they led, which, as the novel's incendiary title seems to imply, were depicted by Kramer as having descended into decadence. For taking on his own, he was attacked by his own.

But when AIDS hit, when the cause became critical, it was Kramer who took the lead. In the early 1980s, when nearly no one else was facing facts or doing a thing to stop the scourge, Kramer joined his protests on paper to his protests on the streets. His activism took many forms, including letters to the editors of local and national newspapers, op-ed essays and articles, plays and speeches, grassroots organizing and, in time, political theater.

In 1981 Kramer cofounded the Gay Men's Health Crisis (GMHC). The idea was for GMHC first to draw attention to AIDS, and then to enlist political, financial, and medical support for those so afflicted. But before long, Kramer, never known for his patience, or for that matter for his affability, was disappointed and disheartened. By 1983 he was writing as if he were at the end of his tether—to wit, "1,112 and Counting"—and he quit GMHC, insisting that it had become impotent and ineffectual. This did not, however, signal the end of either his commitment or his career as an activist. On the contrary, Kramer's frustration stoked his fury. In 1987 he helped found another organization, one of the most famous—or, if you prefer, infamous—grassroots action groups ever: the AIDS Coalition to Unleash Power, known to all in the know as ACT UP.

ACT UP had a clearer goal than did GMHC—and it was more ready to take risks to reach that goal. Its primary purpose was to force the pharmaceutical industry and, more important, the Food and Drug Administration to provide greater access to experimental AIDS drugs. To this end, ACT UP in general (it had tens of thousands of members and one hundred chapters), and Kramer in particular, became synonymous with histrionics. For example, Kramer was capable of standing in the street, megaphone in his hand, screaming, "President Reagan, your son is gay!" (Kramer's rage against prominent politicians who refused even to acknowledge AIDS was boundless.) As Michael Specter summarized it in *The New Yorker*, "Larry Kramer may be responsible for more public arrests than anyone since the height of the civil rights movement: AIDS activists who tried to dump the ashes of a young friend onto the South Lawn of the White House, protesters who shut down the floor of the New York Stock Exchange, surrounded the Food and Drug Administration headquarters, and chained themselves to the gates at the headquarters of the pharmaceutical giant Hoffman-La Roche and to the Golden Gate Bridge." Members of ACT UP adopted inflammatory slogans ("SILENCE = DEATH"); arrived by the thousands at St. Patrick's Cathedral to protest the Catholic Church's stand against AIDS education, condom distribution, and abortion; and entered the studio of the *CBS Evening News* to shout out, smack in the middle of the broadcast, "Fight AIDS, not Arabs!"

Still, for all his heady political activism—years later, Kramer remembered the early days of GMHC and ACT UP as being "euphoric"— the main weapon in his arsenal was his way with words. Here is another example, an open letter he wrote in 1988 to Dr. Anthony Fauci, a leading AIDS researcher and high-ranking official at the National Institutes of Health. The letter was published first in the *Village Voice* and then in the *San Francisco Examiner*, and it began like this:

> I have been screaming at the National Institutes of Health since I first visited your Animal House of Horrors in 1984. I called you monsters then and I called you idiots in my play *The Normal Heart* and now I call you murderers. You are responsible for supervising all government-funded AIDS-treatment research programs. In the name of right, you make decisions that cost the lives of others. I call the decisions you are making acts of murder.

Kramer's enraged invective did not exactly endear him to others; he was widely considered contradictory, controversial, contentious, and sometimes downright obnoxious. Withal, once AIDS struck, he was relentless in his defense of the gay community, and in his offense against those who would deny that the disease was a plague. As Specter wrote, the fear that Kramer unleashed "helped transform gay life," and his actions "helped revolutionize the American practice of medicine," including the FDA's accelerated approval of investigational new drugs. Even his former foe, Dr. Fauci, came to conclude that "Larry helped change medicine in this country. And he helped change it for the better." What is clear is this: when Kramer wrote "1,112 and Counting," AIDS was tantamount to a death sentence. A quarter century later, it was a manageable disease—a transformation for which he in good measure was responsible.

A postscript: leadership can be exercised through case law when the case is a landmark. *Goodridge v. Department of Public Health* was an appellate court case in the state of Massachusetts that dealt with same-sex marriage. It was decided in 2003 by Chief Justice Margaret Marshall. The result of her pathbreaking ruling—which declared the prohibition of gay marriage to be a violation of the state's constitution—was that Massachusetts became the first state in the union legally to permit gay marriage. Marshall's ruling read in part as follows:

> Marriage is a vital social institution. The exclusive commitment of two individuals to each other nurtures love and mutual support: it brings stability to our society. For those who choose to marry, and for their children, marriage provides an abundance of legal, financial, and social benefits. In return it imposes weighty legal, financial, and social obligations. The question before us is whether, consistent with the Massachusetts Constitution, the Commonwealth may deny the protections, benefits, and obligations conferred by civil marriage to two individuals of the same sex who wish to marry. We conclude that it may not. The Massachusetts Constitution affirms the dignity and equality of all individuals. It forbids the creation of second-class citizens. In reaching our conclusion we have given full deference to the arguments made by the Commonwealth. But it has failed to identify any constitutionally adequate reason for denying civil marriage

to same-sex couples. . . . Barred access to the protections, benefits, and obligations of coeval marriage, a person who enters into an intimate, exclusive union with another of the same sex is arbitrarily deprived of membership in one of our community's most rewarding and cherished institutions. That exclusion is incompatible with the constitutional principles of respect for individual autonomy under the law.

3

LEADERS
IN ACTION

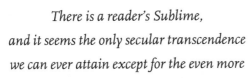

*There is a reader's Sublime,
and it seems the only secular transcendence
we can ever attain except for the even more
precarious transcendence we call
"falling in love."*

—HAROLD BLOOM

T HE VOICES IN Part 3 are familiar. They belong to men and women who exercised leadership so forcefully and to such enduring effect that they are immortal. Most of these leaders held formal positions of high authority, for example, Queen Elizabeth I and President Abraham Lincoln. But some held such positions only later in life, after the leadership for which they became legendary was past. Lenin, Mandela, and Havel belong in this category—their main claim to fame was the work they accomplished before they became heads of state. Indeed, some of the leaders who speak to us here never held such high positions, yet they are of immense historical importance; these include Truth, Gandhi (though for a time he was a leader of his party), and King (though for a time he was leader of the Southern Christian Leadership Conference).

The words that follow were spoken, written, or, in some cases (as with Elizabeth, Lincoln, and Churchill), first put on paper and then delivered in a formal oration. Not every syllable still lingers. But in total this literature of leaders in action belongs securely in the pantheon of classics.

∾

QUEEN ELIZABETH I
1533–1603

For some obvious and some less obvious reasons, there has been a paucity of women leaders overall. The inevitable result is that women leaders who were indisputably great are few in number, and the number of great women leaders whose way with words is part of our literary legacy is fewer still.

Queen Elizabeth I of England was such a *rara avis*, a bird so rare that there has never been another quite like her. This is not to say that her accomplishments are inarguable. They are not—some historians consider her reign rather flawed. But it must be said that during the time in which she lived, royals who were in positions of power and authority were overwhelmingly kings and not queens, and that for nearly 45 years (1558–1603), she ruled so memorably, so remarkably, that ever since her era has been known simply as "the Elizabethan era." Among her prodigious gifts, she was a writer, of poems and prayers, essays and translations—and public documents. From girlhood on, she put pen to paper as gladly as she did often, and during her long reign she continued the habit, which resulted in a significant literary achievement. As Leah Marcus and her coeditors noted, included was "a series of speeches that are often remarkable for their beauty and power."

The two that follow are her most famous. The first, known as the "Spanish Armada Speech," was delivered by the queen to the English army at Tilbury Fort in 1588. It was occasioned by the battle between English forces and the supposedly stronger Spanish fleet that had been dispatched to vanquish Elizabeth's regime and return England to the Catholic faith. The second is "The Golden Speech," which was delivered to members of the House of Commons in 1601. What was expected to be an ordinary oration on the economy was instead a farewell, in which the queen announced that this Parliament would be her last.

Exactly what she said on each of the two occasions cannot be known for certain—both speeches were formally recorded only after the fact and in versions that were slightly different. But what we do know for sure is that Queen Elizabeth I was a formidable wordsmith, as exacting in the substance of her words as in the felicity of their style.

SPEECH TO THE TROOPS AT TILBURY
1588

My loving people, we have been persuaded by some that are careful of our safety to take heed how we commit ourself to armed multitudes for fear of treachery, but, I assure you, I do not desire to live to distrust my faithful and loving people. Let tyrants fear. I have always so behaved myself that, under God, I have placed my chiefest strength and safeguard in the loyal hearts and goodwill of my subjects. And therefore I am come amongst you, as you see, at this time not for my recreation and disport but being resolved in the midst and heat of the battle to live or die amongst you all, to lay down for my God, and for my kingdom, and for my people my honor and my blood even in the dust.

I know I have the body but of a weak and feeble woman, but I have the heart and stomach of a king and of a king of England, too, and think foul scorn that Parma or Spain or any prince of Europe should dare to invade the borders of my realm, to which rather than any dishonor shall grow by me, I myself will take up arms, I myself will be your general, judge, and rewarder of every one of your virtues in the field. I know already for your forwardness you have deserved rewards and crowns, and we do assure you in the word of a prince they shall be duly paid you. In the meantime, my Lieutenant General shall be in my stead, than whom never prince commanded a more noble or worthy subject, not doubting but by your obedience to my General, by your concord in the camp, and your valor in the field, we shall shortly have a famous victory over those enemies of my God, of my kingdoms, and of my people.

THE GOLDEN SPEECH
[THE TOWNSHEND VERSION]
1601

Master Speaker, we have heard your declaration and perceive your care of our state by falling into the consideration of a grateful acknowledgment of such benefits as you have received, and that your coming is to present thanks unto us, which I accept with no less joy than your loves can have desire to offer such a present.

I do assure you there is no prince that loveth his subjects better or whose love can countervail our love. There is no jewel, be it of never so rich a price, which I set before this jewel, I mean your love. For I do more esteem of it than of any treasure or riches, for that we know how to prize, but love and thanks I count unvaluable.

And though God hath raised me high, yet this I count the glory of my crown, that I have reigned with your loves. This makes me that I do not so much rejoice that God hath made me to be a Queen as to be a Queen over so thankful a people. Therefore, I have cause to wish nothing more than to content the subjects, and that is a duty which I owe; neither do I desire to live longer days than that I may see your prosperity, and that's my only desire.

And as I am that person that still (yet under God) hath delivered you, so I trust (by the almighty power of God) that I still shall be His instrument to preserve you from envy, peril, dishonor, shame, tyranny, and oppression, partly by means of your intended helps, which we take very acceptably because it manifests the largeness of your loves and loyalty to your Sovereign.

Of myself I must say this: I was never any greedy, scraping grasper, nor a strait, fast-holding prince, nor yet a waster. My heart was never set on worldly goods but only for my subjects' good. What you do bestow on me, I will not hoard it up but receive it to bestow on you again. Yea, my own proprieties I count yours and to be expended for your good, and your eyes shall see the bestowing of all for your good. Therefore render unto them from me, I beseech you, Master Speaker, such thanks as you imagine my heart yieldeth but my tongue cannot express.

(Note: all this while we kneeled, whereupon her Majesty said:)

Master Speaker, I would wish you and the rest to stand up, for I shall yet trouble you with longer speech.

(So we all stood up and she went on with her speech, saying:)

Master Speaker, you give me thanks, but I doubt me that I have more cause to thank you all than you me, and I charge you to thank them of the Lower House from me, for had I not received a knowledge from you, I might have fallen into the lapse of an error only for lack of true information.

Since I was Queen, yet did I never put my pen unto any grant but that upon pretext and semblance made unto me it was both good and beneficial to the subject in general, though a private profit to some of my ancient servants who had deserved well at my hands. But the contrary being found by experience, I am exceedingly beholding to such subjects as would move the same at the first. And I am not so simple to suppose but that there are some of the Lower House whom these grievances never touched, and for them I think they spake out of zeal for their countries and not out of spleen or malevolent affection as being parties grieved. And I take it exceeding gratefully from them because it gives us to know that no respects or interests had moved them other than the minds they bear to suffer no diminution of our honor and our subjects' loves unto us, the zeal of which affection, tending to ease my people and knit their hearts unto me, I embrace with a princely care. For above all earthly treasure, I esteem my people's love, more than which I desire not to merit.

That my grants should be grievous to my people and oppressions privileged under color of our patents, our kingly dignity shall not suffer it. Yea when I heard it, I could give no rest unto my thoughts until I had reformed it. Shall they think to escape unpunished that have thus oppressed you and have been respectless of their duty and regardless of our honor? No, Master Speaker, I assure you were it not more for conscience-sake than for any glory or increase of love that I desire, these errors, troubles, vexations, and oppressions done by these varlets and lewd persons (not worthy the name of subjects) should not escape without condign punishment. But I perceive they dealt with me like physicians who, administering a drug, make it more acceptable by giving it a good, aromatical savor, or when they give pills do gild them all over.

I have ever used to set the Last Judgment Day before my eyes, as so to rule as I shall be judged to answer before a higher Judge, to whose judgment seat I do appeal, that never thought was cherished in my heart that tended not to my peoples' good. And now if my kingly bounty have been abused and my grants turned to the hurt of my people, contrary to my will and meaning, or if any in authority under me have neglected or perverted what I have committed to them, I hope God will not lay their culps and offences to my charge who, though there were danger in repealing our grants, yet what danger would I not rather incur for your good than I would suffer them still to continue?

I know the title of a king is a glorious title, but assure yourself that the shining glory of princely authority hath not so dazzled the eyes of our understanding but that we well know and remember that we also are to yield an account of our actions before the great Judge.

To be a king and wear a crown is a thing more glorious to them that see it than it is pleasing to them that bear it. For myself, I was never so much enticed with the glorious name of a king or royal authority of a queen as delighted that God had made me His instrument to maintain

His truth and glory and to defend this kingdom, as I said, from peril, dishonor, tyranny, and oppression.

There will never queen sit in my seat with more zeal to my country, care for my subjects, and that sooner with willingness will venture her life for your good and safety than myself, for it is not my desire to live nor reign longer than my life and reign shall be for your good. And though you have had and may have many princes more mighty and wise sitting in this seat, yet you never had or shall have any that will be more careful and loving.

Shall I ascribe anything to myself and my sexly weakness? I were not worthy to live then, and of all most unworthy of the great mercies I have had from God, who hath ever yet given me a heart which never yet feared foreign or home enemy. I speak it to give God the praise as a testimony before you and not to attribute anything to myself; for I, O Lord, what am I whom practices and perils past should not fear? or what can I do? *(These words she spake with a great emphasis:)*

That I should speak for any glory, God forbid.

This, Master Speaker, I pray you deliver to the House, to whom heartily commend me, and so I commit you all to your best fortunes and further counsels. And I pray you, Master Comptroller, Master Secretary, and you of my Council, that before these gentlemen depart into their countries you bring them all to kiss my hand.

Comment

The story of Queen Elizabeth I not only defies convention—it defies imagination. She was the daughter of King Henry VIII and Anne Boleyn. Her father was a ferocious figure, larger than life; her mother was executed for adultery, incest, and treason before her daughter was three. Elizabeth ascended to the throne by a route best described as tortuous. At first she was declared a bastard. Later she was cut out of the succession by her brother, Edward VI. And after that she was imprisoned for nearly a year and almost executed by her half-sister, Mary Tudor, a Catholic who suspected her putative rival of Protestant sympathies.

Elizabeth's reign was equally tumultuous, fraught with peril and promise, intrigue and incident, trouble and triumph. As queen, she presided over, though she pointedly did not formally sanction, the beheading of a different Mary, this one Mary Stuart, Queen of Scotland, also a staunch Catholic, whose very existence threatened Elizabeth's rule. She further claimed one of the most storied victories in English military history (over the Spanish Armada) and, by some sort of alchemy, created a climate that is famed forever for the flourishing of English drama, in particular the plays of William Shakespeare and Christopher Marlowe.

Given the singularity of her situation—not only was she commander in chief, but she was head of the English church, and in every other aspect a woman in a royal role that was intended to be, expected to be, and ordained to be filled by a man—Elizabeth chose her words with care, especially on great public occasions. Again, she was nearly by nature a writer, whose public performances, her speeches and prayers in particular, were the medium that was the message. They were her way of communicating with and connecting to her subjects.

Recent feminist scholars have established the importance of women in history and have enabled us to see Elizabeth as a woman in a man's world more clearly than before. Her speeches provide particular grist for this mill, as is made plain by Mary Beth Rose in an essay titled "Gender and the Construction of Royal Authority in the Speeches of Elizabeth I." Rose cites one of the great modern authorities on Elizabeth, J. E. Neale, and concurs that her "political achievement constitutes an awe-inspiring victory over the odds." But unlike Neale, Rose goes on to locate the queen's strength in her "verbal powers," which enable her to "define her authority and legitimize her actions in gendered terms." Rather than play down her womanhood or pretend that it did not exist as an issue, Elizabeth defiantly used speech to proclaim her female self, while at the same time denying that it diminished her capacities. Not that this precluded her from presuming as well to don a male mantle—not at all. She authoritatively and unambiguously asserted her God-given right, her divine right, to rule.

The queen seems to have felt that she had to address, over and over again, the issue of gender. This was in light of her father's famous—or infamous—attempts to produce a son as his legal heir (his six wives notwithstanding, Henry VIII had only one legitimate son, who died in boyhood). And it was in light of a Renaissance culture that, like Western culture for hundreds of years more, assumed that women should be subordinate to men, and that they belonged properly in the private sphere, not in the public one. The queen's spinsterhood further exacerbated the gender issue, for it meant that she would not, could not produce a successor to the throne. This lack of an obvious heir struck fear into the hearts of many, who were convinced it would further exacerbate civil strife and lead some day to civil war.

The queen's womanhood plays a prominent part in both of the speeches quoted here. Paramount among her tasks, particularly at Tilbury, was to persuade her audience that despite her own exceptional case, the social order—ordained by God and arranged so that women were subordinate to men—remained undisturbed. Indeed, Elizabeth went so far as to claim the contrary. She claimed that she, a woman, was chosen by God to serve as his emissary, and that she, a "weak" woman, was better able than a man to serve her country, even at this military moment. Her logic was that she alone could conflate the power of a man with the purity of a woman, in particular this woman, the virgin queen.

The short address delivered by Elizabeth I directly on the battlefield at Tilbury is considered by scholars to be the most memorable and daring of her queenly reign. For her performance, she famously fastened a silver breastplate over her white velvet dress, and held in her hand a commander's baton. "I know I have the body but of a weak and feeble woman," she declared, "but I have the heart and stomach of a king, and of a king of England, too."

Some 15 years later, as her reign was drawing to a close, many of the queen's problems and plaints persisted. But by this time she was admired and even adored by her subjects, to a degree that was nearly unprecedented. Her response was in kind. As noted by Donald Stump and Susan Felch, in her final major speech, "The Golden Speech," the speech that "ought to be set in letters of gold," she gave her people what they wanted: "repeated assurances of love for her subjects, care for their welfare, devotion to God, and commitment to imperial justice." On this occasion, very different from the one at Tilbury, though Elizabeth took another tone, she returned nevertheless to the issue of gender. This time, though, the queen had merely to remind her listeners: "Though you have had and may have many princes more mighty and wise sitting in this seat, yet you never had or shall have any that will be more careful and loving."

Clearly now, toward the end of her time on the throne, Elizabeth felt free to claim a capacity that was more typically associated with women than with men, that is, the capacity for caring, compassion, and concern. Rose notes that as her days on the throne dwindled in number, the queen began "to view the loving dialogue between herself and her subjects not merely as a manifestation of her power, but as a source of it." Done with having to prove that her might was the equal of a man's, she allowed herself finally to become more fully female, and in so doing discovered a different source of strength altogether.

As Queen Elizabeth I spoke, so Queen Elizabeth I led. As George P. Rice, Jr., put it, "The mature Elizabeth brought to the rostrum the happy combination of natural endowment and careful training needed for success in public speaking." Her public performances were characterized by "logical reasoning through close argumentation"; simultaneously, she played to her subjects by saying what they wanted to hear in a way that they could grasp. To read the Tilbury and Golden Speeches is to concur: "On those two occasions Elizabeth represented herself at her royal best and through them added luster to the annals of English eloquence."

~

SOJOURNER TRUTH
1797–1883

ABRAHAM LINCOLN
1809–1865

The three speeches that follow are connected, and they flow from the first to the second, and from the second to the third. All are short, and they are so deeply etched on America's collective consciousness that even now, long after reciting from memory has ceased to be considered the mark of a good education, their lines linger.

Sojourner Truth was the name she chose. The name she was born with was Isabella Baumfree, one of 13 children born to James and Elizabeth Baumfree, slaves on an estate located 95 miles north of New York City. Though she remained illiterate all her life, Truth nonetheless managed to attain her freedom (in 1826) before she was legally entitled to do so, and in the ensuing decades to become one of the nineteenth century's best-known civil rights activists. She was, along with Harriet Tubman, one of the two most famous African American women of her time.

The speech that follows—known colloquially as "Ain't I a Woman?"— is the one for which Truth is best remembered. She delivered it on May 28, 1851, at a Women's Rights Convention in Akron, Ohio. Though her focus is on the plight of women, underpinning her plaint is her experience as a *black* woman who had long been at the service of white men. Moreover, the last line, in which Truth depicts white men as being trapped between slaves on the one hand and women (black and white) on the other, is as vivid an image as we have of the inexorable entwining of the two great rights revolutions of the nineteenth and twentieth centuries: the struggle for equality by African Americans and by women.

There are several versions of Truth's speech—exactly what she said we will never know. One version, recorded years later by Frances Gage, is heavily in the vernacular; others are rendered simply in modern American dialect. The version that follows is by Marius Robinson, who attended the convention in Akron and worked with Truth. It appeared in the June 21, 1851, issue of the *Anti-Slavery Bugle*.

Notwithstanding Abraham Lincoln's genius for the English language, he too was of humble origin, the son of uneducated farmers. He grew up in a small, long-since-legendary log cabin and was formally schooled for less than two years. An autodidact, the sixteenth president of the United States was first a country lawyer, then a state legislator and congressman from Illinois before going on to win the White House. In his capacity as commander in chief, he led during the deadliest war in American history—for the purpose of preserving the Union. And in his capacity as chief executive, he signed the Emancipation Proclamation, which ended slavery on American soil forever. His second term in office had barely begun when his life was cut short at the hand of an assassin.

Lincoln has long been judged to be among the greatest of American presidents, not least because he was so literate a leader, so adroit at using the English language to enlist others in his cause. The Bible was paramount among Lincoln's literary influences, with Shakespeare close behind. Fred Kaplan wrote that Lincoln was so familiar with the Bard that quotations from his plays "came as naturally to him as breathing." During the Civil War in particular, Shakespeare's history plays "had a special purchase [for Lincoln], even more than they had always had, as exemplars of the drama of national destiny . . . the clashing of ambitions and wills, and the attempt to assert contradictory national visions."

Lincoln's literary gift was recognized in his own time. But to those of us who have come since, his language is among the most important of his legacies, as in the two speeches that follow, each of them a national treasure. The first is the "Gettysburg Address," delivered on November 19, 1863. Lincoln's ostensible purpose was to dedicate a newly opened military cemetery. However, given the circumstances, he thought it important to expand on the occasion to reaffirm, reinvigorate, and even ennoble the war effort. He distinguished not at all between the dead of the North and those of the South and, as was his habit, he drew on the Bible, its content and cadence, to signal redemption and rebirth. The president had another purpose as well. As James McPherson has pointed out, he used his speech to signal: "The new birth of freedom that Lincoln spoke of at Gettysburg referred to the imminent abolition of slavery."

The second speech is Lincoln's second inaugural address. It was delivered on March 4, 1865, and was said to be his favorite. Once again the Bible permeates the text, which was in keeping with Lincoln's learning and leaning, and with the temper of his time.

SOJOURNER TRUTH
AIN'T I A WOMAN?
1851

I want to say a few words about this matter. I am a woman's rights. I have as much muscle as any man, and can do as much work as any man. I have plowed and reaped and husked and chopped and mowed, and can any man do more than that? I have heard much about the sexes being equal. I can carry as much as any man, and can eat as much too, if I can get it. I am as strong as any man that is now. As for intellect, all I can say is, if a woman have a pint, and a man a quart—why can't she have her little pint full? You need not be afraid to give us our rights for fear we will take too much,—for we can't take more than our pint'll hold. The poor men seem to be all in confusion, and don't know what to do. Why children, if you have woman's rights, give it to her and you will feel better. You will have your own rights, and they won't be so much trouble. I can't read, but I can hear. I have heard the bible and have learned that Eve caused man to sin. Well, if woman upset the world, do give her a chance to set it right side up again. The Lady has spoken about Jesus, how he never spurned woman from him, and she was right. When Lazarus died, Mary and Martha came to him with faith and love and besought him to raise their brother. And Jesus wept and Lazarus came forth. And how came Jesus into the world? Through God who created him and the woman who bore him. Man, where was your part? But the women are coming up blessed be God and a few of the men are coming up with them. But man is in a tight place, the poor slave is on him, woman is coming on him, he is surely between a hawk and a buzzard.

ABRAHAM LINCOLN

·········· **GETTYSBURG ADDRESS** ··········

1863

Four score and seven years ago our fathers brought forth on this continent, a new nation, conceived in Liberty, and dedicated to the proposition that all men are created equal.

Now we are engaged in a great civil war, testing whether that nation, or any nation so conceived and so dedicated, can long endure. We are met on a great battle-field of that war. We have come to dedicate a portion of that field, as a final resting place for those who here gave their lives that that nation might live. It is altogether fitting and proper that we should do this.

But, in a larger sense, we can not dedicate—we can not consecrate—we can not hallow—this ground. The brave men, living and dead, who struggled here, have consecrated it, far above our poor power to add or detract. The world will little note, nor long remember what we say here, but it can never forget what they did here. It is for us the living, rather, to be dedicated here to the unfinished work which they who fought here have thus far so nobly advanced. It is rather for us to be here dedicated to the great task remaining before us—that from these honored dead we take increased devotion to that cause for which they gave the last full measure of devotion—that we here highly resolve that these dead shall not have died in vain—that this nation, under God, shall have a new birth of freedom—and that government of the people, by the people, for the people, shall not perish from the earth.

SECOND INAUGURAL ADDRESS

1865

Fellow-Countrymen:

At this second appearing to take the oath of the Presidential office there is less occasion for an extended address than there was at the first. Then a statement somewhat in detail of a course to be pursued seemed fitting and proper. Now, at the expiration of four years, during which public declarations have been constantly called forth on every point and phase of the great contest which still absorbs the attention and engrosses the energies of the nation, little that is new could be presented. The progress of our arms, upon which all else chiefly depends, is as well known to the public as to myself, and it is, I trust, reasonably satisfactory and encouraging to all. With high hope for the future, no prediction in regard to it is ventured.

On the occasion corresponding to this four years ago all thoughts were anxiously directed to an impending civil war. All dreaded it, all sought to avert it. While the inaugural address was being delivered from this place, devoted altogether to *saving* the Union without war, urgent agents were in the city seeking to *destroy* it without war—seeking to dissolve the Union and divide effects by negotiation. Both parties deprecated war, but one of them would *make* war rather than let the nation survive, and the other would *accept* war rather than let it perish, and the war came.

One-eighth of the whole population were colored slaves, not distributed generally over the Union, but localized in the southern part of it. These slaves constituted a peculiar and powerful interest. All knew that this interest was somehow the cause of the war. To strengthen, perpetuate, and extend this interest was the object for which the insurgents would rend the Union even by war, while the Government claimed no right to do more than to restrict the territorial enlargement of it. Neither party expected for the war the magnitude or the duration which it has already attained. Neither anticipated that the *cause* of the conflict might cease with or even before the conflict itself should cease. Each looked for an easier triumph, and a result less fundamental and astounding. Both read the same Bible and pray to the same God, and each invokes His aid against the other. It may seem strange that any men should dare to ask a just God's assistance in wringing their bread from the sweat of other men's faces, but let us judge not, that we be not judged. The prayers of both could not be answered. That of neither has been answered fully. The Almighty has His own purposes. "Woe unto the world because of offenses; for it must needs be that offenses come, but woe to that man by whom the offense cometh." If we shall suppose that American slavery is one of those offenses which, in the providence of God, must needs come, but which, having continued through His appointed time, He now wills to remove, and that He gives to both North and South this terrible war as the woe due to those by whom the offense came, shall we discern therein any departure from those divine attributes which the believers in a living God always ascribe to Him? Fondly do we hope, fervently do we pray, that this mighty scourge of war may speedily pass away. Yet, if God wills that it continue until all the wealth piled by the bondsman's two hundred and fifty years of unrequited toil shall be sunk, and until every drop of blood drawn with the lash shall be paid by another drawn with the sword, as was said three thousand years ago, so still it must be said "the judgments of the Lord are true and righteous altogether."

With malice toward none, with charity for all, with firmness in the right as God gives us to see the right, let us strive on to finish the work we are in, to bind up the nation's wounds, to care for him who shall have borne the battle and for his widow and his orphan, to do all which may achieve and cherish a just and lasting peace among ourselves and with all nations.

Comment

Though different in the extreme, these three speeches are of a piece. Sojourner Truth, born a slave, and later a militant abolitionist and a fierce feminist, was the necessary, the inevitable, precursor to Abraham Lincoln.

In some sense, Lincoln was the son of Truth, the product of her political intention. "Ain't I a Woman?" was, symbolically at least, as significant a literary prelude to the Civil War and the end of slavery as was Martin Luther King's "Letter from a Birmingham Jail" to the modern civil rights movement. Abolitionism was the social movement that led ultimately to the Civil War—and to the end of American slavery. Lincoln's leadership, literary and otherwise, must, in other words, be seen in context. Great as he was, he could not have led as he did even a few years earlier. The soil had to be prepared by, among others, women such as Sojourner Truth, an activist; Harriet Beecher Stowe, a novelist; and the Grimké sisters, Sarah and Angelina, preeminent nineteenth-century crusaders who, like Truth, had the fortitude to declare themselves both against slavery and for the rights of women. (Among British abolitionists, who preceded by several decades their American counterparts, women played an even more prominent role as writers, public speakers, initiators of boycotts, and signers of petitions.)

The descriptions of Sojourner Truth start with her startling presence. She was, in a word, formidable. Suzanne Fitch and Roseann Mandziuk wrote:

> Part of the fascination with Sojourner Truth in her own time was due to her physical presence. She stood close to six feet tall and was thin and very dark-skinned. Her dress was often Quaker-like, and she always wore a turban head-dress. Another feature remembered by those who knew her was her gestures. Her long, bony fingers would help make her point as she admonished her listeners and opponents alike for their laziness toward, or opposition to, her causes.

Others remembered Truth's low voice—so low that some thought it masculine—which she used to advantage, to sing as well as to speak.

Her appearance, along with the words she spoke and the voice she intoned, mattered as much as it did because in the prime of her life, Truth became a preacher—a prophet, some called her. This was not, of course, a formal designation. Rather, she assumed for herself the mantle of someone chosen—chosen to speak to various audiences about various causes. Her crusades drew upon her experience: as a slave, as a woman of color, as a woman in full, and as a person of faith. In addition, she knew the tricks of the consummate performer: songs and stories, jokes and jousts, accessible anecdotes, and the Bible. "Shock was another of her strategies," adds biographer Margaret Washington. "Few speakers used satire more skillfully. . . . Sojourner's biting parody and lambasting of [in this case black] male leaders as narrow, greedy, sexist, and un-Christian undoubtedly stunned her listeners. Just as she wanted whites to 'feel' what the enslaved felt, she wanted to jolt her race into a sense of urgency."

It happened that Truth was the perfect foil for the man who became president while she was in her prime. Who could have known? Who could have known that a man as similarly tall, thin, and formidable a presence, Abraham Lincoln, would, in the not distant future, sign, as Truth put it years later, "the death-warrant of slavery." Nevertheless, history had joined them, this particular black woman to that particular white man, years before they met, which in fact they did, in the White House, after she was vindicated by history and he became president.

President Abraham Lincoln's "Gettysburg Address" is not only an exemplar of the leadership literature, it is also, as Garry Wills points out in his important book *Lincoln at Gettysburg*, a cultural artifact. Wills sets the scene by setting this particular cemetery experience in the context of nineteenth-century cemetery experiences generally, and by touching briefly on Lincoln's political persona.

Soon after its dedication (in 1831), Mount Auburn, a cemetery in Cambridge, Massachusetts, became one of America's principal cultural institutions. It was the first in a series of such burying grounds—the model for the so-called rural cemetery movement. In time, cemeteries were dedicated in rather elaborate ceremonies, in which entire communities were involved. They were, according to Wills, "the supreme locus of liminality in the nineteenth century," the "borderland between life and death, time and eternity, past and future."

It should be added, as Wills did, that this national preoccupation with death suited Lincoln perfectly, for he was himself "funereal, almost to the point of caricature." As one of Lincoln's closest associates had put it, "melancholy dripped from him as he walked," a demeanor that coincided both with what was culturally encouraged and with the mood of the moment at Gettysburg.

The "Gettysburg Address" was delivered only after what was intended to be the high point of the occasion: a long speech (it lasted two hours) in the classical tradition, given by Edward Everett, a scholar, diplomat, and orator of high repute. The president's remarks were, in contrast, remarkably brief. Lincoln spoke for no more than three minutes and uttered less than 300 words, unwilling as he was to waste so much as a single syllable, and prepared as he was to say what he wanted—no more, no less.

The war that had begun two years earlier and was long and bloody beyond imagining had chastened the president. By the time he spoke at Gettysburg, where just a few months earlier some 50,000 men had been killed or wounded in a grim, gruesome battle three days long, he was a changed man: more empathetic and sympathetic; more democratic, conciliatory, and inspirational. His choice of biblical rhetoric and reference was deliberate. It allowed him to move from the particular to the universal, and to appeal to what he had elsewhere called "the better angels of our nature."

Not only was Lincoln a skilled and experienced orator, but he was also something of an actor, mimic, and raconteur. Thus the text met its match in the man. This president was as equipped as any other to deliver to the American people a great speech of high public purpose. As Jonathan Raban put it, "The Gettysburg Address redefined the purpose and meaning of the nation with such richness and precision, and with such breathtaking economy, that it has become a classic of American literature, at least as great a piece of writing as 'Moby-Dick' or the very best poems in 'Leaves of Grass.'"

By the time President Lincoln delivered his second inaugural address, he had every reason to anticipate that the Civil War was nearly over. In fact, recent events had seemed to vindicate his leadership. An editorial in the *Chicago Tribune* confirmed that the president had "slowly and steadily risen in the respect, confidence, and admiration of the people," which is why, at least in the North, the mood on the day of the inaugural was somewhat celebratory. For the first time, Inauguration Day was thought of as a national holiday, which explains why it was expected that Lincoln would use the occasion to, as Ronald White, Jr., put it, "speak a strong word about both his own personal success and the impending victory of union forces."

What the assembled got instead was vintage Lincoln, another major address that was as short as it was sober, as literate and ultimately memorable as any of his others. The president's second inaugural address consisted of 703 words, and so, though he spoke slowly, it took him no more than six or seven minutes to deliver the speech in its entirety.

African Americans were pleased with what they heard, and they responded in kind. However, the rest of the audience was underwhelmed. There were nearly no cheers and only intermittent applause, and when the speech was over, it was clear that the response was, at best, mixed. As none other than Stephen A. Douglas (Lincoln's opponent in the great debates) put it, "there was a leaden stillness about the crowd," probably because Lincoln's address was "more like a sermon than a state paper." For years to come, Lincoln's second inaugural address would be overshadowed by the words he spoke at Gettysburg; in fact, only relatively recently has the second speech been judged to be as great as, if not greater than, the fabled one that preceded it.

The biblical references in the second inaugural address are, again, obvious and numerous. The president asked God to end the war between North and South, and to rejoin what tragically had been sundered. Though the nature of his private faith remains uncertain, President Lincoln used the occasion to enlist the Almighty in delivering the South as well as the North from death and destruction, in establishing between the two warring sides a measure of conciliation, and in achieving "a just, and a lasting peace, among ourselves, and with all nations."

In the last year of his life, President Abraham Lincoln received Sojourner Truth at the White House. Though there is debate about exactly what transpired—the president was remembered by the white woman who accompanied Truth as being less than welcoming—Truth herself seems to have been satisfied. In an account published in the *Standard* shortly after the visit took place, and based on "Sojourner's own account of her visit," she reports: "I am proud to say that I never was treated by any one with more kindness and cordiality than was shown to me by that great and good man, Abraham Lincoln. . . . He took my little book, and with the same hand that signed the death-warrant of slavery, he wrote as follows:

'For Aunty Sojourner Truth,
Oct. 29, 1864 A. Lincoln.'"

~

V. I. LENIN
1870–1924

Lenin, who was among the greatest of all revolutionary leaders and the founder of the Soviet state, was born Vladimir Ilyich Ulyanov. He was the son of an educator and the younger brother of Alexander, who was executed for trying to assassinate the tsar, Alexander III.

Lenin followed in his brother's footsteps. As a young man, he joined a secret political society, moved from the smaller city in which he worked as a lawyer to a much larger one, St. Petersburg, and became an ardent Marxist. At age 25, he was arrested for his political activities and thrown into prison. Fourteen months later, he was released—and sent into exile.

Russia, meanwhile, was becoming increasingly unstable. By the second half of the nineteenth century, some 23 million serfs had been freed and left to fend for themselves, the monarchy was showing signs of stress, and revolutionaries were starting to gather, if only in the distance. Russia was far behind Western Europe in its level of development, so most of the early revolutionists were agrarian socialists. But as the century came to a close, the debate was increasingly dominated by Marxists, who during the next decade or two quarreled mainly among themselves about how exactly the Russian Revolution should start, what exactly it should look like, and who exactly should lead the charge. Among the many questions was the role of the proletariat, which, though an important figure in Marxist theory, had so far played no part in (Russian) Marxist practice.

Into this hotbed of political activity stepped Lenin, who was as disciplined as he was determined. As the debate among Russian Marxists evolved from the purely theoretical to the possibly practical, he became not only a prominent proselytizer, but also a leading theoretician and energetic organizer.

The door was wide open, for by the start of the twentieth century, Russia's communists had gone nearly nowhere. A first congress had taken place two years earlier (in 1898), which had resulted in the choice of a name: the Russian Social-Democratic Labor Party. But, as Robert Service has pointed out, in every other aspect the party was an empty shell:

"No party program; no central party apparatus; no list of affiliated local party groups; no principles of party structure and organization."

For Lenin, this was a vacuum waiting to be filled. From his various perches in Germany, Switzerland, and elsewhere in Europe, he gathered about him like-minded Russian émigrés, edited an important Marxist newspaper, *Iskra (Spark)*, and penned pieces on how to make a revolution. His work culminated in the 1902 pamphlet titled *What Is to Be Done?*, which still stands as the best of its kind. *What Is to Be Done?* is a manual. It is a manual on how exactly to overthrow the old in favor of the new—which is to say, it picks up where *The Communist Manifesto* left off.

WHAT IS TO BE DONE?
1902

I could go on analysing the Rules, but I think that what has been said will suffice. A small, compact core of the most reliable, experienced, and hardened workers, with responsible representatives in the principal districts and connected by all the rules of strict secrecy with the organisation of revolutionaries, can, with the widest support of the masses and without any formal organisation, perform *all* the functions of a trade union organisation, in a manner, moreover, desirable to Social-Democracy. Only in this way can we secure the *consolidation* and development of a *Social-Democratic* trade union movement, despite all the gendarmes.

It may be objected that an organisation which is so [loose] that it is not even definitely formed, and which has not even an enrolled and registered membership, cannot be called an organisation at all. Perhaps so. Not the name is important. What is important is that this "organisation without members" shall do everything that is required, and from the very outset ensure a solid connection between our future trade unions and socialism. Only an incorrigible utopian would have a *broad* organisation of workers, with elections, reports, universal suffrage, etc., under the autocracy.

The moral to be drawn from this is simple. If we begin with the solid foundation of a strong organisation of revolutionaries, we can ensure the stability of the movement as a whole and carry out the aims both of Social-Democracy and of trade unions proper. If, however, we begin with a broad workers' organisation, which is supposedly most "accessible" to the masses (but which is actually most accessible to the gendarmes and makes revolutionaries most accessible to the police), we shall achieve neither the one aim nor the other; we shall not eliminate our rule-of-thumb methods, and, because we remain scattered and our forces are constantly broken up by the police, we shall only make trade unions of the Zubatov and Ozerov type the more accessible to the masses.

What, properly speaking, should be the functions of the organisation of revolutionaries? We shall deal with this question in detail. First, however, let us examine a very typical argument advanced by our terrorist, who (sad fate!) in this matter also is a next-door neighbour to the Economist. *Svoboda* [*Freedom*], a journal published for workers, contains in its first issue an article entitled "Organisation", the author of which tries to defend his friends, the Economist workers of Ivanovo-Voznesensk. He writes:

> "It is bad when the masses are mute and unenlightened, when the movement does not come from the rank and file. For instance, the students of a university town leave for their homes during the summer and other holidays, and immediately the workers' movement comes to a standstill. Can a workers' movement which has to be pushed on from outside be a real force? No, indeed. . . . It has not yet learned to walk, it is still in leading-strings. So it is in all matters. The students go off, and everything comes to a standstill. The most capable are seized; the cream is skimmed and the milk turns sour. If the 'committee' is arrested, everything comes to a standstill until a new one can be formed. And one never knows what sort of committee will be set up next—it may be nothing like the former. The first said one thing, the second may say the very opposite. Continuity between yesterday and tomorrow is broken, the experience of the past does not serve as a guide for the future. And all because no roots have been struck in depth, in the masses; the work is carried on not by a hundred fools, but by a dozen wise men. A dozen wise men can be wiped out at a snap, but when the organisation embraces masses, everything proceeds from them, and nobody, however he tries, can wreck the cause."

The facts are described correctly. The picture of our amateurism is well drawn. But the conclusions are worthy of *Rabochaya Mysl* [the name of a journal translated as *Worker's Thought*], both as regards their stupidity and their lack of political tact. They represent the height of stupidity, because the author confuses the philosophical and social-historical question of the "depth" of the "roots" of the movement with the technical and organisational question of the best method in combating the gendarmes. They represent the height of political tactlessness, because, instead of appealing from bad leaders to good leaders, the author appeals from the leaders in general to the "masses." This is as much an attempt to drag us back organisationally as the idea of substituting excitative terrorism for political agitation drags us back politically. Indeed, I am experiencing a veritable *embarras de richesses*, and hardly know where to begin to disentangle the jumble offered up by *Svoboda*. For clarity, let me begin by citing an example. Take the Germans. It will not be denied, I hope, that theirs is a mass organisation, that in Germany everything proceeds from the masses, that the working-class movement there has learned to walk. Yet observe how these millions value their "dozen" tried political leaders, how firmly they cling to them. Members of the hostile parties in parliament have often taunted the socialists by exclaiming: "Fine democrats you are indeed! Yours is a working-class movement only in name; in actual fact the same clique of leaders is always in evidence, the same [August] Bebel and the same [Karl] Liebknecht, year in and year out, and that goes on for decades. Your supposedly elected workers' deputies are more permanent than the officials appointed by the Emperor!" But the Germans only smile with contempt at these demagogic attempts to set the "masses" against the "leaders", to arouse bad and ambitious instincts in the former, and to rob the movement of its solidity and stability by undermining the confidence of the masses in their "dozen wise men". Political thinking is sufficiently developed among the Germans, and they have accumulated sufficient political experience to understand that without the "dozen" tried and talented leaders (and talented men are not born by the hundreds), professionally trained, schooled by long experience, and working in perfect harmony, no class in modern society can wage a determined struggle. The Germans too have had demagogues in their ranks who have flattered the "hundred fools", exalted them above the "dozen wise men", extolled the "horny hand" of the masses, and . . . have spurred them on to reckless "revolutionary" action and sown distrust towards the firm and steadfast leaders. It was only by stubbornly and relentlessly combating all demagogic elements within the socialist movement that German socialism has managed to grow and become as strong as it is. Our wiseacres, however, at a time when Russian Social-Democracy is passing through a crisis entirely due to the lack of sufficiently trained, developed, and experienced leaders to guide the spontaneously awakening masses, cry out, with the profundity of fools: "It is a bad business when the movement does not proceed from the rank and file."

"A committee of students is of no use; it is not stable." Quite true. But the conclusion to be drawn from this is that we must have a committee of professional *revolutionaries*, and it is immaterial whether a student or a worker is capable of becoming a professional revolutionary. The conclusion you draw, however, is that the working-class movement must not be pushed on from outside! In your political innocence you fail to notice that you are playing into the hands of our Economists and fostering our amateurism. Wherein, may I ask, did our students "push on" our workers? *In the sense* that the student brought to the worker the fragments of political knowledge he himself possesses, the crumbs of socialist ideas he has managed to acquire (for the principal intellectual diet of the present-day student, legal Marxism, could furnish only the rudiments, only scraps of knowledge). There has never been too much of *such* "pushing on from outside"; on the contrary, there has so far been all too little of it in our movement, for we have been stewing too assiduously in our own juice; we have bowed far too slavishly to the elementary "economic struggle of the workers against the employers and the government". We professional revolutionaries must and will make it our business to engage in *this kind* of "pushing on" a hundred times more forcibly than we have done hitherto. But the very fact that you select so hideous a phrase as "pushing on from outside"—a phrase which cannot but rouse in the workers (at least in the workers who are as unenlightened as you yourselves) a sense of distrust towards all who bring them political knowledge and revolutionary experience from outside, which cannot but rouse in them an instinctive desire to resist *all* such people—proves you to be demagogues, and *demagogues* are the worst enemies of the working class.

And, please—don't hasten howling about my "uncomradely methods" of debating. I have not the least desire to doubt the purity of your intentions. As I have said, one may become a demagogue out of sheer political innocence. But I have shown that you have descended to demagogy, and I will never tire of repeating that demagogues are the worst enemies of the working class. The worst enemies, because they arouse base instincts in the masses, because the unenlightened worker is unable to recognise his enemies in men who represent themselves, and sometimes sincerely so, as his friends. The worst enemies, because in the period of disunity and vacillation, when our movement is just beginning to take shape, nothing is easier than to employ demagogic methods to mislead the masses, who can realise their error only later by bitter experience. That is why the slogan of the day for the Russian Social-Democrat must be—resolute struggle against *Svoboda* and *Rabocheye Dyelo* [the name of a journal translated as *The Worker's Cause*], both of which have sunk to the level of demagogy. We shall deal with this further in greater detail.

"A dozen wise men can be more easily wiped out than a hundred fools." This wonderful truth (for which the hundred fools will always applaud you) appears obvious only because in the very midst of the argument you have skipped from one question to another. You began by talking and continued to talk of the unearthing of a "committee", of the unearthing of an "organisation", and now you skip to the question of unearthing the movement's "roots" in their "depths". The fact is, of course, that our movement cannot be unearthed, for the very reason that it has countless thousands of roots deep down among the masses; but that is not the point at issue. As far as "deep roots" are concerned, we cannot be "unearthed" even now, despite all our amateurism, and yet we all complain, and cannot but complain, that the "*organisations*" are being unearthed and as a result it is impossible to maintain continuity in the movement. But since you raise the question of *organisations* being unearthed and persist in your opinion, I assert that it is far more difficult to unearth a dozen wise men than a hundred fools. This position I will defend, no matter how much you instigate the masses against me for my "anti-democratic" views, etc. As I have stated repeatedly, by "wise men", in connection with organisation, I mean *professional revolutionaries*, irrespective of whether they have developed from among students or working men. I assert: (1)

that no revolutionary movement can endure without a stable organisation of leaders maintaining continuity; (2) that the broader the popular mass drawn spontaneously into the struggle, which forms the basis of the movement and participates in it, the more urgent the need for such an organisation, and the more solid this organisation must be (for it is much easier for all sorts of demagogues to side-track the more backward sections of the masses); (3) that such an organisation must consist chiefly of people professionally engaged in revolutionary activity; (4) that in an autocratic state, the more we *confine* the membership of such an organisation to people who are professionally engaged in revolutionary activity and who have been professionally trained in the art of combating the political police, the more difficult will it be to unearth the organisation; and (5) the *greater* will be the number of people from the working class and from the other social classes who will be able to join the movement and perform active work in it.

Comment

In theory, revolutions start when those at the bottom make a move against those at the top. Revolutions are, after all, by definition, the overthrow of those *with* power, authority, and influence by those *without*. But in practice, revolutions are usually instigated by a small cadre of leaders who, though they lack formal political authority, do wield personal power and influence. *What Is to Be Done?* drives this point home—repeatedly. Lenin anticipates that the action will be driven by a small band of hard-core revolutionaries, leaders who are trained and primed to overthrow the existing order.

His pamphlet on how to make a revolution was the product of years of plotting and planning how to get from point A to point B, how to get from an entrenched, enduring Russian monarchy to a world ruled by workers. It was also Lenin's claim to fame: his ideas on what revolutionists should be like and what strategies and tactics they should employ. *What Is to Be Done?* was, in short, a personal statement as well as a political one, intended to set its author apart from, and over and above, all the other Russian Marxists who inevitably were vying for the position of leader of the pack.

Lenin's assertive tone, which veered often into sarcasm, disputatious-ness, even combativeness, confirms the contention. No one has judged *What Is to Be Done?* to be especially well written. But the prose is fluent and forceful, and it is nothing if not forward leaning. In no uncertain terms, Lenin tells Russian Marxists what to do and when and how to do it.

The importance of Marxist theory to Marxist practice is central to Lenin's argument. "There can be no revolutionary movement without a revolutionary theory," he declared. This served not only to bolster his own leading role as preeminent theoretician, but also to make clear to his small, select reading audience that belonging to the revolutionary vanguard requires intellectual rigor as well as political daring. Lenin's emphasis on theory served other purposes as well. For one of his tasks in *What Is to Be Done?* was to differentiate between traditional, orthodox Marxism, as orig-inally outlined by Marx and Engels in *The Communist Manifesto*, and Russian Marxism. In addition, Lenin thought it important to distinguish between leftist politics in countries such as Germany and leftist politics in Russia, where the circumstances were different altogether.

It was also up to Lenin to determine the role of the worker, who was supposedly central to communism but who remained of marginal im-portance in Russia well into the twentieth century. Lenin was taken with a phrase that was first used by Marx, "the dictatorship of the proletariat." But he also believed, and for good reason, that Russian workers, who in any case were still few in number in what remained largely an agrarian society, lacked revolutionary consciousness. They would never seize power of their own accord—certainly not in Lenin's lifetime. Enlisting them in his cause would therefore require indoctrination and, particu-larly, leadership by an elite core of revolutionaries who, while alienated from the ruling classes, nevertheless had the intellect and drive to create change.

Arguably, *What Is to Be Done?* is, more than anything else, testimony to the importance of revolutionary leadership. Lenin argues over and over again for the need to cultivate and educate "professional revolutionaries." This band of brothers (comrades)—small in number and hardened to the core—would instruct on theory and lead in practice. Such centralization, such command and control and clandestine activity were, Lenin argued, the critical components of the Russian revolutionary movement.

The publication of *What Is to Be Done?* did not go unnoticed. Lenin was already prominent in certain circles. Moreover, his strident (if paradoxical) advocacy of strong top-down leadership attracted attention, in particular from his competitors, other leading Marxists who were more democratically disposed. But not until Lenin spearheaded the Russian Revolution (1917) did his pamphlet receive widespread scrutiny. Nor did the attention wane on his death, several years later. For his successor as leader of the Bolshevik Party and the still fledgling Soviet Union was Stalin, who, not surprisingly, praised *What Is to Be Done?* as a model of revolutionary rectitude.

Lenin's legacy is legend. He influenced an array of other leaders, with Mao Zedong being perhaps the most important example, imbuing them at great remove with ideas similar to his own, and with the same revolutionary zeal. Here is Mao in 1942, on the occasion of the opening of the Party School of the Central Committee of the Communist Party of China: "There must be a revolutionary party because the world contains enemies who oppress the people and the people want to throw off enemy oppression. . . . We are Communists, we want to lead the people in overthrowing the enemy and so we must keep our ranks in good order [and] we must march in step."

But the precise nature of Lenin's legacy, including his literary legacy, remains a subject of some dispute. Specifically, there has long been a debate between those who think that his theory and practice were in keeping with the liberal West, and those who, in contrast, think that his theory and practice were more in keeping with the controlling and sometimes despotic East. Here it will suffice to say that while *What Is to Be Done?* does insist that a small cadre of revolutionary leaders be in the vanguard, in complete control, it does not seem to sanction the brutal, tyrannical, totalitarian leadership that Stalin came to connote.

When Lenin died at age 53 in 1924, Russians were bereft: 900,000 people came to view his casket during the four days and nights after his passing, and on the sixth day his body was embalmed and exhibited in the Lenin Mausoleum. It rests there to this day.

~

MAHATMA GANDHI
1869–1948

Idiosyncratic in his personal life, peripatetic in his political life, and fertile in his creative life, Mohandas Gandhi, known as Mahatma Gandhi, had as great and enduring an impact on how leaders lead *and* on how followers follow as anyone else in the twentieth century. (The honorific "Mahatma," bestowed on Gandhi during the 1920s, means "Great Soul.") While he is associated most closely with India's ultimately successful nationalist movement against British colonial rule, it was, in fact, South Africa where Gandhi developed his political skills, honed his political ideas, and adopted the abstemious personal habits for which he was known to the end of his life.

By his own testimony, Gandhi was changed forever by an experience shortly after his arrival in South Africa in 1893: he was thrown off a train on account of the color of his skin. The trauma transformed him. During the two decades that followed, he remained in South Africa, becoming newly politically involved; adopting a life of extreme simplicity, self-sufficiency, and self-purification; and experiencing a deep religious awakening and personal transformation.

It was also in South Africa that he conceived of *satyagraha*, both as principle and as political practice. Gandhi translated *satyagraha* as "truth-force." But in time it came to mean something more concrete: nonviolent resistance to achieve conflict resolution through conciliation, as opposed to conquest.

In addition to being a thinker, activist, and source of moral suasion, Gandhi was an author, and a prolific one at that (his collected works take up 90 volumes), who wrote ostensibly to teach. Judith Brown noted, "Even when he was writing in his autobiography about his own personal transformations and struggles, his aim was to teach his readers. He wrote, 'It is not my purpose to attempt a real autobiography. I simply want to tell the story of my numerous experiments with truth,' because he hoped that this would 'not be without benefit to the reader.'"

The three selections included here—"Conditions for Becoming a *Satyagrahi*" (1909), "*Satyagraha*—Not 'Passive Resistance'" (c. 1917), and "The

Essential Law of *Satyagraha*" (1919)—all pertain to *satyagraha*, and they are ordered chronologically. To read them is to conclude that Gandhi wrote not only to "benefit" his readers, but also for his own ends, to further refine his political philosophy. He thought to improve his practice by improving his theory—which in good part explains why what began as a spiritual exercise evolved over the years into leadership as powerful and persuasive as any other.

CONDITIONS FOR BECOMING A *SATYAGRAHI*
1909

The *satyagraha* campaign in the Transvaal has lasted so long and has been so conducted that we have been able to see—learn—a great many things from it. Many have had personal experience of it. This much at least has been realized by everyone—that, in a struggle of this kind, there is no room for defeat. If, on any occasion, we fail, we shall discover that the failure was due to some deficiency in the *satyagrahi* and did not argue the inefficacy of *satyagraha* as such. The point needs to be carefully grasped. No such rule can be applied to physical fighting. When two armies engage in such fighting, the defeat of either will not necessarily be the result of the inferior fighting quality of the troops. The combatants may have a high morale, and yet, insufficiency in other matters may lead to defeat. For instance, one side may have better arms than the other, or may be favourably placed in the battlefield, or may command superior technical skill. There are many such extraneous factors which account for the victory or defeat of the parties to a physical fight. But such factors offer no difficulties to those fighting the battle of *satyagraha*. Their deficiency alone can come in their way. Moreover, in the usual kind of fighting, all the members of the losing side should be deemed to have been defeated, and in fact they do think that way. In *satyagraha*, the victory of a single member may be taken to mean the victory of all, but the defeat of the side as a whole does not spell defeat for the person who has not himself yielded. For instance, in

Mahatma Gandhi: *Essential Writings*, edited with an Introduction by Judith Brown (OWC, 2008): pp. 309–311, 315–316 and 324–330. Reproduced by permission of Oxford University Press.

the Transvaal fight, even if a majority of Indians were to submit to the obnoxious Act, he who remains unyielding will be victorious indeed, for the fact remains that he has not yielded.

That being so, it is necessary to inquire as to who can offer so admirable a battle—one which admits of no defeat—which can have only one result. The inquiry will enable us to understand some of the results of the Transvaal campaign, and to decide how and by whom a campaign of this kind can be fought elsewhere or on some other occasion.

If we inquire into the meaning of *satyagraha*, we find that the first condition is that anyone who wants to engage in this kind of fighting should show a special regard for truth—should have the strength that flows from truthfulness. That is to say, such a man should depend on truth alone. . . . It is absurd to suggest that *satyagraha* is being resorted to only by those who are deficient in physical strength or who, finding physical strength unavailing, can think of no alternative but *satyagraha*. Those who hold such a view, it may be said, do not know what this fight means. *Satyagraha* is more potent than physical strength, which is as worthless as straw when compared with the former. Essentially, physical strength means that a man of such strength fights on the battlefield with little regard for his body, that is to say, he knows no fear. A *satyagrahi*, on his part, gives no thought whatever to his body. Fear cannot touch him at all. That is why he does not arm himself with any material weapons, but continues resistance till the end without fear of death. This means that the *satyagrahi* should have more courage than the man who relies on physical strength. Thus, the first thing necessary for a *satyagrahi* is pursuit of truth, faith in truth.

He must be indifferent to wealth. Wealth and truth have always been in conflict with each other, and will remain so till the end of time. We have found from many examples of Indians in the Transvaal that he who clings to wealth cannot be loyal to truth. This does not mean that a *satyagrahi* can have no wealth. He can, but he cannot make his wealth his God. Money is welcome if one can have it consistently with one's pursuit of truth; otherwise one must not hesitate even for a moment to sacrifice it as if it were no more than dirt on one's hand. No one who has not cultivated such an attitude can practise *satyagraha*. Moreover, in a land where one is obliged to offer *satyagraha* against the rulers, it is not likely that the *satyagrahi* will be able to own wealth. The power of a king may be unavailing against an individual. But it can touch his property, or play on his fear of losing it. The king bends the subjects to his will by threatening them with loss of property or physical harm. Therefore, under the rule of a tyrannical king, for the most part, it is only those who make themselves accomplices in his tyranny who can retain or amass wealth. Since a *satyagrahi* cannot allow himself to be an accomplice in tyranny, he must, in such circumstances, be content to think himself rich in his poverty. If he owns any wealth, he must hold it in some other country.

A *satyagrahi* is obliged to break away from family attachments. This is very difficult to do. But the practice of *satyagraha*, if *satyagraha* is to be worthy of its name, is like walking on the edge of a sword. In the long run, even the breaking away from family attachments will prove beneficial to the family. For, the members of the family will come to feel the call for *satyagraha*, and those who have felt such a call will have no other desire left. When faced with suffering of any kind—loss of wealth or imprisonment—one need not be concerned about the future of one's family. He who has given us teeth will provide us with food to eat. If He provides for such dangerous creatures as the snake, the scorpion, the tiger and the wolf, He is not likely to be unmindful of mankind. It is not a pound of millets or a handful of corn that we hanker after, but the delights of the palate; not just the clothes that we need to enable us to bear cold, but garments of brocaded silk. If we abandon all this restless craving, there will hardly be any need for anxiety as to the means for maintaining one's family.

In this connection, it is worth while to bear in mind that many of these things have to be sacrificed even if physical force is resorted to. One is obliged to suffer hunger and thirst, to bear heat and cold, to sacrifice family bonds, to put up with pecuniary loss. The Boers went through all this when they resorted to physical force. The one great difference between the physical resistance that they offered and our resistance based on truth is that the game they played was in the nature of a gamble. Physical strength, moreover, has made them proud. Their partial success made them forgetful of their former condition. Having fought with deadly arms against a deadly enemy, they are bearing hard upon us as deadly tyrants. When a *satyagrahi* wins in battle, his success cannot but be beneficial to him and to others. A *satyagrahi*, if he is to remain loyal to truth, can never be a tyrant.

This inquiry, then, leads at last to the conclusion that he alone can offer *satyagraha* who has true faith in religion. "The name of Rama on the lips, and a dagger under the arm"—that is no faith. It is no religion to speak in its name and to do exactly the opposite of what it teaches. But anyone who has true religion and faith in him can offer *satyagraha*. In other words, he who leaves everything to God can never know defeat in this world. Such men are not defeated in fact simply because people say that they are defeated. So also one cannot claim success simply because people believe that one has succeeded. There can be no arguing about this; if you know the difference, you know it, else you don't.

This is the real nature of *satyagraha*. The Transvaal Indians have partially understood it. Having done so, they have been faithful to it in practice, again partially. Even so, we have been able to taste its priceless sweetness. He who has sacrificed everything for *satyagraha* has gained everything, for he lives in contentment. Contentment is happiness. Who has ever known any happiness other than this? Every other kind of happiness is but a mirage. The nearer we approach it, the farther it recedes.

We hope that every Indian will think of the matter this way and make himself a *satyagrahi*. If we learn the use of the weapon of *satyagraha*, we can employ it to overcome all hardships originating from injustice. It is not here in South Africa alone that the weapon is useful; it will be more so in our home-country. Only we must know its true nature, which is easy to do, and yet difficult. Men of great physical strength are rare. Rarer still must be those who derive their strength from truth.

SATYAGRAHA—NOT 'PASSIVE RESISTANCE'
C. 1917

The force denoted by the term "passive resistance" and translated into Hindi as *nishkriya pratirodha* is not very accurately described either by the original English phrase or by its Hindi rendering. Its correct description is "*satyagraha*." *Satyagraha* was born in South Africa in 1908. There was no word in any Indian language denoting the power which our countrymen in South Africa invoked for the redress of their grievances. There was an

English equivalent, namely, "passive resistance," and we carried on with it. However, the need for a word to describe this unique power came to be increasingly felt, and it was decided to award a prize to anyone who could think of an appropriate term. A Gujarati-speaking gentleman submitted the word "*satyagraha*," and it was adjudged the best.

"Passive resistance" conveyed the idea of the Suffragette Movement in England. Burning of houses by these women was called "passive resistance" and so also their fasting in prison. All such acts might very well be "passive resistance" but they were not "*satyagraha*." It is said of "passive resistance" that it is the weapon of the weak, but the power which is the subject of this article can be used only by the strong. This power is not "passive" resistance; indeed it calls for intense activity. The movement in South Africa was not passive but active. The Indians of South Africa believed that Truth was their object, that Truth ever triumphs, and with this definiteness of purpose they persistently held on to Truth. They put up with all the suffering that this persistence implied. With the conviction that Truth is not to be renounced even unto death, they shed the fear of death. In the cause of Truth, the prison was a palace to them and its doors the gateway to freedom.

Satyagraha is not physical force. A *satyagrahi* does not inflict pain on the adversary; he does not seek his destruction. A *satyagrahi* never resorts to firearms. In the use of *satyagraha*, there is no ill-will whatever.

Satyagraha is pure soul-force. Truth is the very substance of the soul. That is why this force is called *satyagraha*. The soul is informed with knowledge. In it burns the flame of love. If someone gives us pain through ignorance, we shall win him through love. . . . Nonviolence is a dormant state. In the waking state, it is love. Ruled by love, the world goes on. In English there is a saying, "Might is Right." Then there is the doctrine of the survival of the fittest. Both these ideas are contradictory to the above principle. Neither is wholly true. If ill-will were the chief motive-force, the world would have been destroyed long ago; and neither would I have had the opportunity to write this article nor would the hopes of the readers be fulfilled. We are alive solely because of love. We are all ourselves the proof of this. Deluded by modern Western civilization, we have forgotten our ancient civilization and worship the might of arms.

We forget the principle of non-violence, which is the essence of all religions. The doctrine of arms stands for irreligion. It is due to the sway of that doctrine that a sanguinary war is raging in Europe.

THE ESSENTIAL LAW
OF *SATYAGRAHA*
1919

I feel that the time has now arrived to examine the meaning of *satyagraha*. The word was newly coined some years ago, but the principle which it denotes is as ancient as time. This is the literal meaning of *satyagraha*— insistence on truth, and force derivable from such insistence. In the present movement, we are making use of *satyagraha* as a force: that is to say, in order to cure the evil in the shape of the Rowlatt legislation, we have been making use of the force generated by *satyagraha*, that is, insistence on truth. One of the axioms of religion is, there is no religion other than truth. Another is, religion is love. And as there can be only one religion, it follows that truth is love and love is truth. We shall find too, on further reflection, that conduct based on truth is impossible without love. Truth-force then is love-force. We cannot remedy evil by harbouring ill-will against the evil-doer. This is not difficult of comprehension. It is easy enough to understand. In thousands of our acts, the propelling power is truth or love. The relations between father and son, husband and wife, indeed our family relations are largely guided by truth or love. And we therefore consciously or unconsciously apply *satyagraha* in regulating these relations.

If we were to cast a retrospective glance over our past life, we would find that out of a thousand of our acts affecting our families, in nine hundred and ninety-nine we were dominated by truth, that in our deeds, it is not right to say we generally resort to untruth or ill-will. It is only where a conflict of interests arises, then arise the progeny of untruth, viz., anger, ill-will, etc., and then we see nothing but poison in our midst. A little hard thinking will show us that the standard that we apply to the regulation of domestic relations is the standard that should be applied to regulate the relations between rulers and the ruled, and between man and man. Those men and women who do not recognize the domestic tie are considered to be very like brutes or barbarous, even though they in form have the human body. They have never known the law of *satyagraha*. Those who recognize the domestic tie and its obligations have to a certain extent gone beyond that brute stage. But if challenged, they would say "what do we care though the whole universe may perish so long as we guard the family interest?" The measure of their *satyagraha*, therefore, is less than that of a drop in the ocean.

When men and women have gone a stage further, they would extend the law of love, i.e., *satyagraha*, from the family to the village. A still further stage away from the brute life is reached when the law of *satyagraha* is applied to provincial life, and the people inhabiting a province regulate their relations by love rather than by hatred. And when as in Hindustan we recognize the law of *satyagraha* as a binding force even between province and province and the millions of Hindustan treat one another as brothers and sisters, we have advanced a stage further still from the brute nature.

In modern times, in no part of the earth have the people gone beyond the nation stage in the application of *satyagraha*. In reality, however, there need be no reason for the clashing of interest between nation and nation, thus arresting the operation of the great law. If we were not in the habit generally of giving no thought to our daily conduct, if we did not accept local custom and habit as matters of course, as we accept the current coin, we would immediately perceive that to the extent that we bear ill-will towards other nations or show disregard at all for life, to that extent we disregard the law of *satyagraha* or love, and to that extent we are still not free from the brute nature. But there is no religion apart from that which enables us entirely to rid ourselves of the brute nature. All religious sects and divisions, all churches and temples, are useful only so long as they serve as a means towards enabling us to recognize the universality of *satyagraha*. In India we have been trained from ages past in this teaching and hence it is that we are taught to consider the whole universe as one family. I do wish to submit as a matter of experience that it is not only possible to live the full national life, by rendering obedience to the law of *satyagraha*, but that the fullness of national life is impossible without *satyagraha*, i.e., without a life of true religion. That nation which wars against another has to an extent disregarded the great law of life. I shall never abandon the faith I have that India is capable of delivering this truth to the whole world, and I wish that all Indians, men and women, whether they are Hindus or

Mahomedans, Parsis, Christians or Jews, will share with me this un-quenchable faith.

Comment

In 1848 the American writer Henry David Thoreau published an essay titled "Civil Disobedience." He famously began, "That government is best which governs least," but then he took a tone more extreme. He claimed that individual power should supersede institutional power. "Must the citizen even for a moment, or in the least degree, resign his conscience to the legislator?" Thoreau asked. "I think that we should be men first, and subjects afterward." In his life as in his work, Thoreau was clear. He at least should, and would, resist any government to which he had a major objection.

Gandhi was without question an intellectual original, a product of his particular time and circumstance. But he himself acknowledged being influenced not only by masters of Indian philosophy, but also by Western thinkers such as Tolstoy, Ruskin, and especially Thoreau. Though it is not known for certain when Thoreau came to Gandhi's attention—whether it was before or after his experiment with nonviolent resistance—Gandhi acknowledged Thoreau as a "great writer, philosopher, poet, and withal a most practical man." Whatever its precise provenance, Gandhi took *satyagraha*—nonviolent resistance, or civil disobedience, or militant nonviolence (the various translations, while similar, do not mean precisely the same thing)—to a different place altogether. If only because of the numbers involved and the size of his canvas, what Gandhi did was new.

There were two turning points in Gandhi's life as a leader. The first was when he tested *satyagraha* as a tactic; the second was when he applied it to enduring effect. The test took place in South Africa in 1906, where in response to South Africa's new anti-Indian measures (the so-called Black Act), Gandhi spoke to a crowd of 3,000 Indians and launched his first major campaign. Years later, he acknowledged that the moment was critical: "A mission . . . came to me in 1906, namely, to spread truth and non-violence among mankind."

When Gandhi returned to India in 1915, after two decades in South Africa, he applied *satyagraha* to the Indian experience, to India's colonial subjugation. In the beginning, right after his return, he led a life of the mind, but soon he became politically involved and invested. He protested, fasted (his famous fasts were both a spiritual exercise and a political tactic), got himself arrested, and was finally imprisoned. Gandhi was preparing the soil, preparing himself and his followers for what would become the legendary salt *satyagraha* (1930), the mass protest against the British for their imposition of a salt tax. This was the second major turning point—after the salt *satyagraha*, the British raj was never the same. Although colonial rule formally came to an end only in 1947, Gandhi's decision to launch a nationwide, nonviolent protest against the colonialists was crucial. It provided clear evidence that Indians in countless and constantly growing numbers were willing to risk arrest in the interest of independence.

Underpinning his work in both South Africa and India was Gandhi's outrage at inequity and injustice. In South Africa, it was the ill-treatment of the Indian minority at the hands of local whites; in India, it was colonialism, the subjugation of the Indian majority to the British minority. As one expert pointed out, Eknath Easwaran, the India into which Gandhi was born had been under foreign domination for centuries. But, "remarkably, for the last hundred years of this period, it lay in the grip not of an ordinary conqueror, but of a mercantile operation, the British East India Company [which was] licensed by the Crown to pursue its fortunes by virtually any means it liked, including raising its own armies and waging war."

In part because of his legacy to leaders of the American civil rights movement, Gandhi has become, perhaps, more closely associated with marches and protests than with collaboration and cooperation. But the ideas and ideals that constitute *satyagraha* make it clear that Gandhi's work is much more about conciliation than about conflict, much more about surmounting strife than about inciting it. *Satyagraha* evolved over time, becoming more complex and sophisticated, and ending finally as a rather complex amalgam that included truth, nonviolence (*ahimsa*), self-suffering, and even coercion. For while *satyagraha* is more about resolving conflict while maintaining peace than it is about anything else, it does potentially bring harm, for example, to shop owners whose businesses are being boycotted. Hence the variation on nonviolent resistance: militant nonviolence.

Among the most famous of Gandhi's disciples was Martin Luther King, Jr., who remembered his discovery of *satyagraha* as a "profoundly significant" experience. In fact, King was so impressed by Gandhi that in 1959 he traveled to India on a pilgrimage of sorts, to visit with his family. However, Gandhi's impact was not only on *leaders* of the American civil rights movement, but on *followers* as well. As King's close colleague, John Lewis, recalled it, in the 1960s he and other civil rights leaders trained students to resist nonviolently. Their instructions included some do's and some don'ts. Students were, for example, told that they must not, under any circumstances, "strike back nor curse if abused." On the other hand, they were supposed to be "friendly and courteous at all times." And they were to "remember the teachings of Jesus Christ, Mahatma Gandhi and Martin Luther King. Love and nonviolence is the way."

Gandhi is so rich and complex a figure that he is a prism through which we see ourselves. As David Shulman has pointed out, one can always read Gandhi, "in his iconic loincloth and spectacles, as a kind of utopian romantic." Or, in contrast, one can see him as a "wily politician and hard-headed manipulator of traditional Hindu images of power." Or following Wendy Doniger, a leading authority on Hinduism, we can understand Gandhi as, again in Shulman's words, "embodying a modernist, spruced-up version of the medieval Tantric ritualist and magician, mesmerized by the possibility of enhancing his own inner strength, and thus his effect on the world, by classic methods such as frequent fasting and abstinence, severe chastity tests . . . and Yogic meditation."

Gandhi was, not incidentally, an intellectual leader as well as a spritual and political one. He had a profound impact on, among others, prominent Western philosophers such as John Rawls and Ronald Dworkin (both American), and he inspired psychographer Erik Erikson to write one of his most important books, *Gandhi's Truth*. Erikson, a well-known disciple of Freud's, described *satyagraha* as involving "a double conversion: the hateful person, by containing his egoistic hate and by learning to love the opponent as human, will confront the opponent with an enveloping technique that will force, or rather permit, him to regain his latent capacity to trust and to love." A dream, perhaps, a dream that can become real only some of the time. Still, *satyagraha* will find expression so long as life is unfair and politics is practiced as remediation.

∽

WINSTON CHURCHILL
1874–1965

Before he became prime minister of England in 1940, Winston Churchill had been in public service for decades, as a military man and as a civilian. He had always been highly positioned, although he was not always so highly thought of. In fact, shortly before he came into his own, with his staunch opposition to Hitler transforming him into one of the great hero leaders of the Western world, his fortunes, as Geoffrey Wheatcroft observed, "had sunk as low as he would ever know." Churchill had long been known for a career that resembled nothing so much as Snakes and Ladders, that "nursery board game where a shake of the dice leads to either a brisk ascent or a downward slither." Though he entered Parliament as young as 25 and was named home secretary at 34, by the time the First World War was over, he had been humiliated, blamed for a major defeat, and forced to slowly and steadily climb his way back to being respectable, only to be defeated again, this time politically, over, of all things, his opposition to Indian independence, particularly Mahatma Gandhi. The mid-1930s were not, then, a propitious time for Churchill as he warned, over and over again and nearly alone, of the danger named Hitler.

The speeches that follow were delivered during this period. They were, in other words, delivered during a period in which Churchill did *not* play an obvious leadership role. In fact, until the late 1930s, he had few followers, not even members of his own party, the Conservatives, who, as John Lukacs wrote, "distrusted Churchill, that maverick, for many reasons." And so it was that his repeated warnings about Hitler the dictator and about Germany rearming and preparing for war while Britain was not were discounted to the point of being ignored.

Though Churchill in wartime is the role for which he is most widely admired, during the prewar period he was, arguably, still more remarkable. About Hitler, Churchill was clairvoyant. His proclivity to predict, in tandem with his brilliant literary style (he wrote all his own speeches) and golden tongue (though he was not in a conventional sense a strong speaker), allowed him to address to great oratorical effect, if not to great political influence, that most famous of English-speaking assemblies, the House of Commons.

The two speeches included here put both Churchill's political prescience and his brilliance as wordsmith on dazzling display. As the legendary American broadcaster Edward R. Murrow put it, when there was little else to fight with, Churchill "mobilized the English language and sent it into battle." The first speech was delivered in the House of Commons on November 12, 1936. Aptly titled "Adamant for Drift," it was described by editor Robert Rhodes James as being among Churchill's "most brilliant and devastating." The second, "The Threat to Czechoslovakia," was delivered on March 24, 1938, and is referred to by James as "historic and tragically prophetic."

———— ADAMANT FOR DRIFT ————
1936

What would have been said, I wonder, if I could two years ago have forecast to the House the actual course of events? Suppose we had then been told that Germany would spend for two years £800,000,000 a year upon warlike preparations; that her industries would be organised for war, as the industries of no country have ever been; that by breaking all Treaty engagements she would create a gigantic air force and an army based on universal compulsory service, which by the present time, in 1936, amounts to upwards of thirty-nine divisions of highly equipped troops, including mechanised divisions of almost unmeasured strength and that behind all this there lay millions of armed and trained men, for whom the formations and equipment are rapidly being prepared to form another eighty divisions in addition to those already perfected. Suppose we had then known that by now two years of compulsory military service would be the rule, with a preliminary year of training in labour camps; that the Rhineland would be occupied by powerful forces and fortified with great skill, and that Germany would be building with our approval, signified by treaty, a large submarine fleet.

Suppose we had also been able to foresee the degeneration of the foreign situation, our quarrel with Italy, the Italo-German association, the Belgian declaration about neutrality—which, if the worst interpretation of it proves to be true, so greatly affects the security of this country—and the disarray of the smaller Powers of Central Europe. Suppose all that had been forecast—why, no one would have believed in the truth of such a nightmare tale. Yet just two years have gone by and we see it all in broad daylight. Where shall we be this time two years? I hesitate now to predict. . . .

No doubt as a whole His Majesty's Government were very slow in accepting the unwelcome fact of German rearmament. They still clung to the policy of one-sided disarmament. It was one of those experiments, we are told, which had to be, to use a vulgarism, "tried out", just as the experiments of non-military sanctions against Italy had to be tried out. Both experiments have now been tried out, and Ministers are accustomed to plume themselves upon the very clear results of those experiments. They are held to prove conclusively that the policies subjected to the experiments were all wrong, utterly foolish, and should never be used again, and the very same men who were foremost in urging those experiments are now foremost in proclaiming and denouncing the fallacies upon which they were based. They have bought their knowledge, they have bought it dear, they have bought it at our expense, but at any rate let us be duly thankful that they now at last possess it. . . .

Look at the Tank Corps. The tank was a British invention. This idea, which has revolutionised the conditions of modern war, was a British idea forced on the War Office by outsiders. Let me say they would have just as hard work today to force a new idea on it. I speak from what I know. During the War we had almost a monopoly, let alone the leadership, in tank warfare, and for several years afterwards we held the foremost place. To England all eyes were turned. All that has gone now. Nothing has been done in "the years that the locust hath eaten" to equip the Tank Corps with new machines. The medium tank which they possess, which in its day was the best in the world, is now looking obsolete. Not only in numbers for there we have never tried to compete with other countries—but in quality these British weapons are now surpassed by those of Germany, Russia, Italy and the United States. All the shell plants and gun plants in the Army, apart from the very small peace-time services, are in an elementary stage. A very long period must intervene before any effectual flow of munitions can be expected, even for the small forces of which we dispose. Still we are told there is no necessity for a Ministry of Supply, no emergency which should induce us to impinge on the normal course of trade. If we go on like this, and I do not see what power can prevent us from going on like this, some day there may be a terrible reckoning, and those who take the responsibility so entirely upon themselves are either of a hardy disposition or they are incapable of foreseeing the possibilities which may arise.

Now I come to the greatest matter of all, the air. We received on Tuesday night, from the First Lord of the Admiralty, the assurance that there is no foundation whatever for the statement that we are "vastly behind hand" with our Air Force programme. It is clear from his words that we are behind hand. The only question is, what meaning does the First Lord attach to the word "vastly"? He also used the expression, about the progress of air expansion, that it was "not unsatisfactory". One does not know what his standard is. His standards change from time to time. . . .

Owing to past neglect, in the face of the plainest warnings, we have now entered upon a period of danger greater than has befallen Britain since the U-boat campaign was crushed; perhaps, indeed, it is a more grievous period than that, because at that time at least we were possessed of the means of securing ourselves and of defeating that campaign. Now we have no such assurance. The era of procrastination, of half-measures, of soothing and baffling expedients, of delays, is coming to its close. In its place we are entering a period of consequences. We have entered a period in which for more than a year, or a year and a half, the considerable preparations which are now on foot in Britain will not, as the Minister clearly showed, yield results which can be effective in actual fighting strength; while during this very period Germany may well reach the culminating point of her gigantic military preparations, and be forced by financial and economic stringency to contemplate a sharp decline, or perhaps some other exit from her difficulties. It is this lamentable conjunction of events which seems to present the danger of Europe in its most disquieting form. We cannot avoid this period; we are in it now. Surely, if we can abridge it by even a few months, if we can shorten this period when the German Army will begin to be so much larger than the French Army, and before the British Air Force has come to play its complementary part, we may be the architects who build the peace of the world on sure foundations.

Two things, I confess, have staggered me, after a long Parliamentary experience, in these Debates. The first has been the dangers that have so swiftly come upon us in a few years, and have been transforming our position and the whole outlook of the world. Secondly, I have been staggered by the failure of the House of Commons to react effectively against those dangers. That, I am bound to say, I never expected. I never would have believed that we should have been allowed to go on getting into this plight, month by month and year by year, and that even the Government's own confessions of error would have produced no concentration of Parliamentary opinion and force capable of lifting our efforts to the level of emergency. I say that unless the House resolves to find out the truth for itself it will have committed an act of abdication of duty without parallel in its long history.

THE THREAT TO CZECHOSLOVAKIA
1938

The Prime Minister, in what I think it is not presumptuous for me to describe as a very fine speech, set before us the object which is in all our minds—namely, how to prevent war. A country like ours, possessed of immense territory and wealth, whose defences have been neglected, cannot avoid war by dilating upon its horrors, or even by a continuous display of pacific qualities, or by ignoring the fate of the victims of aggression elsewhere. War will be avoided, in present circumstances, only by the accumulation of deterrents against the aggressor. If our defences are weak, we must seek allies; and, of course, if we seek allies, alliances involve commitments. But the increase of commitments may be justified if it is followed by a still greater increase of deterrents against aggression. . . .

I must say that I myself have not felt during this crisis that there is an immediate danger of a major land war breaking out over Czechoslovakia. I know it is very rash to make such a statement, but . . . are they not getting all they want without it? Are they not achieving a long succession of most important objectives without firing a single shot? Is there any limit to the economic and political pressure which, without actually using military force, Germany will be able to bring to bear upon this unhappy State? She can be convulsed politically, she can be strangled economically, she is practically surrounded by superior forces, and, unless something is done to mitigate the pressure of circumstances, she will be forced to make continuous surrenders, far beyond the bounds of what any impartial tribunal would consider just or right, until finally her sovereignty, her independence, her integrity, have been destroyed. Why, then, should the rulers of Germany strike a military blow? Why should they incur the risk of a major war? . . .

But the story of this year is not ended at Czechoslovakia. It is not ended this month. The might behind the German Dictator increases daily. His appetite may grow with eating. The forces of law and freedom have for a long time known nothing but rebuffs, failures and humiliations. Their influence would be immensely increased by any signs of concerted action and initiative and combination. . . .

Do not let anyone suppose that this is a mere question of hardening one's heart and keeping a stiff upper lip, and standing by to see Czechoslovakia pole-axed or tortured as Austria has been. Something more than that particular kind of fortitude will be needed from us. It is not only Czechoslovakia that will suffer. Look at the States of the Danube Basin. First and foremost there is Yugoslavia. That is a most powerful and virile State, three-quarters of whose martial people are undoubtedly in the fullest sympathy with the democracy of France and Great Britain, and are animated by an ardent hatred of Nazi or Fascist rule. They have a rooted desire to maintain themselves in their independence. Is nothing being done to ascertain what Yugoslavia would do, assuming that Great Britain and France were prepared to interest themselves in the problems of the Danube Basin? Yugoslavia might well be gained, and I am told that the effect of that on Bulgaria would probably be to draw her into the same orbit. Then there is Rumania, so directly menaced by the potential German movement to the East. These three countries if left alone, and convinced that there is no will power operating against the Dictators, will fall one by one into the Nazi grip and system. What then will be the position of Greece and Turkey?

I ask these questions, hoping that they may be carefully considered. Is it not possible that decided action by France and Great Britain would rally the whole of these five States as well as Czechoslovakia, all of whom have powerful armies, who together aggregate 75,000,000 of people, who have several millions of fighting men already trained, who have immense resources, who all wish to dwell in peace within their habitations, who individually may be broken by defeat and despoiled, but who, united, constitute an immense resisting power? Can nothing be done to keep them secure and free and to unite them in their own interests, in French and British interests and, above all, in the interests of peace? Are we really going to let the whole of these tremendous possibilities fall away without a concerted effort of any kind? If we do, let us not suppose for a moment that we shall ourselves have escaped our perils. On the contrary, we shall have multiplied our perils, for a very obvious reason:

At present Germany might contemplate a short war, but, once she has laid hands on these countries and extended her power to the Black Sea, the Nazi régime will be able to feed itself indefinitely, however long war may last, and thus we may weaken the deterrent force against war of that blockade to which the hon. Member who has just spoken referred. We should have removed another of the deterrents that stand between us and war. The Nazification of the whole of the Danube States is a danger of the first capital magnitude to the British Empire. Is all to go for nothing? Is it all to be whistled down the wind? If so, we shall repent in blood and tears our improvidence and our lack of foresight and energy.

I have set the issue before the House in terms which do not shirk realities. It has been said by almost all speakers that, if we do not stand up to the Dictators now, we shall only prepare the day when we shall have to stand up to them under far more adverse conditions. Two years ago it was safe, three years ago it was easy, and four years ago a mere dispatch might have rectified the position. But where shall we be a year hence? Where shall we be in 1940?

Comment

When Churchill sent a message, as he did in both of these speeches, he was hard to hear for several reasons, not least among them that he was not, certainly not till toward the end of the decade, the best messenger. Again, this time in the words of Churchill biographer Paul Addison, "Opinions of Churchill were perhaps more uniformly dismissive in the 1930s than at any previous time. Stripped of the dignity of office, ageing and restless and full of apocalyptic warnings about the end of Empire, he looked less like a statesman than a ham actor whose melodramatics were out of date."

But this was not only about personality, it was about politics, about strong differences of opinion among generally well-intentioned men who saw the world differently. So far as European politics was concerned, among the British political elite, there were at least two major divides: the first between the majority who considered the greatest threat to be communism (the Soviet Union), and the minority who believed that it was fascism (Germany and, to a lesser extent, Italy); the second between the majority who were persuaded that Hitler could and should be appeased, and the minority who thought, as Churchill perfectly put it, that Hitler's "appetite may grow with eating." In both these debates, which became the more fraught as the decade came to a close, Churchill, who was on the outs anyway, was among the minority.

Meanwhile, as Churchill repeatedly reminded anyone who was willing to listen, Hitler was forging ahead, standing astride the European continent in a manner and with a swagger that just a few years earlier were almost inconceivable. Each of his major moves was more outrageous than the last. In 1936, the Nazis remilitarized the Rhineland, an outright violation of the Treaty of Versailles. In early 1938, they simply annexed the whole of Austria. And in late 1938, they occupied the Sudetenland, a part of Czechoslovakia that was all too easily ceded to Hitler by Chamberlain and French Prime Minister Edouard Daladier. But even before this series of miserable events, Churchill's sense of foreboding was strong. Asked in 1936, "Mr. Churchill, is there going to be a war?" he went so far as to reply, "Certainly, a very terrible war in which London will be bombed and Buckingham Palace will be razed to the ground, and the lions and tigers will escape from the zoo and roam through streets of London attacking people." Of course, nothing the Nazis did during this period, and nothing Churchill said during this period, stopped Chamberlain from going so far as to fly to Germany three times in a single year (1938) in a desperate if doomed attempt at appeasement.

From Churchill's perspective, the problem lay not only with Hitler, but also with Britain's refusal to recognize the threat that he posed and to respond to it properly. This explains why Churchill addressed, over and over again, what was, as he saw it, his country's appalling lack of military readiness. (In the face of the increasingly sophisticated and powerful German Luftwaffe, Churchill fixed on the Royal Air Force. As early as 1934, he warned that air mastery by one power over another would lead to the "absolute subjugation" of the weaker by the stronger.) And this explains why as early as 1935 he recommended a "grand alliance," a coalition of European nations anchored by an ironclad and publicly declared Anglo-French military agreement. One would have thought that the idea would be as persuasive as it was familiar—peace in Europe secured by a balance of power.

In March 1939, German troops marched into Prague, and Czechoslovakia collapsed. Hitler, having annexed what remained of Czechoslovakia to the German Reich, was triumphant. Chamberlain, having suffered a humiliating and ultimately mortal blow to his policy of appeasement, was discredited. And Churchill, having been proved right all along—Hitler's appetite did, it turned out, "grow with eating"—was vindicated. In September 1939, Chamberlain offered Churchill the same post he had held some 25 years earlier, First Lord of the Admiralty, Chief of the British Navy. And by May 1940, in the wake of the military disaster that followed Hitler's invasion of Norway, Chamberlain was out and Churchill was in. Churchill remained British prime minister for the duration, until Germany was brought to its knees and the war in Europe was over.

How could Churchill see what others could not? How could he foretell the future while England—and Europe—famously "slept"? History could, of course, have turned out differently. Hitler's string of successes during the 1930s and early 1940s could have been otherwise, the result, perhaps, of mistakes made within Germany or greater resistance without. But as it happened, events did unfold as Churchill had predicted they would—which is why his capacity as visionary poses so intriguing, even important a question.

Lukacs suggests that one explanation for Churchill's foresightedness was his "exceptional knowledge and comprehension of Europe, of the history and character of many of its nations." Churchill was especially clever on the matter of the German national character. On the one hand, he had long admired Germans, in particular their military prowess. But on the other hand, he had long been put off by Prussian military rigidity, a trait that he had come to know years earlier, while visiting Germany as still rather a young man.

Another observer, Carlo D'Este, whose book about Churchill is tellingly titled *Warlord*, explains his astuteness in matters of war and peace by pointing to his early years, the years during which Winston was first socialized and then trained, to his apparent pleasure, in the military arts. He describes Churchill as a young boy drilling his toy soldiers in imaginary battles, Churchill as an older boy engaged in youthful military adventures, and Churchill during adolescence, when his "interest in soldiering [took] a more practical turn." Finally there was Churchill as a young man at Sandhurst, then known as the Royal Military College, which trained gentlemen cadets to be junior army officers.

These explanations notwithstanding, there *are* times when a man (or woman) seems, for whatever elusive reasons, to meet the moment perfectly. During the 1930s, the years in which Churchill delivered his most prescient speeches, the man was ready, but the moment was not ripe. However, when Chamberlain was disgraced and Hitler prevailed, things changed. Then the moment *was* ripe—and Churchill was ready, willing, and altogether able. "We shall not flag or fail," Churchill proclaimed in June 1940, evoking Shakespeare. "We shall go on to the end, we shall fight in France, we shall fight on the seas and oceans, we shall fight with growing confidence and growing strength in the air, we shall defend our island, whatever the cost may be, we shall fight on the beaches, we shall fight on the landing grounds. We shall fight in the fields and in the streets, we shall fight in the hills; we shall never surrender."

∾

MARTIN LUTHER KING, JR.
1929–1968

"I have a dream that one day this nation will rise up and live out the true meaning of its creed. . . . I have a dream that my four little children will one day live in a nation where they will not be judged by the color of their skin but by the content of their character. I have a dream today!" So flow perhaps the most memorable lines of the most memorable speech ever delivered by *any* American. (In 2008, more than 95 percent of American teenagers were able to identify the speaker.) Known now as the "I Have a Dream Speech," it was delivered by Martin Luther King, Jr., on the steps of the Lincoln Memorial on August 28, 1963.

Several months before, however, King had delivered another document, this one in writing, that was arguably more important. His "Letter from Birmingham Jail," dated April 16, 1963, was literally written in the cell where King was confined after his arrest for leading a nonviolent protest in Birmingham, Alabama. King thought Birmingham "the most segregated city in America." He further believed, "If we can crack Birmingham, we can crack the South." Moreover, the local commissioner for public safety, "Bull" Connor, described by *Time* as an "arch-segregationist," was King's perfect foil. Bound and determined to defend the status quo against King and his kind, and willing to this end to use strong-arm tactics including fire hoses and attack dogs, Connor came to symbolize the last bastion of brutality in defense of segregation.

King was one among more than 50 people arrested in Birmingham on Good Friday, April 12. Satisfied for a while to stay in his cell, the better to draw attention to his case and his cause, King used his time behind bars to write an extended essay. He framed it in the form of a letter addressed to eight white clergy, in which he justified loudly and clearly and once and for all the legitimacy of his crusade. This "prison epistle," as Jonathan Bass has called it, invokes the Bible, philosophers and theologians, and other famous figures past and present. But more than anything else it invokes, and did evoke, the fury that fueled the leadership of Martin Luther King, Jr.

--------- LETTER FROM BIRMINGHAM JAIL ---------

1963

My Dear Fellow Clergymen:

While confined here in the Birmingham city jail, I came across your recent statement calling my present activities "unwise and untimely." Seldom do I pause to answer criticism of my work and ideas. If I sought to answer all the criticisms that cross my desk, my secretaries would have little time for anything other than such correspondence in the course of the day, and I would have no time for constructive work. But since I feel that you are men of genuine good will and that your criticisms are sincerely set forth, I want to try to answer your statements in what I hope will be patient and reasonable terms.

I think I should indicate why I am here in Birmingham, since you have been influenced by the view which argues against "outsiders coming in." I have the honor of serving as president of the Southern Christian Leadership Conference, an organization operating in every southern state, with headquarters in Atlanta, Georgia. We have some eighty-five affiliated organizations across the South, and one of them is the Alabama Christian Movement for Human Rights. Frequently we share staff, educational and financial resources with our affiliates. Several months ago the affiliate here in Birmingham asked us to be on call to engage in a nonviolent direct-action program if such were deemed necessary. We readily consented, and when the hour came we lived up to our promise. So I, along with several members of my staff, am here because I was invited here. I am here because I have organizational ties here.

But more basically, I am in Birmingham because injustice is here. Just as the prophets of the eighth century B.C. left their villages and carried their "thus saith the Lord" far beyond the boundaries of their home towns, and just as the Apostle Paul left his village of Tarsus and carried the gospel of Jesus Christ to the far corners of the Greco-Roman world, so am I compelled to carry the gospel of freedom beyond my own home town. Like Paul, I must constantly respond to the Macedonian call for aid.

Moreover, I am cognizant of the interrelatedness of all communities and states. I cannot sit idly by in Atlanta and not be concerned about what happens in Birmingham. Injustice anywhere is a threat to justice everywhere. We are caught in an inescapable network of mutuality, tied in a single garment of destiny. Whatever affects one directly, affects all indirectly. Never again can we afford to live with the narrow, provincial "outside agitator" idea. Anyone who lives inside the United States can never be considered an outsider anywhere within its bounds.

You deplore the demonstrations taking place in Birmingham. But your statement, I am sorry to say, fails to express a similar concern for the conditions that brought about the demonstrations. I am sure that none of you would want to rest content with the superficial kind of social analysis that deals merely with effects and does not grapple with underlying causes. It is unfortunate that demonstrations are taking place in Birmingham, but it is even more unfortunate that the city's white power structure left the Negro community with no alternative.

In any nonviolent campaign there are four basic steps: collection of the facts to determine whether injustices exist; negotiation; self-purification; and direct action. We have gone through all of these steps in Birmingham. There can be no gainsaying the fact that racial injustice engulfs this community. Birmingham is probably the most thoroughly segregated city in the United States. Its ugly record of brutality is widely known. Negroes have experienced grossly unjust treatment in the courts. There have been more unsolved bombings of Negro homes and churches in Birmingham than in any other city in the nation. These are the hard, brutal facts of the case. On the basis of these conditions, Negro leaders sought to negotiate with the city fathers. But the latter consistently refused to engage in good-faith negotiation. . . .

You may well ask: "Why direct action? Why sit-ins, marches and so forth? Isn't negotiation a better path?" You are quite right in calling for negotiation. Indeed, this is the very purpose of direct action. Nonviolent direct action seeks to create such a crisis and foster such a tension that a community which has constantly refused to negotiate is forced to confront the issue. It seeks to so dramatize the issue that it can no longer be ignored. My citing the creation of tension as part of the work of the nonviolent-resister may sound rather shocking. But I must confess that I am not afraid of the word "tension." I have earnestly opposed violent tension, but there is a type of constructive, nonviolent tension which is necessary for growth. Just as Socrates felt that it was necessary to create a tension in the mind so that individuals could rise from the bondage of myths and half-truths to the unfettered realm of creative analysis and objective appraisal, we must see the need for nonviolent gadflies to create the kind of tension in society that will help men rise from the dark depths of prejudice and racism to the majestic heights of understanding and brotherhood. . . .

We know through painful experience that freedom is never voluntarily given by the oppressor; it must be demanded by the oppressed. Frankly, I have yet to engage in a direct-action campaign that was "well timed" in the view of those who have not suffered unduly from the disease of segregation. For years now I have heard the word "Wait!" It rings in the ear of every Negro with piercing familiarity. This "Wait" has almost always meant "Never." We must come to see, with one of our distinguished jurists, that "justice too long delayed is justice denied."

We have waited for more than 340 years for our constitutional and God-given rights. The nations of Asia and Africa are moving with jetlike speed toward gaining political independence, but we still creep at horse-and-buggy pace toward gaining a cup of coffee at a lunch counter. Perhaps it is easy for those who have never felt the stinging darts of segregation to say, "Wait." But when you have seen vicious mobs lynch your mothers and fathers at will and drown your sisters and brothers at whim; when you have seen hate-filled policemen curse, kick and even kill your black brothers and sisters; when you see the vast majority of your twenty million Negro brothers smothering in an airtight cage of poverty in the midst of an affluent society; when you suddenly find your tongue twisted and your speech stammering as you seek to explain to your six-year-old daughter why she can't go to the public amusement park that has just been advertised on television, and see tears welling up in her eyes when she is told that Funtown is closed to colored children, and see ominous clouds of inferiority beginning to form in her little mental sky, and see her beginning to distort her personality by developing an unconscious bitterness toward white people; when you have to concoct an answer for a five-year-old son who is asking: "Daddy, why do white people treat colored people so mean?"; when you take a cross-country drive and find it necessary to sleep night after night in the uncomfortable corners of your automobile because no motel will accept you; when you are humiliated day in and day out by nagging signs reading "white" and "colored"; when your first name becomes "nigger," your middle name becomes "boy" (however old you are) and your last name becomes "John," and your wife and mother are never given the respected title "Mrs."; when you are harried by day and haunted by night by the fact that you are a Negro, living constantly at tiptoe stance, never quite knowing what to expect next, and are plagued with inner fears and outer resentments; when you go forever fighting a degenerating sense of "nobodiness" then you will understand why we find it difficult to wait. There comes a time when the cup of endurance runs over, and men are no longer willing to be plunged into the abyss of despair. I hope, sirs, you can understand our legitimate and unavoidable impatience.

You express a great deal of anxiety over our willingness to break laws. This is certainly a legitimate concern. Since we so diligently urge people to obey the Supreme Court's decision of 1954 outlawing segregation in the public schools, at first glance it may seem rather paradoxical for us consciously to break laws. One may want to ask: "How can you advocate breaking some laws and obeying others?" The answer lies in the fact that there are two types of laws: just and unjust. I would be the first to advocate obeying just laws. One has not only a legal but a moral responsibility to obey just laws. Conversely, one has a moral responsibility to disobey unjust laws. I would agree with St. Augustine that "an unjust law is no law at all." . . .

Of course, there is nothing new about this kind of civil disobedience. It was evidenced sublimely in the refusal of Shadrach, Meshach and Abednego to obey the laws of Nebuchadnezzar, on the ground that a higher moral law was at stake. It was practiced superbly by the early Christians, who were willing to face hungry lions and the excruciating pain of chopping blocks rather than submit to certain unjust laws of the Roman Empire. To a degree, academic freedom is a reality today because Socrates practiced civil disobedience. In our own nation, the Boston Tea Party represented a massive act of civil disobedience.

We should never forget that everything Adolf Hitler did in Germany was "legal" and everything the Hungarian freedom fighters did in Hungary was "illegal." It was "illegal" to aid and comfort a Jew in Hitler's Germany. Even so, I am sure that, had I lived in Germany at the time, I would have aided and comforted my Jewish brothers. If today I lived in a Communist country where certain principles dear to the Christian faith are suppressed, I would openly advocate disobeying that country's antireligious laws.

I must make two honest confessions to you, my Christian and Jewish brothers. First, I must confess that over the past few years I have been gravely disappointed with the white moderate. I have almost reached the regrettable conclusion that the Negro's great stumbling block in his stride toward freedom is not the White Citizen's Counciler or the Ku Klux Klanner, but the white moderate, who is more devoted to "order" than to justice; who prefers a negative peace which is the absence of tension to a positive peace which is the presence of justice; who constantly says: "I agree with you in the goal you seek, but I cannot agree with your methods of direct action"; who paternalistically believes he can set the timetable for another man's freedom; who lives by a mythical concept of time and who constantly advises the Negro to wait for a "more convenient season." Shallow understanding from people of good will is more frustrating than absolute misunderstanding from people of ill will. Lukewarm acceptance is much more bewildering than outright rejection.

I had hoped that the white moderate would understand that law and order exist for the purpose of establishing justice and that when they fail in this purpose they become the dangerously structured dams that block the flow of social progress. I had hoped that the white moderate would understand that the present tension in the South is a necessary phase of the transition from an obnoxious negative peace, in which the Negro passively accepted his unjust plight, to a substantive and positive peace, in which all men will respect the dignity and worth of human personality. Actually, we who engage in nonviolent direct action are not the creators of tension. We merely bring to the surface the hidden tension that is already alive. We bring it out in the open, where it can be seen and dealt with. Like a boil that can never be cured so long as it is covered up but must be opened with its ugliness to the natural medicines of air and light, injustice must be exposed, with all the tension its exposure creates, to the light of human conscience and the air of national opinion before it can be cured.

In your statement you assert that our actions, even though peaceful, must be condemned because they precipitate violence. But is this a logical assertion? Isn't this like condemning a robbed man because his possession of money precipitated the evil act of robbery? Isn't this like condemning Socrates because his unswerving commitment to truth and his philosophical inquiries precipitated the act by the misguided populace in which they made him drink hemlock? Isn't this like condemning Jesus because his unique God-consciousness and never-ceasing devotion to God's will precipitated the evil act of crucifixion? We must come to see that, as the federal courts have consistently affirmed, it is wrong to urge an individual to cease his efforts to gain his basic constitutional rights because the quest may precipitate violence. Society must protect the robbed and punish the robber.

I had also hoped that the white moderate would reject the myth concerning time in relation to the struggle for freedom. I have just received a letter from a white brother in Texas. He writes: "All Christians know that the colored people will receive equal rights eventually, but it is possible that you are in too great a religious hurry. It has taken Christianity almost two thousand years to accomplish what it has. The teachings of Christ take time to come to earth." Such an attitude stems from a tragic misconception of time, from the strangely rational notion that there is something in the very flow of time that will inevitably cure all ills. Actually, time itself is neutral; it can be used either destructively or constructively. More and more I feel that the people of ill will have used time much more effectively than have the people of good will. We will have to repent in this generation not merely for the hateful words and actions of the bad people but for the appalling silence of the good people. . . .

But though I was initially disappointed at being categorized as an extremist, as I continued to think about the matter I gradually gained a measure of satisfaction from the label. Was not Jesus an extremist for love: "Love your enemies, bless them that curse you, do good to them that hate you, and pray for them which despitefully use you, and persecute you." Was not Amos an extremist for justice: "Let justice roll down like waters and righteousness like an ever-flowing stream." Was not Paul an extremist for the Christian gospel: "I bear in my body the marks of the Lord Jesus." Was not Martin Luther an extremist: "Here I stand; I cannot do otherwise, so help me God." And John Bunyan: "I will stay in jail to the end of my days before I make a butchery of my conscience." And Abraham Lincoln: "This nation cannot survive half slave and half free." And Thomas Jefferson: "We hold these truths to be self-evident, that all men are created equal . . ." So the question is not whether we will be extremists, but what kind of extremists we will be. Will we be extremists for hate or for love? Will we be extremists for the preservation of injustice or for the extension of justice? In that dramatic scene on Calvary's hill three men were crucified. We must never forget that all three were crucified for the same crime—the crime of extremism. Two were extremists for immorality, and thus fell below their environment. The other, Jesus Christ, was an extremist for love, truth and goodness, and thereby rose above his environment. Perhaps the South, the nation and the world are in dire need of creative extremists. . . .

I hope the church as a whole will meet the challenge of this decisive hour. But even if the church does not come to the aid of justice, I have no despair about the future. I have no fear about the outcome of our struggle in Birmingham, even if our motives are at present misunderstood. We will reach the goal of freedom in Birmingham, and all over the nation, because the goal of America is freedom. Abused and scorned though we may be, our destiny is tied up with America's destiny. Before the pilgrims landed at Plymouth, we were here. Before the pen of Jefferson etched the majestic words of the Declaration of Independence across the pages of history, we were here. For more than two centuries our forebears labored in this country without wages; they made cotton king; they built the homes of their masters while suffering gross injustice and shameful humiliation—and yet out of a bottomless vitality they continued to thrive and develop. If the inexpressible cruelties of slavery could not stop us, the opposition we now face will surely fail. . . .

Never before have I written so long a letter. I'm afraid it is much too long to take your precious time. I can assure you that it would have been much shorter if I had been writing from a comfortable desk, but what else can one do when he is alone in a narrow jail cell, other than write long letters, think long thoughts and pray long prayers?

If I have said anything in this letter that overstates the truth and indicates an unreasonable impatience, I beg you to forgive me. If I have said anything that understates the truth and indicates my having a patience that allows me to settle for anything less than brotherhood, I beg God to forgive me.

I hope this letter finds you strong in the faith. I also hope that circumstances will soon make it possible for me to meet each of you, not as an integrationist or a civil rights leader but as a fellow clergyman and a Christian brother. Let us all hope that the dark clouds of racial prejudice will soon pass away and the deep fog of misunderstanding will be lifted from our fear-drenched communities, and in some not too distant tomorrow the radiant stars of love and brotherhood will shine over our great nation with all their scintillating beauty.

Yours for the cause of Peace and Brotherhood,
Martin Luther King, Jr.

Comment

The Birmingham campaign against segregation and for fair practices was among the most sensational of the civil rights movement. On the one hand, it involved a series of protests that, in keeping with the practice of Mahatma Gandhi, were deliberately nonviolent. But on the other hand, the Southern Christian Leadership Conference (SCLC), which spearheaded the campaign, was consciously confrontational. Beginning in 1962, staggered boycotts had caused downtown Birmingham businesses to decline precipitously, and by spring 1963 there were sit-ins and kneel-ins, marches and protests. Moreover, when the campaign flagged through fear of local authorities, outsiders were brought in, most prominently the by now renowned leader of the civil rights movement, the Reverend Martin Luther King, Jr.

King and his small band of activists had been forewarned: if they dared to engage in mass demonstrations without a permit, Birmingham officials would serve them with an injunction. So King knew full well that his mere presence in Birmingham would further roil the local waters, and that if he did anything that was in the least confrontational, he would probably provoke the police to arrest him immediately. This was why, atypically, he hesitated on that Good Friday morning, why he retreated to his bedroom to pray before emerging to tell his closest associates, "The path is clear to me. I've got to march. I've got so many people depending on me, I've got to march."

King's preeminent biographer, Taylor Branch, described what happened shortly thereafter, after King and some 50 other protesters left the Zion Hill Baptist Church to march for racial justice while singing the movement anthem, "We Shall Overcome." Branch wrote that without warning, "a detective seized King by the back of his belt, lifted him to his toes, and shoved him toward a paddy wagon. . . . After lock-up, they separated [King] from everyone else and refused his requests to make phone calls or talk with his lawyers. King disappeared into solitary confinement, 'the hole,' sealed off from his fellow prisoners and the outside world alike." Bull Connor, meanwhile, was telling reporters, "King was getting what he wanted."

King anticipated the reaction to this series of events—up to a point. The mainstream media were overwhelmingly censorious, in the North as well as the South. (*Time* referred to the Birmingham march as "a poorly timed protest"; the *Washington Post* called it of "doubtful utility.") And Birmingham locals were generally angry and unhappy. Even the city's blacks were divided, with some being in favor of the deliberate disturbances, and others opposed to what they considered an unnecessary exacerbation of local tensions. To King, though, the most disappointing response was from clergy, black and white, who not only did not support him, but left him to twist in the wind in his hour of need. As Gayraud Wilmore has pointed out, the problem was not confined to Birmingham. It was a larger issue: "But it must be conceded that the black church in its national institutional form—almost as much as the white church—was more of a sympathetic spectator than a responsible participant in the events that marked the progress of the movement."

A public statement by eight white clergy that condemned the local demonstrations as "unwise and untimely" was, by all accounts, the most painful of the numberless rebukes directed at King during his stay in Birmingham. These particular clergy were known for being relatively liberal and more sympathetic than most to King's cause, yet they invoked their religious authority against the strongest weapon in his tactical arsenal, civil disobedience. Thus King was being attacked not only by his enemies, but also by his purported friends. This explains his decision to address "Letter from Birmingham Jail" to these eight men in particular (although his intended audience was of course far larger). And this explains his particular anger at white moderates, at what he referred to as the "appalling silence of the good people." Bass has documented that King had been intending for a while to write a piece along the lines of the prison epistle. He was just waiting for "the perfect moment, the appropriate place, the right immediate audience in the eight Birmingham clergy, and an impassioned press corps."

The "Letter" was written under miserable conditions. The only light in King's cell came from a small opening high on the wall; even securing paper on which to write presented a problem. Nevertheless, King persevered and produced in the end a miraculous manifesto—leadership literature that will endure forever.

King's "Letter" makes several points. But more than anything else, it is a defense of the civil rights movement, in particular its timing, as in now and not later, and its use of nonviolent resistance or, in King's words, "nonviolent direct action" or, to be perhaps even more precise, militant nonviolence. King spoke to issues that included negotiation and extremism, moderation and violence, the role of the church, and the importance of the American dream. In the end, though, the document seems somehow more personal than it does political. King clearly was as angry as he was ardent, as earthbound as heaven-sent. He was clear-eyed about what had to happen, *always* has to happen if power is to be redistributed: "We know through painful experience that freedom is never voluntarily given by the oppressor; it must be demanded by the oppressed." Note the words *never* and *demand.* These are not the words of a patient man, but rather of one whose "cup of endurance" has run over, who is no longer willing to be told "wait" when it nearly always means "never," and who, while begging for forgiveness for any offense he might commit, was nevertheless hell-bent on creating change in the here and now, no matter the opposition, no matter the risk.

King chose to address these particular members of the white clergy because in challenging them, he was, ironically, challenging the very gradualism with which he is associated to this day. The "Letter" is evidence that, notwithstanding the Reverend Martin Luther King, Jr.'s reputation as a man of moderation, this was a leader who was dedicated to something that was more akin to revolution than to evolution.

~

NELSON MANDELA
1918–

He became, ultimately, an international icon. After decades of service and suffering, Nelson Mandela became a symbol of survival against all odds, of the oppressed taking on the oppressor, of conciliation in the wake of conflict, of personal peace in place of political vengeance.

Mandela was high-born: his father was a chief, and his mother came from a ruling family. He was also the first in his family to attend school, becoming a lawyer and engaging briefly in the practice of law. Even as a young man he was politically active, imbued with growing fervor for the proposition that apartheid—the strict legal racial segregation that since 1948 had been the policy in South Africa—had somehow to be brought to an end. In 1944 Mandela joined the African National Congress (the ANC, founded in support of black Africans), and beginning in 1948 he actively resisted the ruling National Party.

Mandela was arrested for the first time in 1956 and charged with treason. Though he was acquitted after a long trial, he was rearrested in 1962, and this time sentenced to five years in prison. The turning point came in 1964, when, as the result of the arrests of others on charges in which Mandela was implicated, he was a defendant in what came to be known as the Rivonia Trial. The trial lasted two years and ended with a sentence of life imprisonment for Nelson Mandela, among seven others. For the next 27 years of his life, he remained incarcerated.

On the occasion of his inauguration as president of the Democratic Republic of South Africa in May 1994, Nelson Mandela spoke in the conciliatory tones for which he has since become best known: "The time for healing of the wounds has come. The moment to bridge the chasms that divide us has come. The time to build is upon us." But his signal contribution to the leadership literature was not made then, nor was its content conciliatory. Rather, his literary legacy is a statement made years earlier, at the Rivonia Trial.

At the beginning of the case for the defense, Mandela was given permission to, in effect, deliver a speech. Selected by the other accused to provide a framework for the proceedings to follow, Mandela addressed various issues, some personal, most political, not least among them the ANC's connection to communism. Primarily, though, Mandela sought to explain, and to justify, the party's strategic shift from nonviolence to violence. He wanted to make clear why, in the wake of the Sharpeville shootings (in which scores of black African protesters had been shot by the police), ANC leaders had made a deliberate decision to change course: in 1961 they established a military wing, Umkhonto we Sizwe (Spear of the Nation), to which Mandela repeatedly refers.

Mandela's speech from the dock at the Rivonia Trial was identified by Anthony Sampson, his authorized biographer, as the "most effective of Mandela's whole political career." It established him as leader not only of the ANC but, by reaching a wide audience, of the worldwide opposition to apartheid. The statement is Mandela's manifesto—his impassioned explanation of why, when all else fails, the oppressed have no choice but to take on their oppressors, by any means necessary.

———— I AM PREPARED TO DIE ————
PRETORIA SUPREME COURT
1964

I am the First Accused.

I hold a Bachelor's Degree in Arts and practised as an attorney in Johannesburg for a number of years in partnership with Oliver Tambo. I am a convicted prisoner serving five years for leaving the country without a permit and for inciting people to go on strike at the end of May 1961.

At the outset, I want to say that the suggestion made by the State in its opening that the struggle in South Africa is under the influence of foreigners or communists is wholly incorrect. I have done whatever I did, both as an individual and as a leader of my people, because of my experience in South Africa and my own proudly felt African background, and not because of what any outsider might have said. . . .

Having said this, I must deal immediately and at some length with the question of violence. Some of the things so far told to the Court are true and some are untrue. I do not, however, deny that I planned sabotage. I did not plan it in a spirit of recklessness, nor because I have any love of violence. I planned it as a result of a calm and sober assessment of the political situation that had arisen after many years of tyranny, exploitation, and oppression of my people by the Whites.

I admit immediately that I was one of the persons who helped to form Umkhonto we Sizwe, and that I played a prominent role in its affairs until I was arrested in August 1962.

In the statement which I am about to make I shall correct certain false impressions which have been created by State witnesses. Amongst other things, I will demonstrate that certain of the acts referred to in the evidence were not and could not have been committed by Umkhonto. I will also deal with the relationship between the African National Congress and Umkhonto, and with the part which I personally have played in the affairs of both organizations. I shall deal also with the part played by the Communist

Party. In order to explain these matters properly, I will have to explain what Umkhonto set out to achieve; what methods it prescribed for the achievement of these objects, and why these methods were chosen. I will also have to explain how I became involved in the activities of these organizations.

I deny that Umkhonto was responsible for a number of acts which clearly fell outside the policy of the organisation, and which have been charged in the indictment against us. I do not know what justification there was for these acts, but to demonstrate that they could not have been authorized by Umkhonto, I want to refer briefly to the roots and policy of the organization.

I have already mentioned that I was one of the persons who helped to form Umkhonto. I, and the others who started the organization, did so for two reasons. Firstly, we believed that as a result of Government policy, violence by the African people had become inevitable, and that unless responsible leadership was given to canalize and control the feelings of our people, there would be outbreaks of terrorism which would produce an intensity of bitterness and hostility between the various races of this country which is not produced even by war. Secondly, we felt that without violence there would be no way open to the African people to succeed in their struggle against the principle of white supremacy. All lawful modes of expressing opposition to this principle had been closed by legislation, and we were placed in a position in which we had either to accept a permanent state of inferiority, or to defy the Government. We chose to defy the law. We first broke the law in a way which avoided any recourse to violence; when this form was legislated against, and then the Government resorted to a show of force to crush opposition to its policies, only then did we decide to answer violence with violence.

But the violence which we chose to adopt was not terrorism. We who formed Umkhonto were all members of the African National Congress, and had behind us the ANC tradition of non-violence and negotiation as a means of solving political disputes. We believe that South Africa belongs to all the people who live in it, and not to one group, be it black or white. We did not want an interracial war, and tried to avoid it to the last minute. If the Court is in doubt about this, it will be seen that the whole history of our organization bears out what I have said, and what I will subsequently say, when I describe the tactics which Umkhonto decided to adopt. I want, therefore, to say something about the African National Congress.

The African National Congress was formed in 1912 to defend the rights of the African people which had been seriously curtailed by the South Africa Act, and which were then being threatened by the Native Land Act. For thirty-seven years—that is until 1949—it adhered strictly to a constitutional struggle. It put forward demands and resolutions; it sent delegations to the Government in the belief that African grievances could be settled through peaceful discussion and that Africans could advance gradually to full political rights. But White Governments remained unmoved, and the rights of Africans became less instead of becoming greater. In the words of my leader, Chief Lutuli, who became President of the ANC in 1952, and who was later awarded the Nobel Peace Prize:

> "who will deny that thirty years of my life have been spent knocking in vain, patiently, moderately, and modestly at a closed and barred door? What have been the fruits of moderation? The past thirty years have seen the greatest number of laws restricting our rights and progress, until today we have reached a stage where we have almost no rights at all".....

In 1960 there was the shooting at Sharpeville, which resulted in the proclamation of a state of emergency and the declaration of the ANC as an unlawful organization. My colleagues and I, after careful consideration, decided that we would not obey this decree. The African people were not part of the Government and did not make the laws by which they were governed. We believed in the words of the Universal Declaration of Human Rights, that "the will of the people shall be the basis of authority of the Government", and for us to accept the banning was equivalent to accepting the silencing of the Africans for all time. The ANC refused to dissolve, but instead went underground. We believed it was our duty to preserve this organization which had been built up with almost fifty years of unremitting toil. . . .

. . . I must return to June 1961. What were we, the leaders of our people, to do? Were we to give in to the show of force and the implied threat against future action, or were we to fight it and, if so, how?

We had no doubt that we had to continue the fight. Anything else would have been abject surrender. Our problem was not whether to fight, but was how to continue the fight. We of the ANC had always stood for a non-racial democracy, and we shrank from any action which might drive the races further apart than they already were. But the hard facts were that fifty years of non-violence had brought the African people nothing but more and more repressive legislation, and fewer and fewer rights. It may not be easy for this Court to understand, but it is a fact that for a long time the people had been talking of violence—of the day when they would fight the White man and win back their country—and we, the leaders of the ANC, had nevertheless always prevailed upon them to avoid violence and to pursue peaceful methods. When some of us discussed this in May and June of 1961, it could not be denied that our policy to achieve a non-racial State by non-violence had achieved nothing, and that our followers were beginning to lose confidence in this policy and were developing disturbing ideas of terrorism. . . .

At the beginning of June 1961, after a long and anxious assessment of the South African situation, I, and some colleagues, came to the conclusion that as violence in this country was inevitable, it would be unrealistic and wrong for African leaders to continue preaching peace and non-violence at a time when the Government met our peaceful demands with force.

This conclusion was not easily arrived at. It was only when all else had failed, when all channels of peaceful protest had been barred to us, that the decision was made to embark on violent forms of political struggle, and to form Umkhonto we Sizwe. We did so not because we desired such a course, but solely because the Government had left us with no other choice. In the Manifesto of Umkhonto published on 16 December 1961, which is Exhibit AD, we said:

> "The time comes in the life of any nation when there remain only two choices—submit or fight. That time has now come to South Africa. We shall not submit and we have no choice but to hit back by all means in our power in defence of our people, our future, and our freedom".

. . . I can only say that I felt morally obliged to do what I did. . . .

As far as the Communist Party is concerned, and if I understand its policy correctly, it stands for the establishment of a State based on the principles of Marxism. Although it is prepared to work for the Freedom Charter, as a short term solution to the problems created by white supremacy, it regards the Freedom Charter as the beginning, and not the end, of its programme.

The ANC, unlike the Communist Party, admitted Africans only as members. Its chief goal was, and is, for the African people to win unity and full political rights. The Communist Party's main aim, on the other hand, was to remove the capitalists and to replace them with a working-class government. The Communist Party sought to emphasize class distinctions whilst the ANC seeks to harmonize them. This is a vital distinction.

It is true that there has often been close co-operation between the ANC and the Communist Party. But co-operation is merely proof of a common goal—in this case the removal of white supremacy—and is not proof of a complete community of interests.

The history of the world is full of similar examples. Perhaps the most striking illustration is to be found in the co-operation between Great Britain, the United States of America, and the Soviet Union in the fight against Hitler. Nobody but Hitler would have dared to suggest that such co-operation turned Churchill or Roosevelt into communists or communist tools, or that Britain and America were working to bring about a communist world.

Another instance of such co-operation is to be found precisely in Umkhonto. Shortly after Umkhonto was constituted, I was informed by some of its members that the Communist Party would support Umkhonto, and this then occurred. At a later stage the support was made openly. . . .

It is perhaps difficult for white South Africans, with an ingrained prejudice against communism, to understand why experienced African politicians so readily accept communists as their friends. But to us the reason is obvious. Theoretical differences amongst those fighting against oppression is a luxury we cannot afford at this stage. What is more, for many decades communists were the only political group in South Africa who were prepared to treat Africans as human beings and their equals; who were prepared to eat with us, talk with us, live with us, and work with us. They were the only political group which was prepared to work with the Africans for the attainment of political rights and a stake in society. Because of this, there are many Africans who, today, tend to equate freedom with communism. They are supported in this belief by a legislature which brands all exponents of democratic government and African freedom as communists . . . .

Our fight is against real, and not imaginary, hardships or, to use the language of the State Prosecutor, "so-called hardships". Basically, we fight against two features which are the hallmarks of African life in South Africa and which are entrenched by legislation which we seek to have repealed. These features are poverty and lack of human dignity, and we do not need communists or so-called "agitators" to teach us about these things.

South Africa is the richest country in Africa, and could be one of the richest countries in the world. But it is a land of extremes and remarkable contrasts. The whites enjoy what may well be the highest standard of living in the world, whilst Africans live in poverty and misery. Forty per cent of the Africans live in hopelessly overcrowded and, in some cases, drought-stricken Reserves, where soil erosion and the overworking of the soil makes it impossible for them to live properly off the land. Thirty per cent are labourers, labour tenants, and squatters on white farms and work and live under conditions similar to those of the serfs of the Middle Ages. The other 30 per cent live in towns where they have developed economic and social habits which bring them closer in many respects to white standards. Yet most Africans, even in this group, are impoverished by low incomes and high cost of living. . . .

The Government often answers its critics by saying that Africans in South Africa are economically better off than the inhabitants of the other countries in Africa. I do not know whether this statement is true and doubt whether any comparison can be made without having regard to the cost-of-living index in such countries. But even if it is true, as far as the African people are concerned it is irrelevant. Our complaint is not that we are poor by comparison with people in other countries, but that we are poor by comparison with the white people in our own country, and that we are prevented by legislation from altering this imbalance.

The lack of human dignity experienced by Africans is the direct result of the policy of white supremacy. White supremacy implies black inferiority.

Legislation designed to preserve white supremacy entrenches this notion. Menial tasks in South Africa are invariably performed by Africans. When anything has to be carried or cleaned the white man will look around for an African to do it for him, whether the African is employed by him or not. Because of this sort of attitude, whites tend to regard Africans as a separate breed. They do not look upon them as people with families of their own; they do not realize that they have emotions—that they fall in love like white people do; that they want to be with their wives and children like white people want to be with theirs; that they want to earn enough money to support their families properly, to feed and clothe them and send them to school. And what "house-boy" or "garden-boy" or labourer can ever hope to do this? . . .

Africans want to be paid a living wage. Africans want to perform work which they are capable of doing, and not work which the Government declares them to be capable of. Africans want to be allowed to live where they obtain work, and not be endorsed out of an area because they were not born there. Africans want to be allowed to own land in places where they work, and not to be obliged to live in rented houses which they can never call their own. Africans want to be part of the general population, and not confined to living in their own ghettoes. African men want to have their wives and children to live with them where they work, and not be forced into an unnatural existence in men's hostels. African women want to be with their menfolk and not be left permanently widowed in the Reserves. Africans want to be allowed out after eleven o'clock at night and not to be confined to their rooms like little children. Africans want to be allowed to travel in their own country and to seek work where they want to and not where the Labour Bureau tells them to. Africans want a just share in the whole of South Africa; they want security and a stake in society.

Above all, we want equal political rights, because without them our disabilities will be permanent. I know this sounds revolutionary to the whites in this country, because the majority of voters will be Africans. This makes the white man fear democracy.

But this fear cannot be allowed to stand in the way of the only solution which will guarantee racial harmony and freedom for all. It is not true that the enfranchisement of all will result in racial domination. Political division, based on colour, is entirely artificial and, when it disappears, so will the domination of one colour group by another. The ANC has spent half a century fighting against racialism. When it triumphs it will not change that policy.

This then is what the ANC is fighting. Their struggle is a truly national one. It is a struggle of the African people, inspired by their own suffering and their own experience. It is a struggle for the right to live.

During my lifetime I have dedicated myself to this struggle of the African people. I have fought against white domination, and I have fought against black domination. I have cherished the ideal of a democratic and free society in which all persons live together in harmony and with equal opportunities. It is an ideal which I hope to live for and to achieve. But if needs be, it is an ideal for which I am prepared to die.

Comment

In a book I wrote titled *Followership: How Followers Are Creating Change and Changing Leaders,* I defined followers as "subordinates who have less power, authority, and influence than do their superiors and who therefore usually, but not invariably, fall into line." Moreover, I divided followers into five different groups, one of which I called "Diehards." Diehard followers are as their name implies: prepared to die for their cause, if necessary, whether that cause is an individual, an idea, or both. "Diehards are defined by their dedication, including their willingness to risk life and limb. Being a Diehard is all-consuming. It is who you are. It determines what you do."

At the time of the Rivonia Trial, Mandela was already, in important ways, a leader, in particular of the black African opposition. But in other important ways, in the larger South African context, he was simultaneously a follower, a diehard follower, a powerless person who in opposing the powerful had already, for a decade or more, put his life at risk. Now, by declaring for the world to hear that a "democratic and free society" was "an ideal" for which he was "prepared to die," Mandela raised the stakes still further. By virtually daring the government to sentence him to death, he transformed his near-complete helplessness into a source of strength.

In fact, a sentence of death by hanging—which, given the charges of conspiracy and sabotage, was possible if not probable—was in the end reduced to one of life imprisonment.

Mandela's statement for the defense at the Rivonia Trial was carefully crafted and laboriously prepared. The last draft was finally finished in his own hand, not unlike Martin Luther King, Jr.'s draft of "Letter from Birmingham Jail," written almost exactly one year before. While there are important differences between the two documents, there are strong similarities as well, ranging from the general—the struggle between black people and white people, between those without power and those with—to the specific—both were statements of defiance penned under circumstances that were certain to focus the mind.

Mandela's journey from promulgating a strategy of nonviolence exclusively to promulgating one of violence episodically was apparently acutely, perhaps even painfully, experienced. This was a man who for most of his life had followed in the footsteps of Mahatma Gandhi. This was a man who for all practical purposes was Gandhi's disciple, who was, in the words of one observer, "an unwavering adherent of [Gandhi's] nonviolent philosophy." Like Gandhi, at the start of his career, Mandela was a politicized lawyer. Like Gandhi, he made it his mission in life to stand up for, fight for, human rights. And like Gandhi, his strategy was pointedly and purposely nonviolent. Mandela often alluded to Gandhi, paid him homage, and had a picture of him (among others) hanging in his home. (Mandela was not the only African leader to invoke Gandhi on nonviolent resistance. Postcolonialists like Zambia's Kenneth Kaunda and Ghana's Kwame Nkrumah did the same.)

But when push came to shove, Mandela ditched Mohandas Gandhi for, in effect, Franz Fanon. That is, he, like Fanon (who was roughly his contemporary), came ultimately to conclude that under certain circumstances the use of violence is not only appropriate but necessary. By this time in his life, Mandela had come to believe that it is not wrong to use violence when violence seems to be the only recourse—it is right. In his statement at the Rivonia Trial, this is a theme that reverberates over and over again, as if in defending himself before the current court, and before the court of public opinion, Mandela was, in addition, defending himself before the dictates of his own conscience. "What were we," he asks rhetorically, "the leaders of our people, to do?" Nonviolence had changed nothing, improved nothing, so "we had no doubt that we had to continue the fight. Anything else would have been abject surrender.... I can only say that I felt morally obliged to do what I did."

Mandela could have used the occasion of the Rivonia Trial to engage in debate from the witness box. He chose instead to deliver from the dock a statement that was personal as well as political, that followed the trajectory of his life, beginning with his tribal background and ending with the specter of his own death at the hands of the state. He spoke for fully four hours, and when he was done, the court sat in stunned silence. Mandela, it was said afterward, delivered his last lines without notes. And just before his closing words—"But if needs be, it is an ideal for which I am prepared to die"—he dropped his voice.

Mandela had to have been acutely aware not only of the immediate import of the Rivonia Trial, but of its historical moment as well. Never a great speaker, he was, as it happened, at his best in a courtroom. Biographer Elleke Boehmer writes that "the lawyer's bench and the dock granted him a certain license as a crowd-pleaser, where he learned to mould his wooden tones to fit the smooth modulations of a legal argument." But for all the argumentation, the lines that linger are the last, those that evoke the possibility of his demise and his readiness to die for his cause. This uneasy, uncertain suspension between life and death, which in spite of his long years came to characterize the man, the hero leader, is mythological in its implication. It is also Shakespearean. Small wonder it is said that while he was waiting for the verdict at Rivonia, Mandela thought of the Duke's instruction, incantation, to Claudio, from *Measure for Measure*, "Be absolute for death."

⁓

VACLAV HAVEL
1936–

The end of Communism in Czechoslovakia was, famously, bloodless. It was 1989, and Communism was crumbling everywhere in Eastern Europe. But Czechoslovakia was somehow somewhat different. Czechoslovakia's revolution was the "Velvet Revolution." And Czechoslovakia's first post-Communist president was a playwright.

Vaclav Havel was elected president in 1989, 1990, and 1993 (after the Slovaks declared their independence and the Czech Republic was created), and then one final time, in 1998. But his mark on history was made not as a person in a position of political power or authority, but rather as someone who, on the face of it, was without power or authority altogether. What he had was influence—for Havel will be remembered not for *being* president, but for what he did *before* being president, for what he did during his two decades as a political dissident.

The excerpt that follows, from his essay titled "The Power of the Powerless," is a sample of the literature that was essential to the collapse of Communism in Eastern Europe and the Soviet Union. Widely read and reread in Czechoslovakia and beyond, the extended essay was Havel's analysis of the present and his anticipation of the future.

It was also, curiously and counterintuitively, a harbinger of the twenty-first-century literature on leadership and management. Havel in fact makes plain that the systems and structures he prefers pertain to the political realm—and to the economic one as well. "The Power of the Powerless" thus prefigures the contemporary literature on corporate leadership: it values flattened organizations over hierarchical ones, prefers "self-management" to management from above, advocates providing everyone at every level with "a feeling of genuine responsibility for their collective work," and favors leaders whose authority is derived from their personality, not from their position.

Still, more than anything else, Havel's essay is justification for opposition—and testifies to what, sometimes at least, is its enduring effect.

-------- **THE POWER OF THE POWERLESS** --------
1978

A specter is haunting Eastern Europe: the specter of what in the West is called "dissent." This specter has not appeared out of thin air. It is a natural and inevitable consequence of the present historical phase of the system it is haunting. It was born at a time when this system, for a thousand reasons, can no longer base itself on the unadulterated, brutal, and arbitrary application of power, eliminating all expressions of nonconformity. What is more, the system has become so ossified politically that there is practically no way for such nonconformity to be implemented within its official structures.

Who are these so-called dissidents? Where does their point of view come from, and what importance does it have? What is the significance of the "independent initiatives" in which "dissidents" collaborate, and what real chances do such initiatives have of success? Is it appropriate to refer to "dissidents" as an opposition? If so, what exactly is such an opposition within the framework of this system? What does it do? What role does it play in society? What are its hopes and on what are they based? Is it within the power of the "dissidents"—as a category of sub-citizen outside the power establishment—to have any influence at all on society and the social system? Can they actually change anything?

I think that an examination of these questions—an examination of the potential of the "powerless"—can only begin with an examination of the nature of power in the circumstances in which these powerless people operate.

II

Our system is most frequently characterized as a dictatorship or, more precisely, as the dictatorship of a political bureaucracy over a society which has undergone economic and social leveling. I am afraid that the term "dictatorship," regardless of how intelligible it may otherwise be, tends to obscure rather than clarify the real nature of power in this system. We usually associate the term with the notion of a small group of people who take over the government of a given country by force; their power is wielded openly, using the direct instruments of power at their disposal, and they are easily distinguished socially from the majority over whom they rule. One of the essential aspects of this traditional or classical notion of dictatorship is the assumption that it is temporary, ephemeral, lacking historical roots. Its existence seems to be bound up with the lives of those who established it. It is usually local in extent and significance, and regardless of the ideology it utilizes to grant itself legitimacy, its power derives ultimately from the numbers and the armed might of its soldiers and police. The principal threat to its existence is felt to be the possibility that someone better equipped in this sense might appear and overthrow it.

Even this very superficial overview should make it clear that the system in which we live has very little in common with a classical dictatorship. . . .

The profound difference between our system—in terms of the nature of power—and what we traditionally understand by dictatorship, a difference I hope is clear even from this quite superficial comparison, has caused me to search for some term appropriate for our system, purely for the purposes of this essay. If I refer to it henceforth as a "post-totalitarian" system, I am fully aware that this is perhaps not the most precise term, but I am unable to think of a better one. I do not wish to imply by the prefix "post" that the system is no longer totalitarian; on the contrary, I mean that it is totalitarian in a way fundamentally different from classical dictatorships, different from totalitarianism as we usually understand it. . . .

The issue is the rehabilitation of values like trust, openness, responsibility, solidarity, love. I believe in structures that are not aimed at the technical aspect of the execution of power, but at the significance of that execution in structures held together more by a commonly shared feeling of the importance of certain communities than by commonly shared expansionist ambitions directed outward. There can and must be structures that are open, dynamic, and small; beyond a certain point, human ties like personal trust and personal responsibility cannot work. There must be structures that in principle place no limits on the genesis of different structures. Any accumulation of power whatsoever (one of the characteristics of automatism) should be profoundly alien to it. They would be structures not in the sense of organizations or institutions, but like a community. Their authority certainly cannot be based on long-empty traditions, like the tradition of mass political parties, but rather on how, in concrete terms, they enter into a given situation. Rather than a strategic agglomeration of formalized organizations, it is better to have organizations springing up ad hoc, infused with enthusiasm for a particular purpose and disappearing when that purpose has been achieved. The leaders' authority ought to derive from their personalities and be personally tested in their particular surroundings, and not from their position in any nomenklatura [the communist political elite, generally based on patronage]. They should enjoy great personal confidence and even great lawmaking powers based on that confidence. This would appear to be the only way out of the classic impotence of traditional democratic organizations, which frequently seem founded more on mistrust than mutual confidence, and more on collective irresponsibility than on responsibility. It is only with the full existential backing of every member of the community that a permanent bulwark against creeping totalitarianism can be established. These structures should naturally arise from below as a consequence of authentic social self-organization; they should derive vital energy from a living dialogue with the genuine needs from which they arise, and when these needs are gone, the structures should also disappear. The principles of their internal organization should be very diverse, with a minimum of external regulation. The decisive criterion of this self-constitution should be the structure's actual significance, and not just a mere abstract norm.

Both political and economic life ought to be founded on the varied and versatile cooperation of such dynamically appearing and disappearing organizations. As far as the economic life of society goes, I believe in the principle of self-management, which is probably the only way of achieving what all the theorists of socialism have dreamed about, that is, the genuine (i.e., informal) participation of workers in economic decision making, leading to a feeling of genuine responsibility for their collective work. The principles of control and discipline ought to be abandoned in favor of self-control and self-discipline. . . .

XXII

. . . I know from thousands of personal experiences how the mere circumstance of having signed Charter 77 has immediately created a deeper and more open relationship and evoked sudden and powerful feelings of genuine community among people who were all but strangers before. This kind of thing happens only rarely, if at all, even among people who have worked together for long periods in some apathetic official structure. It is as though the mere awareness and acceptance of a common task and a shared experience were enough to transform people and the climate of their lives, as though it gave their public work a more human dimension that is seldom found elsewhere.

Perhaps all this is only the consequence of a common threat. Perhaps the moment the threat ends or eases, the mood it helped create will begin to dissipate as well. (The aim of those who threaten us, however, is precisely the opposite. Again and again, one is shocked by the energy they devote to contaminating, in various despicable ways, all the human relationships inside the threatened community.)

Yet even if that were so, it would change nothing in the question I have posed.

We do not know the way out of the marasmus of the world, and it would be an expression of unforgivable pride were we to see the little we do as a fundamental solution, or were we to present ourselves, our community, and our solutions to vital problems as the only thing worth doing.

Even so, I think that given all these preceding thoughts on post-totalitarian conditions, and given the circumstances and the inner constitution of the developing efforts to defend human beings and their identity in such conditions, the questions I have posed are appropriate. If nothing else, they are an invitation to reflect concretely on our own experience and to give some thought to whether certain elements of that experience do not—without our really being aware of it—point somewhere further, beyond their apparent limits, and whether right here, in our everyday lives, certain challenges are not already encoded, quietly waiting for the moment when they will be read and grasped.

For the real question is whether the brighter future is really always so distant. What if, on the contrary, it has been here for a long time already, and only our own blindness and weakness has prevented us from seeing it around us and within us, and kept us from developing it?

Comment

Though the collapse of Communism in Eastern Europe and the Soviet Union was a watershed moment in twentieth-century history, it was a surprise, one of the biggest political surprises ever. With few exceptions, even the experts were stunned by the sudden demise of what was at the time one of the world's two superpowers, the Soviet Union, and by the abrupt end of Communism nearly everywhere in Europe. (Since Lenin and then Stalin, Communists had held sway over large swaths of the European continent.)

But, as is usual in these matters, with the benefit of hindsight, the cracks become visible. It is easier to see now than it was then how it happened that a system that seemed strong was in fact weak and vulnerable to attack, at least from within.

Who launched the attacks, and what exactly did they consist of? The charge was led by a few brave souls, dissidents in Eastern Europe and the Soviet Union who put their life and limb, health and welfare at risk in the service of their cause. Prominent among them were writers, hellbent on deploying their pens as weapons to take on and, in time, topple governments that were infinitely more powerful than they.

Those who wrote in opposition were not necessarily writers, or for that matter leaders. Andrei Sakharov, for example, ultimately among the most respected and even revered (outside Russia) of Soviet dissidents, was a brilliant and brilliantly accomplished physicist before turning to politics and publishing (in 1968) his political manifesto, *Progress, Coexistence, and Intellectual Freedom*. Similarly, Alexander Solzhenitsyn, whose slender novel *One Day in the Life of Ivan Denisovich* (1962) was a breakthrough dissident document, and who later wrote *The Gulag Archipelago* (1968), a three-volume masterpiece that exposed the Soviet prison system, studied mathematics before becoming a writer. (Solzhenitsyn began writing after his own seven-year internment in a camp in Siberia.) Vaclav Havel, though, was different. He was an author all along—and he was, nearly all along, a leader.

Havel's presidency, from 1989 to 2003, was not notably successful. As summarized in the *New York Times*, his years in office were "marked by a jovial eccentricity that repelled as well as endeared. He invited the Rolling Stones to the imposing Prague Castle, the office of the president; allowed a large neon-red heart to be erected on a side of the castle; hired women as bodyguards; and drove along the castle's endless corridors in a red pedal scooter. Critics called him a reluctant leader who learned to like power too much." More seriously, Czechoslovakia broke in two, one part Slovakia, the other the Czech Republic, in spite of the president's strong opposition. And, also more seriously, the president alienated many of his own allies by refusing to ban the Communist Party and, similarly, to prosecute those who were probably guilty of political crimes (committed under Communism).

Havel's leadership as president is in sharp contrast to his leadership as dissident. As indicated, it is the latter, not the former, that will stand the test of time. During the 10- to 20-year period that preceded the Velvet Revolution, no one did more than did Vaclav Havel to seed the soil with democratic rhetoric, to articulate the "post-totalitarian" aspirations of Eastern Europeans under Communism, or to hold fast those in opposition, patient in the present in anticipation of the future. Among his signal acts as dissident was to form (along with four others) Charter 77, a human rights and opposition group that took on the government without compunction. For his pains, Havel was repeatedly sentenced to time in prison, his longest incarceration lasting nearly five years (1979–1984), during which he had permission to write one letter to his wife each week. The letters became, in time, a book, *Letters to Olga*, described by *Library Journal* as "a unique and moving document of the struggle by a man of formidable moral strength to preserve his dignity and identity in the most difficult conditions."

Havel began as a playwright. But in the late 1960s, after the dashed hopes of the aborted "Prague Spring," he turned his talents primarily to politics. A decade later, in 1978, the author who had become an activist in addition published an essay titled "The Power of the Powerless." It was a seminal document, one of the single most important pieces of dissident literature during the decade that preceded the Communist crash. As earlier indicated it was also a forerunner: there is a litany of late twentieth- and early twenty-first-century literature on leadership and management that is as ideal in its aspiration as was Havel.

The most immediate impact of "The Power of the Powerless" was, of course, on Czechoslovakia, where it was widely disseminated (in *samizdat*—the underground publishing network) to become in short order the dissidents' rallying cry. But the impact of the essay extended further—to Poland, for example. A member of the now legendary Polish opposition group Solidarity recalled:

> This essay reached us in the Ursus factory in 1979 at a point when we felt we were at the end of the road. . . . We had been speaking on the shop floor, talking to people, participating in public meetings, trying to speak the truth about the factory, the country, and politics. There came a moment when people thought we were crazy. Why were we doing this? Why were we taking such risks? . . . We began to

doubt the purposefulness of what we were doing. Shouldn't we be coming up with other methods, other ways? Then came the essay by Havel. Reading it gave us the theoretical underpinnings for our activity. It maintained our spirits; we did not give up.

Havel's work as a theorist was serious. As his use of the word *specter* in the first line suggests (the word is also in the first line of *The Communist Manifesto*), "The Power of the Powerless" is an intellectual exercise of considerable ambition and heft, a political and philosophical treatise on nothing less than the meaning of political life. Here, for example, is D. Christopher Brooks, writing in the *East European Quarterly*: "A primary thesis that is repeated in a variety of forms throughout Havel's writings, especially the seminal essay 'The Power of the Powerless' is that, 'Individuals can be alienated from themselves only because there is something in them to alienate.' For Havel, this capacity for self-alienation is humanity's inescapable, and fatal, flaw and manifests itself most prominently in the twentieth century."

Havel is a fitting figure for the close of this book because his work as theoretician was indivisible from his work as practitioner. He was both an intellectual leader and a political leader—a writer who wrote to create change and an agent of change at the same time. So when the Communists fell and the time of troubles seemed over forever, it was inevitable, logical somehow, that Havel the hero dissident would become Havel the hero president. Of course, as the years went by, theory was put into practice, idealism succumbed to realism, and Havel morphed into the merely mortal. Still, he will linger as a dissident who thought the impossible in this best of all possible worlds. "The issue," he wrote in "The Power of the Powerless," is the "rehabilitation of values like trust, openness, responsibility, solidarity, love."

Sources

INTRODUCTION

Beam, Alex. *A Great Idea at the Time: The Rise, Fall, and Curious Afterlife of the Great Books.* New York: Public Affairs, 2008.

Burns, James MacGregor. *Leadership.* New York: Harper & Row, 1978.

Donadio, Rachel. "Revisiting the Canon Wars." *New York Times,* September 16, 2007.

Faust, Drew Gilpin. "The University's Crisis of Purpose." *New York Times,* September 6, 2008.

Fish, Stanley. "Think Again." *New York Times,* January 18, 2009.

Kellerman, Barbara. *Followership: How Followers Are Creating Change and Changing Leaders.* Boston: Harvard Business Press, 2008.

MacMillan, Margaret. *Dangerous Games: The Uses and Abuses of History.* New York: Modern Library, 2009.

May, Ernest R., and Richard E. Neustadt. *Thinking in Time: The Uses of History for Decision-Makers.* New York: Free Press, 1986.

PART 1

LAO TSU, *TAO TE CHING*

Selections

Lao Tsu. *Tao Te Ching.* Translated by Gia-Fu Feng and Jane English; introduction by Jacob Needleman. New York: Vintage, 1998, no pagination.

Also See

The Classic of the Way and Virtue: A New Translation of the Tao-Te Ching of Laozi as Interpreted by Wang Bi. Translated by Richard John Lynn. New York: Columbia University Press, 1999.

Chan, Alan. "Laozi." *Stanford Encyclopedia of Philosophy.* Edited by Edward N. Zalta. Summer 2007 edition; http://plato.stanford.edu/archives/fall2008/entries/laozi/.

Keping, Wang. *The Classic of the Dao: A New Investigation.* Beijing: Foreign Languages Press, 1998.

Welch, Holmes. *The Parting of the Way: Lao Tzu and the Taoist Movement.* Boston: Beacon Press, 1957.

Note on Translation

The *Tao Te Ching* has been translated into English many times. The excerpts included here are from a highly praised translation by Gia-Fu Feng and Jane English that is in keeping with the original text, as opposed to one that is politically correct. For example, a line from Chapter 7 reads, "The sage stays behind, thus he is ahead," rather than "The Master stays behind; that is why she is ahead" (from a translation by S. Mitchell).

CONFUCIUS, *ANALECTS*

Selections

Leys, Simon, trans. *The Analects of Confucius.* New York: Norton, 1997, pp. 3–9, 60–65, 99–101.

Also See

Bell, Daniel A. "The Confucian Party." *International Herald Tribune,* May 11, 2009.

Chin, Ann-ping. *The Authentic Confucius: A Life of Thought and Politics.* New York: Scribner's, 2007.

Lau, D. C. *Confucius: The Analects.* Hong Kong: Chinese University Press, 1992.

Riegel, Jeffrey. "Confucius." *The Stanford Encyclopedia of Philosophy.* Edited by Edward N. Zalta. Fall 2008 edition; http://plato.stanford.edu/archives/fall2008/entries/confucius/.

Watson, Burton. *The Analects of Confucius.* New York: Columbia University Press, 2007.

Note on Translation

The translation is by Simon Leys. Of his work as translator of the *Analects,* he wrote: "This is primarily a *writer's* translation; it is addressed not merely to fellow scholars, but first and foremost to nonspecialists—readers who simply wish to enlarge their cultural horizon but have no direct access to the original text." His hope, Leys added, was "to reconcile learning with literature."

PLATO, *THE REPUBLIC*

Selections

Plato. *The Republic.* Translated by Richard W. Sterling and William C. Scott. New York: Norton, 1985, pp. 165–167, 262–270.

Also See

Brown, Eric. "Plato's Ethics and Politics in *The Republic.*" *The Stanford Encyclopedia of Philosophy.* Edited by Edward N. Zalta. Fall 2008 edition; http://plato.stanford.edu/archives/fall2008/edition/plato-ethics-politics/.

Ebenstein, William, and Alan O. Ebenstein. *Great Political Thinkers: From Plato to the Present.* Fort Worth, Tex.: Holt, Rinehart and Winston, 1991.

Ferrari, G. R. F., ed. *The Cambridge Companion to Plato's Republic.* Cambridge, UK, and New York: Cambridge University Press, 2007.

Kraut, Richard. "Plato." *The Stanford Encyclopedia of Philosophy.* Edited by Edward N. Zalta. Fall 2008 edition; http://plato.stanford.edu/archives/fall2008/entries/plato/.

Plato, *The Republic.* Translated by R. E. Allen. New Haven, Conn.: Yale University Press, 2006.

Plato. *Republic.* Translated by Benjamin Jowett. Introduction and notes by Elizabeth Watson Scharffenberger. New York: Barnes & Noble, 2004.

Plato. *The Republic.* Edited by G. R. F. Ferrari. Cambridge, UK, and New York: Cambridge University Press, 2000.

Rosen, Stanley. *Plato's Republic: A Study.* New Haven, Conn.: Yale University Press, 2005.

Note on Translation

The text used here is primarily the work of the master British classicist Benjamin

Jowett, who first published his translation of *The Republic* in 1871. To this day, Jowett's translation is considered remarkably readable—although we now know that he took a certain amount of literary license. To correct for any misinterpretations or misunderstandings of the original, subsequent scholars have made several changes, which are reflected in the excerpts included here.

PLUTARCH, *LIVES*

Selection

Plutarch's Lives, Volume II. The Dryden Translation. Edited with preface by Arthur Hugh Clough; introduction by James Atlas. New York: Modern Library, 2001, pp. 609–611.

Also See

Plutarch. *Greek Lives*. Translated by Robin Waterfield; introduction and notes by Philip A. Stadter. Oxford and New York: Oxford University Press, 1998.

Plutarch. *Roman Lives*. Translated by Robin Waterfield; introduction and notes by Philip A. Stadter. Oxford and New York: Oxford University Press, 1999.

Note on Translation

The following note on the translation is taken directly from the Introductory Note to a limited edition of *Plutarch's Lives* that was edited by Charles W. Eliot and published in 1937 by P. F. Collier & Son. In other words, the centuries-old translation by John Dryden lives on. "The present translation is that made originally by a group of scholars in the end of the seventeenth century and published with a life of Plutarch by Dryden. This, usually referred to simply as the Dryden translation, was revised in 1859 by Arthur Hugh Clough, who corrected it by the standards of modern scholarship, so that it took the place which it still occupies as the best version in English for the purposes of the general reader."

NICCOLÒ MACHIAVELLI, *THE PRINCE*

Selections

Machiavelli, Niccolò. *The Prince*. Translated and with an introduction by Harvey Mansfield. Chicago: University of Chicago Press, 1998, pp. 61–68, 71–73, 87–91, 93–95.

Also See

The following editions of *The Prince*, each with different introductions and translators:

Machiavelli, Niccolò. *The Prince*. Edited, translated, and with an introduction by David Wootton. Indianapolis: Hackett, 1995.

Machiavelli, Niccolò. *The Prince*. Translated with notes by George Bull; introduction by Anthony Grafton. New York: Penguin, 1999.

Machiavelli, Niccolò. *The Essential Writings of Machiavelli*. Translated by Peter Constantine; introduction by Albert Russell Ascoli. New York: Modern Library, 2007.

For a smart, short article on Machiavelli, see

Pierpont, Claudia Roth. "The Florentine." *New Yorker*, September 15, 2008.

Note on Translation

The translation used is by Harvey Mansfield, who wrote that he sought "to be as literal and exact as is consistent with readable English." Mansfield went on to say that since Machiavelli was "one of the greatest and subtlest minds to whom we have access," the translator's responsibility was, insofar as possible, to present Machiavelli in his own words.

THOMAS HOBBES, *LEVIATHAN*
Selection
Hobbes, Thomas. *Leviathan.* http://darkwing.uoregon.edu/-rbear/hobbes/leviathan .html, Chapter 13.
Also See
Girt, Bernard. "Thomas Hobbes." In *The Philosophers: Introducing Great Western Thinkers,* edited by Ted Honderich. Oxford and New York: Oxford University Press, 1999, pp. 49–56.

Lloyd, Sharon A., and Susan Sreedhar. "Hobbes's Moral and Political Philosophy." *The Stanford Encyclopedia of Philosophy.* Edited by Edward N. Zalta. Fall 2008 edition, http://plato.stanford.edu/archives/fall2008/entries/hobbes-moral/.

Missner, Marshall, ed. *Thomas Hobbes, Leviathan.* New York: Pearson Longman, 2008.

Skinner, Quentin. *Hobbes and Republican Liberty.* Cambridge, UK, and New York: Cambridge University Press, 2009.

Sommerville, Johann P. *Thomas Hobbes: Political Ideas in Historical Context.* New York: St. Martin's, 1992.

Sorell, Tom, and Luc Foisneau, eds. *Leviathan after 350 Years.* Oxford, UK, and New York: Oxford University Press, 2004.

Springborg, Patricia, ed. *The Cambridge Companion to Hobbes's Leviathan.* Cambridge, UK, and New York: Cambridge University Press, 2007.

Strauss, Leo. *Natural Right and History.* Chicago: University of Chicago Press, 1953.

Worden, Blair. "Hobbes and the Halo of Power." *New York Review of Books,* July 16, 2009.

JOHN LOCKE, *SECOND TREATISE OF GOVERNMENT*
Selections
http://www.gutenberg.org/dirs/etext05/trgov10.txt.
Also See
Arneil, Barbara. *John Locke and America: The Defence of English Colonialism.* Oxford: Clarendon Press, 1996.

Locke, John. *The Second Treatise of Government.* Edited by Thomas P. Peardon. Indianapolis: Bobbs-Merrill, 1952, pp. 17–19, 84–88, and 96–99.

Locke, John. *Second Treatise of Government.* Edited by C. B. Macpherson. Indianapolis: Hackett Publishing, 1980.

Locke, John. *Two Treatises of Government and A Letter Concerning Toleration.* Edited by Ian Shapiro. New Haven, Conn.: Yale University Press, 2003.

Macpherson, C. B. *The Political Theory of Possessive Individualism: Hobbes to Locke.* Oxford: Clarendon Press, 1962.

Sigmund, Paul E., ed. *The Selected Political Writings of John Locke.* New York: W.W. Norton & Company, 2005.

Tuckness, Alex. "Locke's Political Philosophy." *The Stanford Encyclopedia of Philosophy.* Edited by Edward N. Zalta. Fall 2008 edition; http://plato.stanford.edu/archives/fall2008/entries/locke-political/.

Uzgalis, William. "John Locke." *The Stanford Encyclopedia of Philosophy.* Edited by

Edward N. Zalta. Fall 2008 edition; http://plato.stanford.edu/archives/fall2008/entries/locke/.

THOMAS CARLYLE, *ON HEROES, HERO-WORSHIP, AND THE HEROIC IN HISTORY*; HERBERT SPENCER, *THE STUDY OF SOCIOLOGY*; WILLIAM JAMES, "GREAT MEN AND THEIR ENVIRONMENT"; LEO TOLSTOY, *WAR AND PEACE*

Selections

Carlyle, Thomas. *On Heroes, Hero-Worship, & the Heroic in History*. 1840. Reprint, Berkeley: University of California Press, 1993, pp. 3–4.

James, William. "Great Men and Their Environment." In *Selected Papers on Philosophy*. New York: Dutton, 1917, pp. 173–181, 188–189.

Spencer, Herbert. *The Study of Sociology*. New York: Appleton, 1884, pp. 30–37.

Tolstoy, Leo. *War and Peace*. 1868–1869. Reprint, Oxford University Press, 1983, originally published in 1868–1869, pp. 645–648.

Also See

Bloom, Harold, ed. *Leo Tolstoy's War and Peace*. New York: Chelsea House, 1988.

Goodman, Russell. "William James." *The Stanford Encyclopedia of Philosophy*. Edited by Edward N. Zalta. Fall 2008 edition; http://plato.stanford.edu/archives/fall2008/entries/james/.

Heffer, Simon. *Moral Desperado: A Life of Thomas Carlyle*. London: Weidenfeld and Nicolson, 1995.

Hook, Sidney. *The Hero in History: A Study in Limitation and Possibility*. New York: John Day, 1943.

James, William. *The Will to Believe and Other Essays in Popular Philosophy, and Human Immortality*. New York: Dover, 1956.

Macpherson, Hector. *Herbert Spencer: The Man and His Work*. London: Chapman and Hall, 1900.

Sidorsky, David. "Sidney Hook." *The Stanford Encyclopedia of Philosophy*. Edited by Edward N. Zalta. Fall 2008 edition; http://plato.stanford.edu/archives/fall2008/entries/sidney-hook/.

Spencer, Herbert. *The Study of Sociology*. Introduction by Talcott Parsons. Ann Arbor: University of Michigan, 1961.

Tolstoy, Leo. *War and Peace*. Translated by Richard Pevear and Larissa Volokhonsky. New York: Knopf, 2007.

Wasiolek, Edward. *War and Peace: The Theoretical Chapters*. In Bloom, ed. *Leo Tolstoy's War and Peace*, pp. 87–102.

JOHN STUART MILL, *ON LIBERTY*

Selection

Mill, John Stuart. *On Liberty and Other Essays*. Edited by John Gray. Oxford and New York: Oxford University Press, 1991, pp. 5–9, 18–19, 62–63, 84–85, 127–128.

Also See

Devigne, Robert. *Reforming Liberalism: J. S. Mill's Use of Ancient, Religious, Liberal, and Romantic Moralities*. New Haven, Conn.: Yale University Press, 2006.

Gopnik, Adam. "Right Again: The Passions of John Stuart Mill." *New Yorker*, October 6, 2008.

Justman, Stewart. *The Hidden Text of Mill's* Liberty. Savage, Md.: Rowman & Littlefield, 1991.

Skorupski, John. *Why Read Mill Today?* London and New York: Routledge, 2006.

MAX WEBER, *THE THEORY OF SOCIAL AND ECONOMIC ORGANIZATION*

Selections

Weber, Max, A. M. Henderson, and Talcott Parsons. *Max Weber: The Theory of Social and Economic Organization*. Edited and with an introduction by Talcott Parsons. New York: Free Press, 1947, pp. 328–329, 358–363.

Also See

Bendix, Reinhard. *Work and Authority in Industry*. 1956. Reprint, New Brunswick, N.J.: Transaction, 2001.

Kim Sung Ho. "Max Weber." *The Stanford Encyclopedia of Philosophy*. Edited by Edward N. Zalta. Fall 2008 edition; http://plato.stanford.edu/archives/fall2008/entries/weber/.

Michels, Robert. *Political Parties: A Sociological Study of the Oligarchical Tendencies of Modern Democracy*. 1911. Reprint, New York: Free Press, 1962.

Podolny, Joel, Rakesh M. Khurana, and Marya Hill-Popper. "Revisiting the Meaning of Leadership." *Research in Organizational Behavior*, October 2004.

Weber, Max. *On Charisma and Institution Building: Selected Papers*. Edited by S. N. Eisenstadt. Chicago: University of Chicago Press, 1968.

Willner, Ann Ruth. *The Spellbinders: Charismatic Political Leadership*. New York: Yale University Press, 1984.

Note on the Translation

The translation used here, by A. M. Henderson and the eminent sociologist Talcott Parsons, was the first to appear in English. Because their work was interrupted by the Second World War, this initial translation took years to complete. When the book was finally published, Parsons noted that his translation was no longer alone "in bringing to the English reader some of the more comprehensive and fundamental works by Max Weber."

SIGMUND FREUD, *GROUP PSYCHOLOGY AND THE ANALYSIS OF THE EGO, CIVILIZATION AND ITS DISCONTENTS, MOSES AND MONOTHEISM*

Selections

Freud, Sigmund. *Group Psychology and the Analysis of the Ego*. New York: Norton, 1989, pp. 9–10, 32–35, 76.

Freud, Sigmund. *Civilization and Its Discontents*. Edited and translated by James Strachey. New York: Norton, 1961, pp. 41–43.

Freud, Sigmund. *Moses and Monotheism*. Translated by Katherine Jones. New York: Vintage, 1967, pp. 136–140.

Also See

Freud, Sigmund. *Civilization and Its Discontents*. Edited and translated by James Strachey.

Introduction by Louis Menand and biographical afterword by Peter Gay. New York: Norton, 2005.

Kets de Vries, M. F. R. See his various writings for contemporaneous interpretations of Freud's impact on how to think about leaders and followers.

Roazen, Paul. *Freud: Political and Social Thought.* New York: Knopf, 1968.

Note on Translation

Freud's most frequent translator by far was the Englishman James Strachey. However, Strachey's translations, which were overseen by Freud's daughter, Anna, a highly respected psychotherapist in her own right, are not considered especially felicitous. Menand notes, in fact, that the "peculiarities" of the English translations have themselves been the subject of a substantial literature. Still, the most widely available translations of both *Group Psychology* and *Civilization* are by Strachey, and they are the ones used here. Katherine Jones, the translator of *Moses and Monotheism*, was the wife of Freud's disciple and biographer, Ernest Jones.

MARY PARKER FOLLETT, "THE ESSENTIALS OF LEADERSHIP"; JAMES MacGREGOR BURNS, *LEADERSHIP*

Selections

Graham, Pauline, ed., *Mary Parker Follett—Prophets of Management: A Celebration of Writings from the 1920s.* Preface by Rosabeth Moss Kanter; Introduction by Peter F. Drucker. Boston: Harvard Business School Press, 1995, pp. 168–173. "Essentials of Leadership" was the title of a speech Follett originally delivered in 1933 (the title of Graham's book notwithstanding).

Burns, James MacGregor. *Leadership.* New York: Harper & Row, 1978, pp. 18–23.

Also See

Beschloss, Michael R., and Thomas E. Cronin. *Essays in Honor of James MacGregor Burns.* Englewood Cliffs, N.J.: Prentice-Hall, 1969.

Burns, James MacGregor. *Transforming Leadership.* New York: Grove, 2003.

Follett, Mary Parker, *The New State: Group Organization the Solution of Popular Government.* Introductions by Benjamin R. Barber and Jane Mansbridge. University Park, Pa.: Pennsylvania State University Press, 1998.

Liebmann, George W. *Six Lost Leaders: Prophets of Civil Society.* Lanham, Md.: Lexington, 2001.

Tonn, Joan C. *Mary Parker Follett: Creating Democracy, Transforming Management.* New Haven, Conn.: Yale University Press, 2003.

STANLEY MILGRAM, *OBEDIENCE TO AUTHORITY*; HANNAH ARENDT, *EICHMANN IN JERUSALEM: A REPORT ON THE BANALITY OF EVIL*

Selections

Milgram, Stanley. *Obedience to Authority: An Experimental View.* New York: Harper & Row, 1974, pp. 1–9, 11.

Arendt, Hannah. *Eichmann in Jerusalem: A Report on the Banality of Evil.* Introduction by Amos Elon. New York: Penguin, 2006, pp. 135–138, 148–150.

Also See

Arendt, Hannah. *The Portable Hannah Arendt.* Edited by Peter Baehr. New York: Penguin, 2000.

Blass, Thomas, ed. *Obedience to Authority: Current Perspectives on the Milgram Paradigm.* Mahwah, N.J.: Erlbaum, 2000.

Canovan, Margaret. *Hannah Arendt: A Reinterpretation of Her Political Thought.* Cambridge, UK, and New York: Cambridge University Press, 1992.

Kelman, Herbert C., and Lee V. Diamond. *Crimes of Obedience.* New Haven, Conn.: Yale University Press, 1989.

Kellerman, Barbara. *Followership: How Followers Are Creating Change and Changing Leaders.* Boston: Harvard Business Press, 2008.

Kirsch, Adam. "Beware of Pity: Hannah Arendt and the Power of the Impersonal." *New Yorker,* January 12, 2009.

Young-Bruehl, Elizabeth. *Why Arendt Matters.* New Haven, Conn.: Yale University Press, 2006.

Zimbardo, Philip. *The Lucifer Effect: Understanding How Good People Turn Evil.* New York: Random House, 2007.

Zimbardo, Philip. "When Good People Do Evil." *Yale Alumni Magazine,* January/February 2007.

PART 2

MARY WOLLSTONECRAFT, *A VINDICATION OF THE RIGHTS OF WOMEN*

Selection

Wollstonecraft, Mary. *A Vindication of the Rights of Women.* Edited by Carol Poston New York: Norton, 1988, pp. 7–11, 147–150.

Also See

Bentley, Toni. "A Hyena in Petticoats." *New York Times Book Review,* May 29, 2005, pp. 5–6.

Craciun, Adriana, ed. *Mary Wollstonecraft's A Vindication of the Rights of Women.* London and New York: Routledge, 2002.

Freedman, Estelle B., ed. *The Essential Feminist Reader.* New York: Modern Library, 2007.

Johnson, Claudia L., ed. *The Cambridge Companion to Mary Wollstonecraft.* Cambridge, UK, and New York: Cambridge University Press, 2002. See especially Alan Richardson, "Mary Wollstonecraft on Education," pp. 24–41.

Moers, Ellen. "Vindicating Mary Wollstonecraft." *New York Review of Books,* 23, 2, 1976.

Wollstonecraft, Mary. *A Vindication of the Rights of Women.* Introduction by Katha Pollitt. New York: Modern Library, 2001.

THOMAS PAINE, *COMMON SENSE*

Selection

http://www.ushistory.org/paine/commonsense/.

Also See

Harmer, Harry. *Tom Paine, The Life of a Revolutionary.* London: Haus, 2006.

Larkin, Edward. *Thomas Paine and the Literature of Revolution.* New York: Cambridge University Press, 2005.

Hook, Sidney, ed. *Common Sense, Rights of Man, and Other Essential Writings of Thomas Paine*. New foreword by Jack Fruchtman, Jr. New York: Signet Classic, 2003.

Lepore, Jill. "The Sharpened Quill." *New Yorker*, October 16, 2006, pp. 168–175.

Nelson, Craig. *Thomas Paine: Enlightenment, Revolution, and the Birth of Modern Nations*. New York: Viking, 2006.

Paine, Thomas. *Common Sense*. Edited with an introduction by Isaac Kramnick. New York: Penguin, 1976, pp. 81–90, 100.

ELIZABETH CADY STANTON, *DECLARATION OF SENTIMENTS*

Selection

Freedman, Estelle. *The Essential Feminist Reader*. New York: Modern Library, 2007.

Also See

Buhle, Mari Jo, and Paul Buhle, eds. *The Concise History of Woman Suffrage—Selections from Stanton, Anthony, Gage, and Harper*. Urbana: University of Illinois Press, 2005.

Davis, Sue. *The Political Thought of Elizabeth Cady Stanton: Women's Rights and the American Political Traditions*. New York: New York University Press, 2008.

DuBois, Ellen Carol, ed. *Elizabeth Cady Stanton—Susan B. Anthony: Correspondence, Writings, Speeches*. New York: Schocken, 1981.

DuBois, Ellen Carol, and Richard Cándida Smith, eds. *Elizabeth Cady Stanton, Feminist as Thinker: A Reader in Documents and Essays*. New York: New York University Press, 2007.

Ginzberg, Lori, D. *Elizabeth Cady Stanton: An American Life*. New York: Hill & Wang, 2009.

Gordon, Ann D., ed. *The Selected Papers of Elizabeth Cady Stanton and Susan B. Anthony*. New Brunswick, N.J.: Rutgers University Press, 1997, pp. 75–81.

KARL MARX AND FRIEDRICH ENGELS, *THE COMMUNIST MANIFESTO*

Selection

Marx, Karl, and Friedrich Engels. *The Communist Manifesto*. Introduction by Eric Hobsbawm. London and New York: Verso, 1998, pp. 33–38, 50–51, 75–77.

Also See

Courtois, Stephane, et al. *The Black Book of Communism: Crimes, Terror, Repression*. Cambridge, Mass.: Harvard University Press, 1999.

Marx, Karl, and Friedrich Engels. *The Communist Manifesto*. Introduction by Gareth Stedman Jones. London: Penguin, 2002.

Added Note

The secondary literature on *The Communist Manifesto* is vast and may be consulted under any number of headings, including the names of the two authors and key words such as *communism, socialism, Georg Wilhelm Friedrich Hegel* (German philosopher), *Das Kapital* (published in 1867), which is considered Marx's magnum opus, and twentieth-century histories of the Soviet Union, China, and many other smaller countries, from Cuba to Cambodia.

Note on Translation

Both editions of *The Communist Manifesto* cited here use the original translation, from 1888, by Samuel Moore. This translation had the considerable benefit of being edited by Engels, who for many years lived in England.

W. E. B. DU BOIS, "THE TALENTED TENTH"
Selection

Du Bois, W. E. B. "The Talented Tenth." In Booker T. Washington, et al. *The Negro Problem.* New York: James Pott & Company, 1903.

Also See

Alridge, Derrick, P. *The Educational Thought of W. E. B. Du Bois: An Intellectual History.* New York: Teachers College Press, 2008.

Boxill, Bernard R., ed. *The Negro Problem: Centennial Edition.* Amherst, N.Y.: Humanity, 2003.

Marable, Manning. *Black Leadership: Four Great American Leaders and the Struggle for Civil Rights.* New York: Penguin, 1998.

Peterson, Charles F. *Du Bois, Fanon, Cabral: The Margins of Elite Anti-Colonial Leadership.* Lanham, Md.: Lexington, 2007.

Provenzo, Eugene F., ed. *Du Bois on Education.* Lanham, Md.: Rowman and Littlefield, 2002.

FRANTZ FANON, *THE WRETCHED OF THE EARTH*
Selection

Fanon, Frantz. *The Wretched of the Earth.* Translated by Richard Philcox. Commentary by Jean-Paul Sartre and Homi K. Bhabha. New York: Grove, 2004, pp. 1–7, 235–239.

Also See

Bulhan, Hussein Abdilahi. *Frantz Fanon and the Psychology of Oppression.* New York: Plenum, 1985.

Cheriki, Alice. *Frantz Fanon: A Portrait.* Translated by Nadia Benabid. Ithaca, N.Y.: Cornell University Press, 2006.

Gibson, Nigel C. *Fanon: The Postcolonial Imagination.* Cambridge, UK: Polity, 2003.

Macey, David. *Frantz Fanon: A Biography.* New York: Picador, 2002.

Memmi, Albert. *The Colonizer and the Colonized.* London: Earthscan, 2004.

Silverman, Max, ed. *Frantz Fanon's Black Skin, White Masks: New Interdisciplinary Essays.* Manchester, UK: Manchester University Press, 2005.

Note on Translation

The translation of Fanon from the French is by Richard Philcox, who thought the previous translation of Fanon had "distorted" his voice. So this was his "second chance to be heard," in language that was updated, but that retained what was essential in the original. In a postscript, Philcox wrote that translating Fanon was a challenge, particularly with regard to words as politically charged as *negre* and *noir*, originally translated as *Negro*. In the end, Philcox decided usually to use *black*, though he thought he "lost something in the translation of the word *negre*, for it has both a sting and an embrace, and that is irretrievable."

RACHEL CARSON, *SILENT SPRING*
Selection

Carson, Rachel. *Silent Spring.* With essays by Edward O. Wilson and Linda Lear. Boston: Houghton Mifflin, 2002, pp. 1–13.

Also See

Lytle, Mark Hamilton. *The Gentle Subversive: Rachel Carson, Silent Spring, and the Rise of the Environmental Movement.* New York: Oxford University Press, 2007.

Matthiessen, Peter, ed. *Courage for the Earth: Writers, Scientists, and Activists Celebrate the Life and Writing of Rachel Carson.* Boston: Houghton Mifflin, 2007.

Sideris, Lisa H., and Kathleen Dean Moore, eds. *Rachel Carson: Legacy and Challenge.* Albany: State University of New York Press, 2008.

Waddell, Craig, ed. *And No Birds Sing: Rhetorical Analyses of Rachel Carson's Silent Spring.* Carbondale: Southern Illinois University Press, 2000.

BETTY FRIEDAN, *THE FEMININE MYSTIQUE*

Selection

Friedan, Betty. *The Feminine Mystique.* Introduction by Anna Quindlen. New York: Norton, 2001.

Also See

Horowitz, Daniel. *Betty Friedan and the Making of* The Feminine Mystique: *The American Left, the Cold War, and Modern Feminism.* Amherst: University of Massachusetts Press, 1998.

Sommers, Christina Hoff. "Reconsiderations: Betty Friedan's 'The Feminine Mystique.'" *New York Sun,* September 17, 2008.

SAUL ALINSKY, *RULES FOR RADICALS*

Selection

Alinsky, Saul. *Rules for Radicals: A Practical Primer for Realistic Radicals.* New York: Vintage, 1971, pp. 71–80.

Also See

Alinsky, Saul. *Reveille for Radicals.* New York: Vintage, 1946, 1969.

Sanders, Marion K. *The Professional Radical: Conversations with Saul Alinsky.* New York: Harper & Row, 1965, 1969, 1970.

PETER SINGER, *ANIMAL LIBERATION*

Selection

Singer, Peter. *Animal Liberation.* New York: Ecco, 2002, pp. xx–xxv and 1–9.

Also See

Höchsmann, Hyun. *On Peter Singer.* Belmont, Calif.: Wadsworth, 2002.

Jamieson, Dale, ed. *Singer and His Critics.* Oxford, UK, and Malden, Mass.: Blackwell, 1999. In particular see Jamieson's chapter, "Singer and the Practical Ethics Movement."

Singer, Peter. "Animal Liberation at 30." *New York Review of Books,* May 15, 2003.

LARRY KRAMER, "1,112 AND COUNTING"

Selection

Kramer, Larry. *Reports from the Holocaust: The Making of an AIDS Activist.* New York: St. Martin's, 1989, pp. 33–47.

Also See

Goodridge et al. v. *Department of Public Health, et al. Massachusetts Lawyers Weekly,* May 14, 2008.

Kramer, Larry. *The Tragedy of Today's Gays*. New York: Tarcher/Penguin, 2005.

Long, Thomas L. *AIDS and American Apocalypticism: The Cultural Semiotics of an Epidemic*. Albany: State University of New York Press, 2005.

Mass, Lawrence D., ed. *We Must Love One Another or Die: The Life and Legacies of Larry Kramer*. New York: St. Martin's, 1977.

Morland, Iain, and Annabelle Willcox. *Queer Theory*. Houndmills, UK, and New York: Palgrave Macmillan, 2005. This book also contains "1,112 and Counting," pp. 28–39.

Morris, Charles E., III, ed. *Queering Public Address: Sexualities in American Historical Discourse*. Columbia: University of South Carolina Press, 2007.

Pittinsky, Todd. Oral history interview with Larry Kramer, Harvard University, 2003. Unpublished.

Specter, Michael. "Public Nuisance." *New Yorker*, May 13, 2002.

PART 3

QUEEN ELIZABETH I, "SPEECH TO THE TROOPS AT TILBURY" AND "THE GOLDEN SPEECH"

Selections

The versions of the two speeches used are in Stump, Donald, and Susan M. Felch, eds. *Elizabeth I and Her Age: Authoritative Texts, Commentary and Criticism*. New York: Norton, 2009, pp. 393 (Speech to the Troops at Tilbury) and 503–505 (Golden Speech, the Townshend version).

Also See

Broad, Jacqueline, and Karen Green. *A History of Women's Political Thought in Europe, 1400–1700*. Cambridge, UK, and New York: Cambridge University Press, 2009.

Marcus, Leah S., Janel Mueller, and Mary Beth Rose, eds., *Elizabeth I: Collected Works*. Chicago: University of Chicago Press, 2000.

May, Steven W. *Queen Elizabeth I: Selected Works*. New York: Washington Square Press, 2004.

Rice, George P., Jr. "The Speaker and the Speeches." In Stump and Felch, eds., *Elizabeth I and Her Age*.

Rose, Mary Beth. *Gender and Heroism in Early Modern English Literature*. Chicago: University of Chicago Press, 2002.

SOJOURNER TRUTH, "AIN'T I A WOMAN?"; ABRAHAM LINCOLN, "GETTYSBURG ADDRESS" AND "SPEECH AT THE SECOND INAUGURAL"

Selections

http://en.wikipedia.org/wiki/Ain%27t_I_a_Woman%3F.

http://showcase.netins.net/web/creative/lincoln/speeches/gettysburg.htm.

http://avalon.law.yale.edu/19th_century/lincoln2.asp

Also See

Briggs, John Channing. *Lincoln's Speeches Reconsidered*. Baltimore: Johns Hopkins University Press, 2005.

Fitch, Suzanne Pullon, and Roseann M. Mandziuk. *Sojourner Truth as Orator: Wit, Story, and Song*. Westport, Conn.: Greenwood, 1997.

Fornieri, Joseph R., ed. *The Language of Liberty: The Political Speeches and Writings of Abraham Lincoln*. Washington, D.C.: Regnery, 2009.

Gopnik, Adam. "Angels and Ages." *New Yorker*, May 28, 2007.

Kaplan, Fred. *Lincoln: The Biography of a Writer*. New York: HarperCollins, 2009.

McPherson, James, "Lincoln Off His Pedestal," *New York Review of Books*, September 24, 2009.

Painter, Nell Irvin, ed. *Narrative of Sojourner Truth*. New York: Penguin, 1998.

Painter, Nell Irvin. *Sojourner Truth: A Life, A Symbol*. New York: Norton, 1996.

Raban, Jonathan. "All the President's Literature." *Wall Street Journal*, January 10–11, 2009.

Tackach, James. *Lincoln's Moral Vision: The Second Inaugural Address*. Jackson: University Press of Mississippi, 2002.

Washington, Margaret. *Sojourner Truth's America*. Urbana: University of Illinois Press, 2009.

White, Ronald C., Jr. *Lincoln's Greatest Speech: The Second Inaugural*. New York: Simon & Schuster, 2002.

Wills, Garry. *Lincoln at Gettysburg: The Words That Remade America*. New York: Simon & Schuster, 1992.

V. I. LENIN, *WHAT IS TO BE DONE?*

Selection

http://www.marxists.org/archive/lenin/works/1901/witbd/iv.htm.

Also See

Budgen, Sebastian, Stathis Kouvelakis, and Slavoj Zizek, eds. *Lenin Reloaded: Toward a Politics of Truth*. Durham, N.C.: Duke University Press, 2007.

Fischer, Louis. *The Life of Lenin*. New York: Harper & Row, 1964.

Lih, Lars T. *Lenin Rediscovered: What Is to Be Done? in Context*. Leiden: Brill, 2006.

Service, Robert. *Lenin: A Biography*. Cambridge, Mass.: Harvard University Press, 2000.

Wolfe, Bertram D. *Three Who Made a Revolution*. New York: Dial, 1964.

Note on Translation

There are several translations of *What Is to Be Done?* For this purpose, the differences are slight, so the online version was used, which was first translated by Joe Fineberg in 1929 and then later revised by George Hanna in 1962. A recent translation by Lars T. Lih may be found in his book cited here, *Lenin Rediscovered*.

MAHATMA GANDHI, *ESSENTIAL WRITINGS*

Selections

Brown, Judith M. *Mahatma Gandhi: The Essential Writings*. Oxford and New York: Oxford University Press, 2008, pp. 309–311, 315–316, 324–330.

Also See

Chakrabarty, Bidyut. *Social and Political Thought of Mahatma Gandhi*. London and New York: Routledge, 2006.

Doniger, Wendy. *The Hindus: An Alternative History*. New York: Penguin, 2009.

Erikson, Erik H. *Gandhi's Truth: On the Origins of Militant Nonviolence*. New York: Norton, 1969.

Fischer, Louis, ed. *The Essential Gandhi: An Anthology of His Writings on His Life, Work, and Ideas*. Preface by Eknath Easwaran. New York: Vintage, 1983.

Gandhi, Mahatma. *Gandhi on Non-Violence.* Edited with an introduction by Thomas Merton. New York: New Directions, 2007.

Gandhi, Rajmohan. *Gandhi: The Man, His People, and the Empire.* Berkeley: University of California Press, 2007.

Ganguly, Debjani, and John Docker, eds. *Rethinking Gandhi and Nonviolent Rationality: Global Perspectives.* London and New York: Routledge, 2007.

Haksar, Vinit, "*Satyagraha* and the Right to Civil Disobedience." In Douglas Allen, ed., *The Philosophy of Mahatma Gandhi for the Twenty-First Century.* Lanham, Md.: Lexington, 2008.

Lewis, John. *Walking with the Wind: A Memoir of the Movement.* New York: Simon & Schuster, 1998.

Shulman, David. "A Passion for Hindu Myths." *New York Review of Books,* November 19, 2009.

Thoreau, Henry David. "Civil Disobedience." *The Thoreau Reader.* 1849. http://thoreau .eserver.org/civil.html.

WINSTON CHURCHILL, "ADAMANT FOR DRIFT" AND "THE THREAT TO CZECHOSLOVAKIA"

Selections

http://www.churchill-society-london.org.uk/Locusts.html.

http://www.churchill-society-london.org.uk/Austria.html.

http://www.winstonchurchill.org/learn/speeches/speeches-of-winston-churchill/112-the-danube-basin.

Also See

Addison, Paul. *Churchill: The Unexpected Hero.* Oxford and New York: Oxford University Press, 2005.

D'Este, Carlo. *Warlord: A Life of Winston Churchill at War, 1874–1945.* New York: HarperCollins, 2008.

Gilbert, Martin. *Winston S. Churchill, Volume V, 1922–1939.* London: Heinemann, 1976.

James, Robert Rhodes, ed. *Churchill Speaks: Winston S. Churchill in Peace and War—Collected Speeches, 1897–1963.* New York: Chelsea House, 1980.

Langworth, Richard M., ed. *Churchill by Himself: The Definitive Collection of Quotations.* New York: PublicAffairs, 2008.

Lukacs, John. *Blood, Toil, Tears and Sweat: The Dire Warning.* New York: Basic Books, 2008.

Wheatcroft, Geoffrey. "Churchill and His Myths." *New York Review of Books,* May 29, 2008.

MARTIN LUTHER KING, JR., "LETTER FROM BIRMINGHAM JAIL"

Selection

http://abacus.bates.edu/admin/offices/dos/mlk/letter.html.

Also See

Bass, S. Jonathan. *Blessed Are the Peacemakers: Martin Luther King Jr., Eight White Religious Leaders, and the "Letter from Birmingham Jail."* Baton Rouge: Louisiana State University Press, 2001.

Branch, Taylor. *Parting the Waters: America in the King Years, 1954–63*. New York: Simon & Schuster, 1988.

Dyson, Michael Eric. *I May Not Get There with You: The True Martin Luther King, Jr.* New York: Free Press, 2000.

Wills, Richard Wayne, Sr., *Martin Luther King Jr. and the Image of God*. Oxford and New York: Oxford University Press, 2009.

Wilmore, Gayraud. *Black Religion and Black Radicalism: An Interpretation of the Religious History of African Americans*. Maryknoll, N.Y.: Orbis, 1998.

NELSON MANDELA, "I AM PREPARED TO DIE"
Selection
http://www.anc.org.za/ancdocs/history/mandela/1960s/rivonia.html.
Also See

Boehmer, Elleke. *Nelson Mandela: A Very Short Introduction*. Oxford and New York: Oxford University Press, 2008.

Juckes, Tim J. *Opposition in South Africa: The Leadership of Z. K. Matthews, Nelson Mandela, and Stephen Biko*. Westport, Conn.: Praeger, 1995.

Kellerman, Barbara. *Followership: How Followers Are Creating Change and Changing Leaders*. Boston: Harvard Business Press, 2008.

Lodge, Tom. *Mandela: A Critical Life*. Oxford and New York: Oxford University Press, 2006.

Mandela, Nelson. *Long Walk to Freedom*. Boston: Little, Brown, 1994.

Sampson, Anthony. *Mandela: The Authorized Biography*. New York: Knopf, 1999.

VACLAV HAVEL, "THE POWER OF THE POWERLESS"
Selection
http://www.vaclavhavel.cz/showtrans.php?cat=clanky&val=72_aj_clanky.html&typ=HTML.
Also See

Bilefsky, Dan. "As Playwright, Havel Again Mocks Authority, This Time His Own." *New York Times*, July 26, 2008.

Brooks, D. Christopher. "The Art of the Political: Havel's Dramatic Literature as Political Theory." *East European Quarterly*, Winter 2005.

Goetz-Stankiewicz, Marketa, and Phyllis Carey, eds. *Critical Essays on Vaclav Havel*. New York: G. K. Hall & Co., 1999.

Goldfarb, Jeffrey C. *The Politics of Small Things: The Power of the Powerless in Dark Times*. Chicago: University of Chicago Press, 2006.

Havel, Vaclav, et al. *The Power of the Powerless: Citizens against the State in Central-Eastern Europe*. Edited by John Keane. London: Hutchinson, 1985.

Pontuso, James. *Vaclav Havel: Civic Responsibility in the Postmodern Age*. Lanham, Md.: Rowman & Littlefield, 2004.

Rosenberger, Chandler. "Order from Entropy: Vaclav Havel's Aesthetic of Politics." Paper delivered at Chicago Historical Society, April 2001.

Vladislav, Jan, ed. *Vaclav Havel or Living in Truth: Twenty-Two Essays Published on the Occasion of the Award of the Erasmus Prize to Vaclav Havel*. London and Boston: Faber and Faber, 1986.

About the Author

Barbara Kellerman is the James MacGregor Burns Lecturer in Public Leadership at Harvard University's John F. Kennedy School of Government. Her writing has appeared in the *New York Times*, the *Washington Post*, the *Boston Globe*, the *Los Angeles Times*, and *Harvard Business Review*, and she has appeared on CBS, NBC, NPR, and CNN. Kellerman was ranked by Forbes.com as among the "Top 50 Business Thinkers" (2009) and by *Leadership Excellence* in the top 15 of 100 "Best Minds on Leadership" (2008–2009). She is author and editor of many books on leadership, most recently *Bad Leadership* and *Followership*.

CPSIA information can be obtained at www.ICGtesting.com
Printed in the USA
LVOW04*2002310715

448281LV00006B/43/P

9 780071 633840